# THE MAGNIFICENT BUILDERS

AND THEIR

*Dream Houses*

# THE
# MAGNIFICENT

PUBLISHED BY
AMERICAN HERITAGE PUBLISHING CO.,INC., NEW YORK

BOOK TRADE
DISTRIBUTION BY SIMON AND SCHUSTER, NEW YORK

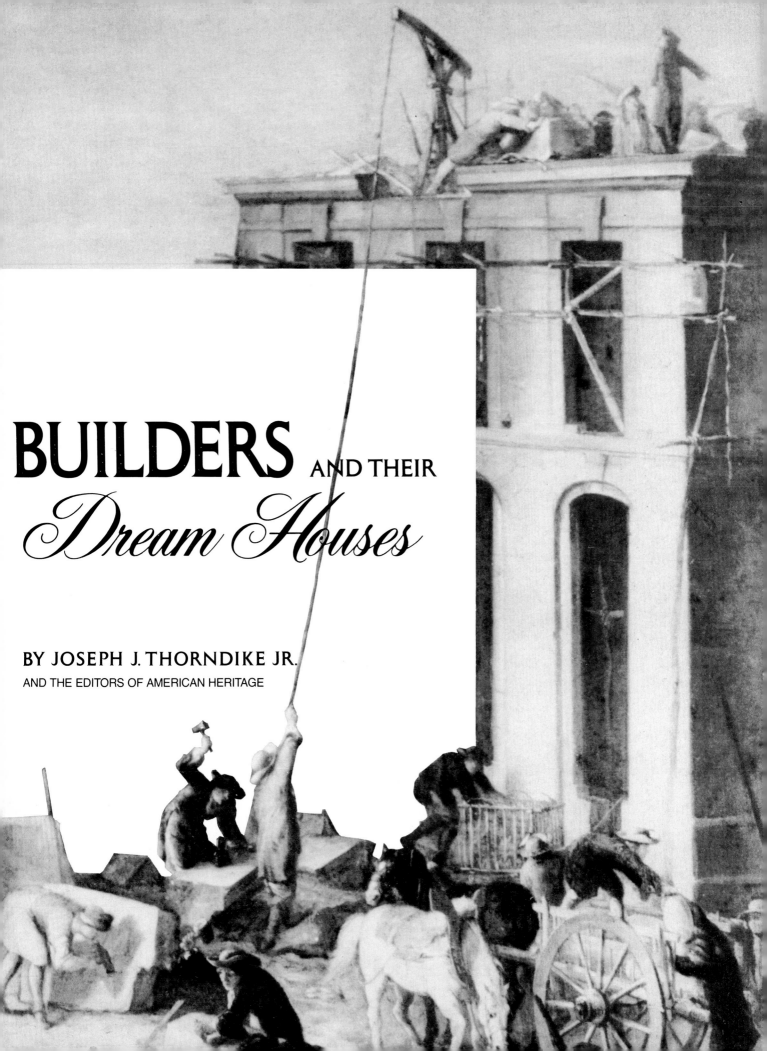

# BUILDERS AND THEIR
## Dream Houses

BY JOSEPH J. THORNDIKE JR.
AND THE EDITORS OF AMERICAN HERITAGE

AMERICAN HERITAGE BOOKS
EDITOR-IN-CHIEF Ezra Bowen

MAGNIFICENT BUILDERS AND THEIR DREAM HOUSES
MANAGING EDITOR Anne Moffat
TEXT EDITOR Richard F. Snow
ART DIRECTOR Murray Belsky
PICTURE EDITOR Gail Nussbaum
FOREIGN PICTURE RESEARCH Rosemary Klein, London
    Gertrudis Feliu, Lausanne
ASSISTANT PICTURE RESEARCHER Gary S. Walther
COPY EDITOR Beatrice Gottlieb
TEXT RESEARCHER Connie Rogers Roosevelt
PRODUCTION MANAGER Carl Ward

AMERICAN HERITAGE PUBLISHING COMPANY, INC.
CHAIRMAN OF THE BOARD Samuel P. Reed
PRESIDENT AND PUBLISHER Rhett Austell
EDITORIAL ART DIRECTOR Murray Belsky
SUBSIDIARY RIGHTS DIRECTOR Beverley Hilowitz

TITLE PAGE: *This detail is taken from a contemporary painting of the building of Versailles by Flemish artist Adam Frans van der Meulen. A more complete view of the work may be seen on pages 12-13.*

## TEXT CREDITS

We are grateful for permission to quote from these copyrighted pages:
—pages 57;60: *Memoirs of Hadrian*, by Marguerite Yourcenar. Copyright 1954 by Marguerite Yourcenar. Reprinted with the permission of Farrar, Straus & Giroux, Inc. and Martin Secker and Warburg Ltd.
—page 95: *Prince of the Renaissance*, by Desmond Seward. Copyright 1973 by Desmond Seward. Published by Macmillan Publishing Co., Inc. and Rainbird Publishing Group Ltd. Reprinted by permission of the publishers.
—page 191: *The Glitter and the Gold* by Consuelo Vanderbilt Balsan. Copyright 1952 by Consuelo Vanderbilt Balsan. Reprinted by permission of Harper & Row, Publishers, Inc.
—page 210: *My Father, Mark Twain* by Clara Clemens. Copyright 1931 by Clara Clemens Gabrilowitsch; renewed 1959 by Clara Clemens Samossoud. Reprinted by permission of Harper & Row, Publishers, Inc.

Library of Congress Cataloging in Publication Data
Thorndike, Joseph J 1913-
The magnificent builders and their dream houses.
Includes index.
1. Architecture, Domestic. 2. Biography.
I. Title.
NA7120.T46 909 78-18371
ISBN 0-8281-3064-7
ISBN 0-8281-3072-8 deluxe
Book Trade Distribution by Simon and Schuster
A Division of Gulf & Western Corporation
New York, New York 10020
Ordering number: 13064—regular edition
                13072—deluxe edition

# CONTENTS

# INTRODUCTION

Plato said: "Every man, before he dies, should do four things: plant a tree, father a son, build a house, and write a book." The urge to build a house is certainly less universal than the urge to father a son but probably more common than the urge to plant a tree or to write a book. In some times and places, such as the American frontier, a man had little choice in the matter: he had to build his own house or sleep outdoors. In settled societies it is a matter of choice, but always there have been those who accepted the challenge. Some have built with their own hands, some with the help of neighbors, some with architect and builders, some (like Louis XIV) with the assistance of thirty-six thousand workmen.

In this book we will be concerned with those men and women who have put a great deal of themselves into their building. We will not be concerned with those who have built whatever seemed to be in fashion or those who meekly took what their architects offered. We will not, for instance, include Baron James de Rothschild of France who, when he saw the enormous country house that his nephew Mayer had built in England, ordered his builder to erect one just like it "only twice as big." We will be concerned with those who knew what they wanted, however different, original, or downright eccentric, and insisted on getting it.

The quality of magnificence, as we see it, lies not so much in the grandeur of the finished structure as in the spirit that created it. There is little magnificence in the rows of mansions that line the streets of the richest American suburbs or expensive villas that rise in posh resorts, each the creation of its architect and its interior decorator. But there is true magnificence in the weird and wonderful tower of stones that a French postman built in his backyard near Hauterives.

Magnitude is not the criterion. The emperor Hadrian employed armies of workmen, both slave and free, to lay out a country estate three quarters the size of Rome. Clarence Schmidt used only his own hands to assemble his private palace out of old doors and automobile parts. But both were inspired and dedicated builders.

Schmidt's junk palace fell victim to fire, as did P. T. Barnum's flamboyant Oriental pavilion called Iranistan at Bridgeport, Connecticut. Other remarkable edifices have suffered destruction less sudden but no less total. The palace of Nonsuch, built by Henry VIII to outshine the royal chateaux of France, fell eventually into the hands of Barbara Villiers, Charles II's mistress, who sold it off piecemeal to pay her gambling debts. It disappeared so completely that in 1959, when the Ministry of Works thought to excavate it, archaeologists had to search out old records before they could even know where to start digging. Having laid bare the foundations, they ran out of money and covered them up again.

The oldest construction on these pages is Persepolis, the ceremonial capital built by Darius the Great of Persia in the sixth century B.C., and burned by Alexander the Great in the fourth century. Its remote location and the blowing sands have protected its ruins now for more than two thousand years while later structures, such as the Golden House of Nero in Rome and Mrs. Astor's mansion on Fifth Avenue, have been pillaged or bulldozed to rubble.

Of all the dream palaces ever built, the one that conjures up the most extravagant visions is the "stately pleasure dome" that Kublai Khan, the Mongol emperor, built at "Xanadu, . . . Where Alph, the sacred river ran,/Through caverns measureless to man/Down to a sunless sea." Coleridge's evocation is no more wondrous than the factual account set down by Marco Polo, who visited Kublai's court in the thirteenth century. The khan was summering in the delicate bamboo pavilion supported by gilded columns with carved dragons on top, and guyed against the winds by two hundred silken cords. The khan rode to the hunt in an outsized howdah borne on the backs of four elephants and accompanied by ten thousand falconers. Of all this splendor nothing remains at Shandu (Xanadu)—on the rather ordinary river Alph 148 miles northwest of Peking—but a gate, set in a fragment of crumbling wall.

Despite the ravages of time, buildings can be as nearly permanent physical monuments as any man can leave. Colbert, the great finance minister of seventeenth-century France, put it to Louis XIV: "Your Majesty knows that, apart from glorious actions of war, nothing celebrates so advantageously the greatness and genius of princes than buildings, and all posterity measures them by the yardstick of these superb edifices which they have erected during their life."

Yet the urge to build is more than the yearning for immortality, more even than the primal nesting urge common to humankind. In its purest form it is a true creative impulse. "Sometimes," said Frederick Church, the builder of Olana, "the desire to build attacks man like a fever—and at it he rushes." It was said of Philip II, the grave, never-resting builder of the Escorial, that he had "the disease of the stone." Those afflicted with the malady cannot stop, as long as they have the energy and the means to keep on building. During a financial crisis in the Hearst publishing empire, Hearst's top executive, John Francis Neylan, had to explain to an angry judge why "the Chief" kept on adding to San Simeon when he was on the edge of bankruptcy. "Money as such bored him . . . . He is a builder . . . . His idea is to build, build, build all the time."

Such was the common impulse of those who appear in these pages.

Joseph J. Thorndike Jr.

# 1 RULERS IN SEARCH OF GLORY

"The duty of the prince is magnificence."
Such was the belief of Charles the Wise.
In following the French king's lead many
rulers have found that the best single way
to assert their power and grandeur was to
build castles and palaces. Some of them,
indeed, such as Louis of France and Philip of
Spain and Henri Christophe, the black king
of Haiti, made palace building one
of the absorbing enterprises of their lives.
The splendid structures that they left
behind now stand as their memorials.

*The Escorial, King Philip II's huge, bleak
monument to the glory of God and the power of
his empire, stands illuminated in the Spanish night.*

# Louis XIV's Versailles

*The Sun King's emblem, a Versailles motif*

When Louis XIV decided to build a chateau at Versailles to house the French court, hardly anyone was pleased. The Duc de Saint-Simon spoke for most of the courtiers when he wrote in his diary: "Versailles, the saddest and most barren of places, with no view, no wood, no water and no earth. . . . It is all shifting sand and marsh, and the air, in consequence, is bad. . . ." Few of the great nobles relished the prospect of giving up the excitements and comforts of Paris for life in a country house, no matter how grand.

Some of his counselors, with considerable prescience, warned the king that it would be a mistake to move the seat of government from Paris and thus isolate it from the people. But Louis was not worried about the people, he was worried about the nobles. He had seen in his youth what trouble they could make if they were left to thrash about in their own provincial lairs or to hatch plots in the salons of Paris. He wanted them where he could watch them, judge them, and keep them under control.

As the plans took shape, Colbert, his indispensable chief of finance, became alarmed. "This mansion," he told the king bluntly, "is concerned more with the pleasures and diversions of Your Majesty than with his glory." Already the tax revenues were being strained: "If Your Majesty desires to discover where in Versailles are the more than 500,000 écus spent there in two years, he will have great difficulty in finding them." Louis was undeterred. He wanted just what Colbert was afraid he wanted: a palace so big and so splendid that it would announce to all the world the power and glory of France and of its ruler, whose emblem was the sun.

Yet underneath these reasons of state, as Colbert suspected, the "Sun King" had other motivations. Louis hated the city; he loved the country. And most of all, he liked to build.

The first problem that came up in the planning of the new chateau was what to do about the hunting lodge which his father had built there. Louis Le Vau, his architect, wanted to tear it down and start afresh, but the king was adamant that the old brick building be left standing. Le Vau's solution was to enclose it on three sides in an "envelope" of honey-colored stone. What the visitor sees first when he approaches Versailles on the road from Paris is the façade of Louis XIII's old hunting lodge, embellished by Le Vau. The entire chateau, stretching two-fifths of a mile from north to south, can be seen only from the gardens on the western side.

From the time construction began in 1668, Louis XIV never missed a chance to visit the site, inspect the work in progress, and consult with Le Vau on the shape of a window or the placement of a terrace. In 1682, when he moved his court to the new chateau, 36,000 men and 6,000 horses were still laboring to get it completed. To the end of his reign, which lasted seventy-two years, Louis never stopped adding to the chateau, changing the rooms, and building new structures on the grounds.

The chateau was laid out in such a way as to place the king, in geography as in everything else, at the center of court life. His private suite (insofar as anything at Versailles could be called private) occupied the second floor of the central section of the old hunting lodge. It included his bedroom, study, reception room, dining room, council chamber, and smaller rooms for his clothes, his books, his medals, his hounds, and his wigs. In the south wing was the apartment of his queen, Marie Thérèse of Spain; in the north wing for many years were the rooms of his mistress, Mme. de Montespan.

The king's bedroom was the site of the great ceremony of *lever* (getting up), which marked the beginning of the royal day. Promptly at eight o'clock the First Valet (there were forty others), having slept in a trundle bed below the gilded balustrade that enclosed the king's own bed, awakened his master with the words "Sir, it is time." At 8:15, after the king had had a rubdown by his masseur and a brief check by his doctor, the First Gentleman of the Bedchamber ceremoniously drew back the curtains of the royal bed. This was a privilege so great that it was rotated among the heads of four great families, each of

*Louis XIV draped himself in ermine for this properly regal Hyacinthe Rigaud portrait.*

11

*The chateau of Vaux-le-Vicomte inspired Louis to build Versailles.*

whom served a year. A similar arrangement, designed to spread the honors, governed the dressing of the royal person. The procedure was split up into small duties, so that one noble offered the king the right sleeve of his shirt while another offered him the left, and so on with each article of dress.

At intervals in this lengthy process the king had a light breakfast and received visitors, beginning with those entitled to the *grande entrée*—the royal family, princes of the blood, and high officers of the crown. Then, while he was being shaved and even while he sat on the *chaise percée*, he received officials of the court, ranging from the Grand Chamberlain and the Grand Master of Ceremonies to the Master Falconer and the Master of the Hunt. Finally the doors of his council chamber were thrown open to "persons of quality," who were always gathered in a throng outside to present petitions for royal favor. At ten the king attended Mass, and at eleven he was ready for business.

A sharp distinction was drawn at the court between men of rank and men of power. Louis's ministers and public officials were chosen for their ability and often had no noble pedigree at all. These were men who met with him almost every morning in the hall adjoining his bedroom, as councils of war and finance and diplomacy and other matters of state. Others, no matter how lofty their lineage or how high their place at the dinner table, were denied any real power in the government. The Duc de Saint-Simon overheard the king on one occasion tell his own brother, the Duc d' Orléans, "Go along now. We are ready for council."

When the council was finished the king proceeded, with his usual train of courtiers, to the dining room for the midday meal. If his brother was there he handed the king his napkin and might be asked to sit down for lunch. But generally the king dined alone, watched at a respectful distance by twenty or thirty courtiers.

In the afternoon, when the weather was fine, the king's pleasure was hunting. To hunt the stag, the boar, and

*The royal carriage makes its way through an army of workmen*

The chateau of Vaux-le-Vicomte, built by Louis XIV's corrupt superintendent of finance, Nicolas Fouquet, both enchanted and enraged the king. Within a month after being entertained there, he had Fouquet imprisoned, and impounded the castle's sumptuous furnishings for his own future chateau, which would be designed by Vaux-le-Vicomte's architect, Louis Le Vau. For his site, the king selected Versailles, where his father had build a hunting lodge—which Louis set out to embellish beyond imagining. Within a decade, Versailles had become the scene of vigorous construction.

*The king forbade the destruction of his father's hunting lodge.*

*in this 1678 painting, while the king's chief minister, Jean Baptiste Colbert, studies the architect's plans.*

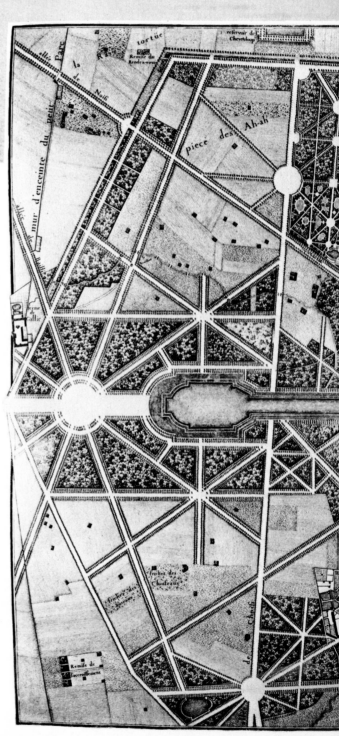

The façade of Versailles, which runs on for more than a quarter mile, is but a small element in what the Duc de Saint-Simon called the Sun King's plan of "tyrannizing over nature . . . subduing it by the force of art and money." As this 1746 map makes clear, Louis's vision included an aggregate of walkways, pools, fountains, and gardens. At right in the map, the village of Versailles surrounds the Place d'Armes, where three avenues converge on the forecourt. Beyond the chateau, a number of meticulously clipped gardens open out into the westward reaches of the complex, which include a cruciform grand canal, with the Grand Trianon sited on its northern arm. Louis Le Vau, the architect who designed much of Versailles, leans on a working drawing in the anonymous portrait shown below.

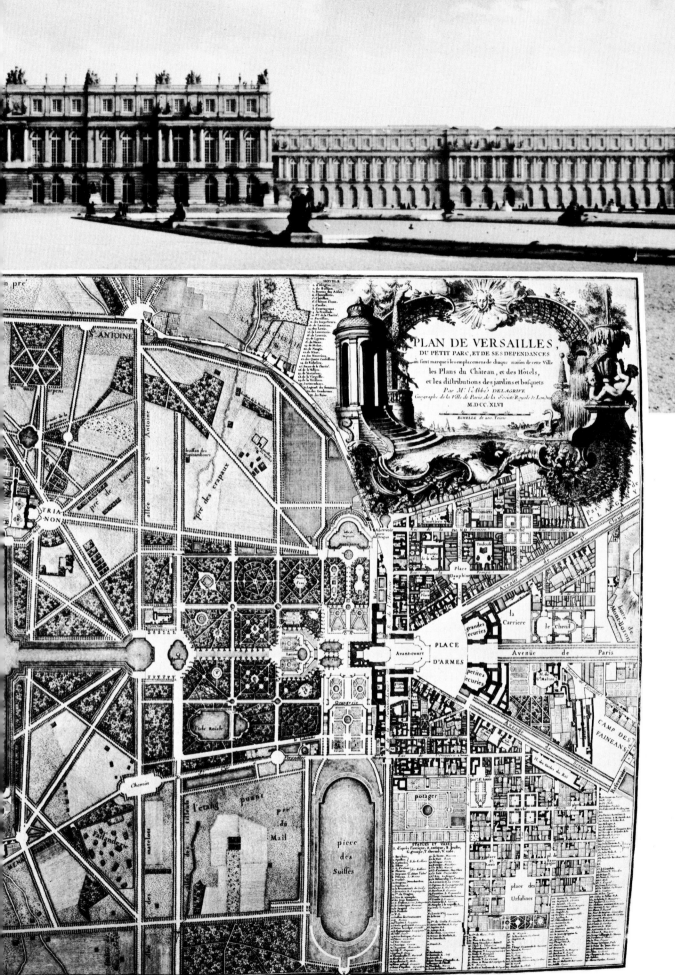

Views like this one of the façade of Versailles from the north garden prompted even so relentlessly cynical an observer as Mark Twain to enthusiasm: "You gaze, and stare, and try to understand that it is real, that it is on the earth, that it is not the Garden of Eden—but . . . you half believe you are the dupe of an exquisite dream."

*Costly as Versailles was, it did offer one advantage to the French economy by convincing Europe that the most exquisite furnishings came from France. As the Louis XIV style—exemplified by the table, commode, and chair at right—became synonymous with elegance, France began a lively export trade. Busiest of the luxury factories was that of the Gobelins, which made not only tapestries, but nearly all the furnishings for the palace. The tapestry at left shows Louis visiting the factory.*

wolf which abounded in the country around the chateau, Louis customarily kept six packs of hounds—a thousand animals in all. His horses were stabled in two handsome buildings with curved fronts that faced the chateau in the east. Designed by Le Vau, these quarters yielded nothing to the chateau itself in spaciousness and elegance of architecture. Surveying the stables, the Elector of Hanover remarked wistfully that he only wished his people housed him as well as Louis XIV housed his horses.

When Louis returned from the hunt or from walking in the gardens, he would usually visit the Marquise de Montespan. In this connection, it may be noted that one of the peculiarities of the design of Versailles is a paucity of corridors. In order to get from one suite to another one had to walk through the intervening rooms. In order to visit Mme. de Montespan Louis was accustomed to pass through the apartment of his previous mistress, Louise de La Vallière. This did not seem to bother the king, who could, without losing his aplomb, toss his pet dog to La Vallière as he passed through. But after a little of this treatment Louise departed for a nunnery, leaving her successor to enjoy the royal favor.

By the time Mme. de Montespan arrived on the scene the poor, sad, dumpy queen was ready to put up with anything Louis did, but La Montespan's husband was not so acquiescent. He was given to storming round the palace, talking pointedly of David and Bathsheba, or attaching a great pair of horns to the roof of his coach. Fortunately for the king's dignity, the Marquis de Montespan consoled himself by seducing a servant girl, dressing her in a soldier's uniform, and enlisting her in his regiment. For this behavior Louis had him put away.

Three times a week during the winter at seven o'clock the courtiers gathered in the magnificent suite of rooms which extended the length of the north side of the main building. These rooms were the particular pride of Charles Le Brun, the talented artist who designed and furnished the interior of the chateau. Late in the reign even they were outdone in splendor by the Hall of

*Duchesse de La Vallière*        *Marquise de Montespan*        *Marquise de Maintenon*

Mirrors, the great mirrored gallery which was added by Versailles's second architect, Jules Hardouin-Mansart. The public rooms were adorned with the treasures of the royal art collection and the products of France's finest manufactories: tapestries from Beauvais and the Gobelin works in Paris, porcelain from Rouen and St. Cloud, carpets from the Savonnerie, furniture clad in silver or inlaid with tortoiseshell and mother-of-pearl. Thousands of candles, reflected back from mirrors and silver and jewels, turned these rooms into a sparkling palace of light, without, however, doing much for the temperature on warm nights or for the quality of the air.

The evening's entertainments had something for almost all tastes: cards, billiards, dancing, concerts, and sometimes plays. But the greatest show of all was put on by the guests themselves. J. H. Plumb, the English historian, describes them: "Stiff-necked, dressed in clothes as bright as a peacock's feathers, the courtiers of Louis XIV moved about Versailles to the strains of Lully and Couperin like great heraldic beasts caught up in a ritual dance—elegant, stylized, yet intensely taut." No wonder they were taut; in that society a duke was judged by the grace of his dancing step, a countess by the wit of her reply to a compliment. If an ambassador's wife unthinkingly took a place at table above a princess of the blood, her country might suffer the disfavor of the French government. Careers might be blighted or fortunes lost by a slip of the tongue. On one occasion, when Mme de Maintenon had succeeded Mme. de Montespan as the royal mistress, Jean Baptiste Racine so far forgot himself as to mention in the royal presence the name of another playwright, Paul Scarron. Scarron, as it happened, had been Mme. de Maintenon's husband. The king froze, turned away, and never spoke to Racine again.

Many of the "great heraldic beasts" of the court were men with ancient titles, vast estates, and power over great regions of France. By keeping them in the golden cage of Versailles, at the pain of incurring royal displeasure, Louis made them little more than personal retainers,

vying with one another for a nod or a favor. It was partly in order to house all these great personages and their households that Versailles needed to be so big. The new south wing of the chateau was given over in large part to the apartments of the royal princes and other of the king's relatives, including his illegitimate children, who all required space for their growing families.

The most elevated member of the royal house, next to the king, was his brother, the Duc d'Orléans, known simply as Monsieur, who was heir to the throne until the birth of a dauphin. Monsieur was a foppish, mincing little man who liked jewels, fancy clothes, and handsome young men. He was married to a massive German wife, Princess Elizabeth Charlotte of the Palatinate, known as Madame. It was Madame's custom to spend her evenings observing the exotic personalities of the court and her afternoons writing vivid, earthy, often hilarious accounts of the goings-on to her German relatives. Louis never let on that he had her mail intercepted and thus obtained an unvarnished view of his court and courtiers. Madame, for her part, never let on that she knew perfectly well that the king read her mail. She was fond of Louis, as he was of her, and used her letters to tell him things that she could not tell him to his face. Comparing the king's new mistress, Mme. de Montespan, with his old mistress, Louise de La Vallière, she wrote: "La Montespan was whiter complexioned than La Vallière; she had a beautiful mouth and fine teeth but her expression was always insolent. One had only to look at her to see that she was scheming something. . . . At least La Vallière was clean in her person, whereas La Montespan was filthy. . . ."

The entire north wing of the chateau was occupied by the nobles, all of whom were allotted rooms of a size and elegance proportionate to their rank, very much as if they were officers of a modern corporation. One whole corridor was known as the *rue des Noailles* because it was occupied by members of that distinguished family. Many of these lodgers had fine houses of their own outside the palace grounds, but they clung jealously to their rooms in

A Ce S.ᵗ Jean de raphaele                    B Ce Jamt du Dominichini

the chateau, even in some cases to tiny, ill-lit cubicles. Saint-Simon, who kept his nook on the top floor for forty years, never gave up complaining about its size and location, but he never gave up the room either. Persons of rank but without real social acceptance might exist in these dim corridors for years on end, so far out of the brilliant scene that hardly anyone remembered they were there. On one occasion, when Madame needed a lady in waiting, someone suggested the Duchesse de Brancas who, separated from her husband, had been holed up in a far corner of the chateau for many lonely years. Appointed to be Madame's lady in waiting, she returned to society as if from exile.

Elsewhere in the chateau accommodations had to be found for the principal officers of government, the ambassadors of foreign countries, and the officials of the court, along with their households and retainers. By the differing counts of chroniclers, there seem to have been between two thousand and five thousand persons in residence at Versailles, not including the servants. The kitchen staff alone numbered fifteen hundred.

In Louis's conception of Versailles the gardens were just as important as the building. They are the work of André Lenôtre, a figure to rank with Le Vau and Le Brun in the team of talented artists who created Versailles. West of the grand terrace of the chateau the gardens stretch for a full mile along either side of a grand canal. Lenôtre liked austere geometrical arrangements of trees, shrubs, and finely patterned stone or pebble walkways. As for flowers, he thought them "fit only for nursemaids to look at from their upstairs windows." Since the king insisted on flowers, Lenôtre had to plant them, but not in nearly as great profusion as they grow in the chateau gardens today. He preferred trees, which he brought to Versailles, often fully grown, in vast quantities. "Six thousand elms from Flanders," was one recorded shipment. The Marquise de Sévigné described "entire leafy forests being ferried to Versailles" on ox-drawn wagons. Hidden away among the trees in the

*Owing largely to redecorating by Louis XV, little remains of Louis XIV's original bedroom, seen in the contemporary drawing at top. The bed has disappeared, and there is now a tapestry instead of paintings by Raphael and Domenichino. But the railing is thought to be authentic, and so is the relief representing France on the wall against which the bed used to stand.*

21

grand design of the gardens are walks, ponds, sculptures, grottoes, arches, gazebos, an outdoor theater, a menagerie, and an aviary for exotic birds.

The greatest glories of this magical landscape are the fountains—fourteen hundred of them, ranging from delicate jets to the spectacular fountain of Apollo, the sun god, rising out of the water in his horse-drawn chariot. Since there was no river at Versailles, water had to be pumped from the Seine by means of the great machine at Marly, a series of fourteen bucket wheels turned by two hundred twenty-three pumps. When Louis walked in the gardens the fountain controls were manned by a force of workmen, so that each sector of the waterworks could be put into action just before the king got there. It was one of Louis's frustrations that he could never get enough water to keep all the fountains running all the time. In 1683 he turned the problem over to Maréchal de Vauban, the chief engineer of the French army, who deployed thirty thousand men to construct an aqueduct from the river Eure. But after three years they had to be called away to fight and they never finished the aqueduct.

The gardens made a perfect setting for the festivals which Louis gave every so often for the diversion of his court and the astonishment of foreign visitors. At one of the first of these splendid affairs, in 1668, the evening began with a promenade through the gardens, the gentlemen on foot, the ladies in carriages. The trees were hung with fruits, and pathside tables were spread with confections to tempt the guests as they passed. Dinner was served in a *salle de verdure*, built especially for the occasion, at little silver tables by the light of hundreds of candles. Before dinner the guests saw a new play written for the occasion by Molière, with intervals of opera and ballet performed to music also written for the occasion by Lully. Afterward there was dancing until nearly dawn, when the sky was lit up by a display of fireworks.

As usual, the king himself was the most interesting part of the show. Beside him at dinner sat Louise de La Vallière, his first recognized mistress, pregnant and in

tears. Louis had eyes only for the the scintillating Marquise de Montespan, who sat at the next table.

The king's lifelong extravaganza was a costly show, but not without its profitable side. Because Louis insisted on the best of everything, Versailles became a showcase of the finest furniture and tapestries and china and silver that French craftsmen with royal patronage could produce. It set the taste of Europe and established France as the source of the beautiful things that every noble family from England to Russia wanted to furnish their palaces. Even Colbert, who had to find the money to pay the royal bills, recognized that Versailles was a boon to the export trade in luxury goods. The palace itself was the envy of every visiting monarch from James II of England to Peter the Great of Russia. Before the end of the reign, palaces bearing the unmistakable mark of Versailles were rising in Vienna, Potsdam, Dresden, Munich, St. Petersburg, and many lesser cities. Even Washington, D.C. owes its design in large part to Versailles.

Both France and the monarchy paid a heavy price for the splendor of Versailles. The cost of the court, combined with the cost of frequent wars, used up every penny that Louis's finance ministers could raise, leaving nothing for more constructive uses. But the splendor was not dimmed until the time of the revolution which, some seventy years after the death of the Sun King, engulfed his great-great-great-grandson.

In the last years of his reign, beset by military defeats and falling revenues, saddened by the deaths of both his son and his grandson, Louis must have had misgivings about the way he had used the wealth of France. For on his deathbed he called for his great-grandson. To the five-year-old boy who would succeed him he gave this last advice: "You are going to be a great king. Do not copy me in my love of building or my love of warfare. . . . Remember your duty and your obligations to God, see that your subjects honor Him. Take good advice and follow it, try to improve the lot of your people, as I, unfortunately, have never been able to do."

*The mill at Le Hameau was one of nine thatch-roofed buildings that made up the fantasy village.*

# A BUCOLIC FANCY

For all its splendor, Versailles
could be one of the least pleasant
places on earth. Courtiers spent
their days under constant observation,
endlessly moving through the thick
reek of unwashed bodies and uncollected
sewage. There was no real escape,
but royalty could—and did—get some
privacy in retreats set on remote
corners of the royal estate.
A century after the Sun King's
time, Marie Antoinette, the wife
of his great-great-great-grandson Louis
XVI, built the most unusual of these:
Le Hameau, an idyllic toy village
where she could divert herself
with mock rural simplicity. There
she milked a herd of prize Swiss
cows in a marble-walled stable
and watched while carefully selected
peasants ground corn and did laundry.
Her cottage had a thatched roof, rude
walls, and wormholes augered into its
timbers; but inside she could eat
cake in rooms every bit as glittering
as those in the main palace.
It was at Le Hameau that the
doomed, silly queen got word, on
the evening of October 5, 1789,
that an angry crowd was on the way
to her make-believe hamlet. She
left immediately, and never returned.

*Marie Antoinette sits with her children in this portrait, one
of more than twenty done of the queen by Elisabeth Vigée-Lebrun.*

*Marie's beguilement with idealized rural life may have
reached its apogee when she ordered four of these Sèvres
porcelain milk pails for the royal dairy at Rambouillet.*

# THE QUEEN'S BOUQUET

*This doorway leads from the Petit Trianon's dining room to a salon.*

Another of Versailles's charming outbuildings that eventually became a hideaway for Marie Antoinette was a delightful little palace called the Petit Trianon. Built by Louis XV as a smaller version of the grand and rather chilly Trianon that Louis XIV himself had put up on the outskirts of his estate, the Petit Trianon eventually inspired copies in places ranging from the estates of American financiers to the holdings of an Iranian merchant prince. The Petit Trianon was to have been a refuge for Louis XV and his mistress Mme. de Pompadour, but she died before the palace was finished. The king transferred his copious affections to his last mistress—the Comtesse du Barry—and it was with her that he first occupied the completed building in 1768. When he died in 1774, his son, Louis XVI, presented the chateau to his own queen, Marie Antoinette, saying, "You love flowers. I have a bouquet to offer you—the Trianon." Determining to play as slight a role as possible in court life, the willful young queen withdrew to the Petit Trianon. There she decreed that the few courtiers chosen to visit her should behave without the usual ceremony: no one was to get up when she entered or left the drawing room. She held court there until the Revolution cut short her feckless reign. Some years later an English visitor made his way to Versailles and "to *le Petit Trianon* . . . which . . . has, in the strange metamorphosis things as well as men have experienced in France, become a common inn."

*The queen slept in this canopied bed.*

*Mme. de Pompadour is shown here in porcelain*

26

*The design of the Petit Trianon marked the end of the vogue for heavily ornamented buildings.*

*This view of Sans Souci, most luxurious of Henri's castles, was published in 1830, a decade after his death.*

*A bust of Henri Christophe*

# Henri Christophe's Sans Souci

On a mountaintop on the north coast of Haiti a gray stone fortress thrusts out, like the prow of a ship, above the port of Cap-Haïtien. There is nothing else like it in the West Indies or anywhere else in the western hemisphere. It is the citadel of La Ferrière, built early in the nineteenth century by Henri Christophe, the black king of Haiti.

The citadel was built to withstand the expected attack of a French landing force. It was meant also to throw back any challenge from the king's enemies in Haiti. But in the event it served neither purpose. The French attack never came, and when his own troops rebelled they found the king, sick and undefended, in his palace of Sans Souci, at the foot of the mountain. Today the palace lies in ruins, but the citadel still stands, a monument to Henri Christophe and to the first and only successful slave rebellion in the Americas.

Henri Christophe was born in 1767, probably to slave parents, on one of the West Indian islands. An official record of the time says that the island was Grenada, which was then French. But the descendants of some of his comrades believed it was St. Kitts (properly St. Christopher), a British island that may have given him his last name. In any case, he ran away from his plantation at twelve and was carried to Saint-Domingue (later Haiti) by a ship captain who, according to one account, sold him to a French naval officer as a manservant.

The French officer was part of a naval force sent by King Louis XVI, at the behest of Benjamin Franklin, to recruit West Indian troops to help the American Revolution. Whether Christophe saw any action is not known, but he probably heard plenty of talk about liberty and rebellion before he was returned to Haiti. Perhaps because of his services in the expeditionary force or perhaps because of his faithful work in the management of an inn at Cap-Haïtien, Christophe found himself in his early twenties one of the colony's few free Negroes.

Saint-Domingue was the French or western part of the island of Hispaniola, whose eastern or Spanish part was

called Santo Domingo. At that time it was the richest of all the French sugar islands. Its population was a fateful mix of 40,000 whites (who owned most of the plantations), 28,000 free mulattos (who also owned some plantations), and 452,000 African slaves. As in the American South, there were kind masters and cruel masters. But the atmosphere of a tropical island, where Frenchmen came to make quick fortunes rather than to make homes, gave free rein to plantation owners who were capable of cutting off the leg of a runaway slave, or shooting one to try out a pistol, or burying one to his neck and using his head as a target for bowling balls.

All the pressures that were pent up in such a caldron of cruelty were brought to the surface after 1789 by the events of the French Revolution. The first trouble came when the National Assembly in Paris granted to all freemen, irrespective of color, the right to vote in elections for the Colonial Assembly. When the mulattos tried to exercise their franchise as freemen, the whites resisted and killed their leaders. The spirit of rebellion spread quickly to the black slaves, who began burning houses and killing the planters' families, often with cruelty that matched or exceeded that of the masters.

Out of this terror rose a black leader named Toussaint, who had been a planter's coachman. A frail, wizened little man with a high, narrow forehead, Toussaint proved himself a master of military maneuver in the jungles and mountain ranges of the island. Soon he was known as L'Ouverture (Opening) because so many villages opened up before his forces. Henri Christophe, by now a young man of massive build and commanding air, joined him as a sergeant.

The war for Haitian independence went on for twelve years, during which Christophe rose to be one of Toussaint's generals, commanding the northern district centered on Cap-Haïtien. In 1802 Napoleon, who had succeeded the men of the French Revolution, sent his brother-in-law, General Charles Victor Emmanuel Leclerc, with a force of twenty-two thousand men to

reassert French control over Haiti. Expecting to find a barbarous, ragtag army, the French were met instead by an imperious Henri Christophe in the full uniform of a French general, leading well-disciplined troops. Christophe could not prevent the French landing, but he burned the city, including his own handsome house, before retreating to join Toussaint in the hills.

In their attempt to subdue the Haitian rebellion the French tried force, deception, and bribery. Toussaint was captured by a ruse and shipped off to France, where he soon died in a cold prison. The blacks were officially freed and then officially enslaved again. Finally yellow fever doomed the French expedition. By 1803 the French had been driven out, and Jean Jacques Dessalines, Toussaint's lieutenant, came to power, with Christophe returned to his old command of the north. As a military commander the fierce Dessalines had won the admiring nickname "Tiger," and when he heard that Napoleon had taken the title of emperor he declared himself an emperor too. But Dessalines had no talent for governing a country, and within three years he was killed in a mutiny by his own troops. A republic was proclaimed, with Port-au-Prince as its capital and a mulatto named Pétion as president. But Christophe refused to give up control of the northern section, centered in Cap-Haïtien, where he assumed the title of governor general. After a few military skirmishes it became apparent that neither government had the power to conquer the other.

The economy of Haiti was in ruins. In the years of revolution the plantation hands had come to feel that the end of slavery meant the end of work. The fields were untended, the crops were unharvested, the treasury was empty. About the only product of value was the gourd, the basic staple of the Haitian diet. In the part of Haiti under his control, Christophe at once declared all gourds the property of the state, gathered them in, and then resold them to the peasants for the coffee crop. The coffee he sold to Europe in return for gold and issued currency, in a unit known then and since as the gourde.

Christophe was determined to prove that a country of ex-slaves could match the countries of Europe in efficiency and prosperity and culture. Engineers, teachers, and doctors were brought from Europe. The cities were rebuilt, the plantations put back in production. No one was allowed to be idle. Before long, Christophe's people got the idea that the ruler was everywhere, riding through their villages on his white horse or spying upon them through a telescope from the terrace of his palace.

It was equally important, Christophe felt, that the ruler and his court be a match for European royalty. Within a year Christophe crowned himself King Henri I and created on the spot a nobility to surround him. There were four princes, eight dukes, twenty-two counts, thirty-seven barons, and fourteen knights. Each rank had its own robes and regalia, yielding nothing in finery to the costumes worn at the French imperial court. Europeans might laugh at some of the titles he bestowed—the Duke of Limonade and the Duke of Marmalade—but they came from the names of plantations, as the proud

domains of France had furnished titles. Foreign visitors who expected to be amused by the spectacle of ignorant ex-slaves strutting around in the trappings of European nobility came away impressed by the standards of courtesy and polite behavior enforced by the king. Henri might be uneducated, but he surrounded himself with educated English advisors. He might be illiterate, but he dictated letters that were as polished and well-phrased as those exchanged by European diplomats.

His palace at the foot of the mountains twenty miles from Cap-Haïtien was built to assert the majesty of the black king and the dignity of the ex-slave country. It was made of bricks plastered over with yellow stucco and roofed with red tile. A mountain stream flowed under the rooms of state on the first floor to keep them cool in the stifling summer heat. The rooms were floored with marble and mahogany and decorated with paintings, sculptures, tapestries, and furniture imported from Europe. There were suites for his queen, Marie Louise, his son and heir Prince Jacques, and his two daughters,

Améthiste and Athénaire, with their servants and tutors.
The king gave his palace the name Sans Souci, the same
as that of the palace of Frederick the Great of Prussia.

If Sans Souci was built to impress the Europeans with
the civilization of free Haiti, the citadel above it was built
to impress them with its impregnable strength. King
Henri's predecessor, Dessalines, had begun to fortify the
peak of La Ferrière, but it was Henri who made it into
the citadel that still stands. The walls rise eighty to one
hundred thirty feet above their bases on the steep mountainside. They are twenty to thirty feet thick. The stones
that went into them had to be hauled up the peak by
teams of mules and, in places so steep that animals could
not get a footing, by sheer manpower. In the embrasures
of the walls stood three hundred sixty-five cannons,
supplied with balls and powder. Food and water for ten
thousand men were stocked to withstand a long siege.

But Henri Christophe, who understood so well the uses
of power, had no sense of its limits. He ignored the
mutterings of the people who had been freed from
slavery only to be impressed into labor as hard as that
which built the pyramids. He displayed a capricious
temper. When he was displeased with his military chief,
Richard, Duke of Marmalade, he assigned him to manual
labor on the walls of the citadel. When through his
telescope he spied a farmer sleeping in the door of his
cabin at midday, he had one of the cannon trained on the
man and blasted him to bits.

So long as the king was himself no one dared challenge
him. But one day in the spring of 1820, as if by
premonition, he went to Mass for the first time in
memory, in the little town of Limonade. As he attempted
to rise from his knees before the altar he crashed forward
to the floor. When he regained consciousness two days
later his right side had been paralyzed by a stroke. In the
next weeks the king made a brave show of ruling as
before. On good days he was carried out to a palace
terrace to issue orders, hear petitions, and receive reports
of his kingdom. But the reports told of defections in the

army, including that of Duke Richard, and of disaffec-
tion among the peasants, who looked with envy on the
easier life to be enjoyed in the republic to the south. By
October rebels controlled the capital, Cap-Haïtien.

On October 7, 1820, King Henri summoned all his
reserves of energy for a demonstration of his powers. For
two hours he had his body massaged with a mixture of
raw rum and red peppers. Then he was dressed in his
parade uniform with the blue coat and the white knee
breeches and the festoons of gold trim. With clenched
jaw he hauled himself to his feet, took a step—and did
not fall. The palace guard was paraded on the terrace.
His white horse was saddled and ready. Determined to
lead the troops in battle again, the king moved slowly,
without help, across the terrace. He was almost to the
horse when he stopped and sank slowly to the pavement.

The next day he tried again. With an equerry
supporting his paralyzed right side, he moved along the
front line of troops, looking into the eyes of each man.
Then, fighting to control his slurred speech, he reminded
them of what he had done to make Haiti respected in the
world. When he was finished, the guard cheered, "Vive
le roi!" and marched off, many of them to join the rebels.
Most of the king's ministers had already left.

Later that evening Henri gave his queen, Marie
Louise, a receipt for gold bullion worth six million dollars
that he had deposited for her in the Bank of England.
Then he said good-by to his family, sent them away, and
put a bullet through his heart. With the help of a few
faithful followers, the heavy body was dragged up the
mountain to the citadel and dumped into a lime pit to
keep it from the pursuing rebels. The queen and the two
princesses were allowed to take ship for England, but the
prince royal was killed. In the course of time Henri's
kingdom was reunited with the republic to the south.
From the day of his death until the present day adven-
turers have picked and pulled at the stones of the fortress
in search of the treasure that the black king was supposed
to have hidden there. None has ever been found.

# Philip II's Escorial

In the spring of 1573 long and melancholy processions began to move, with funeral pomp, across the high central plateau of Spain. By order of Philip II they were escorting the bodies of the royal dead from their separate graves to a final burying place that the king had built to receive them. From the monastery of Yuste, where they had lain for sixteen years, came the bones of Philip's father, the Emperor Charles V. From the royal chapel at Granada came the bodies of his mother, Isabella of Portugal, and his brother, Don Fernando. From Talaveruela in the west came the remains of Doña Leonora, the king's aunt, who had been queen of France. The royal tombs at Valladolid in the north yielded three bodies: another aunt, Mary of Hungary; another brother, Juan, who had died in infancy; and Philip's first wife, Maria of Portugal.

In the processions that conveyed the royal remains rode bishops and priests, bands of monks, and high officials of the Spanish state. They made slow progress, making many stops along the way for village ceremonies. At last they all met at the tomblike palace that Philip had erected on the bleak slopes of the Guadarrama mountains, the Royal Monastery of San Lorenzo of the Escorial. Outside the severe walls of the building they were placed on a catafalque, draped in black brocade, for further long ceremonies.

While the rites were going on a great wind came down from the mountains, tearing off the funeral drapes and scattering them over the bleak landscape. The court chronicler who was present to record the event had no doubt what caused the wind: "Because these things tormented the bad angels and so many pious and holy acts made them angry and envious . . . the princes of Darkness began to stir up the weather and to let loose a wind so fierce and furious that it caused wonder and terror."

For all that the Devil could do, Philip's plan was successfully carried out, and the coffins were disposed in a chapel to await the completion of a marble pantheon.

*A brooding bust of Philip II*

A parchment was placed inside each of the coffins, inscribed with the name, birth date, and date of death of the deceased, together with the date when the body had been moved. The In-gathering of the Royal Corpses was the culmination of Philip's grand project for the Escorial. Now it could be all three things that the king had planned it to be: a tomb, a monastery, and a palace.

Each of these purposes had its separate origin. In his will the Emperor Charles had enjoined Philip to build a proper tomb for their family, the Spanish Hapsburgs, and, since Philip revered his father, this injunction had the force of a command. The second purpose had its origin on the battlefield of St. Quentin, where his army defeated the French on August 10, 1557. Since that was the feast day of Saint Lawrence, Philip vowed then and there to build a great church in memory of that early Christian martyr. At its altar monks of the Hieronymite order would offer prayers in perpetuity for the souls of the royal family.

The third purpose of the Escorial was to serve as seat and symbol of the enduring power of Spain. Philip's own tastes were simple to the point of asceticism, but he was profoundly conscious of his position as head of the most powerful state in Christendom. His palace would have to bespeak his majesty.

Philip went about the choice of a site with the slow care and study that he gave to every problem. A commission, made up of architects, builders, physicians, and religious philosophers, was appointed to conduct the search. Since Philip had recently established his capital in Madrid, the palace should be close enough to that city for easy travel but far enough away to give the king privacy. At length the commission settled on a site thirty miles from Madrid, near the village of El Escorial, which took its name from the heaps of slag (scoria) piled up from worked-out iron mines. Philip, after tramping about the country, studying the wildlife, and tasting the water, gave his approval. The monks who were going to live there were disheartened by the austere aspect of the site

and the cold winds that blew down from the mountains. But austerity was just what Philip wanted.

It is sometimes said that the ground plan of the Escorial derived its inspiration from the gridiron on which its patron saint, Lawrence, was roasted to death by the Romans in the third century. However that may be, the edifice is broken up into rectangular courts and inner buildings, with an extension projecting on one side in the position that the handle of a gridiron would occupy. From the outside it is a great block of pale gray granite, with small windows and scant decoration, rising starkly from the plateau. Only the fine dome of the church, rising above the walls, saves it from looking like a prison.

Philip's first choice for an architect was Juan Bautista de Toledo, who had studied under Michelangelo in Rome and had worked on the plans for St. Peter's. His assistant, and later his successor, was Juan de Herrera. Their royal master kept them both on a tight leash, constantly demanding and rejecting new plans until in the end they were more Philip's than the architects'. He did nothing to lessen the forbidding aspect of the building by deciding, midway in the construction, to double the number of monks in residence and add an extra story to accommodate them.

In the twenty-one years that it took to complete the building, Philip never relaxed his close attention. When the weather was clear he would drive up into the mountains and, sitting on a natural stone seat, watch the work through a spyglass. At other times he could be seen climbing about the scaffolding with his superintendent of construction, Antonio de Villacastin. As the years passed, his ministers despaired at the burden on the king's time, and his subjects groaned at the cost. Fifteen hundred workmen had to be paid. It could never have been done without the steady flow of gold and silver from the mines of the New World.

At last the palace was finished, though Philip would never cease work on the decoration as long as he lived.

*Juan de Herrera, who served as Philip's chief architect for seventeen years, produced hundreds of working drawings, and submitted each to his king's ceaseless scrutiny. Philip approved the cross section of the church, right, and the ingenious mill, center, which funneled water from a reservoir to turn the drive shaft, but demanded that the six finials on the church façade, far right, be replaced with Biblical statues.*

There were four thousand rooms, one hundred miles of corridors, eighty-six staircases. Not until the Pentagon was built in Washington, four centuries later, could any building on earth rival those statistics.

The center of the whole edifice, and its architectural glory, is the church, one of the finest in Christendom. Philip never let the thousands of monks forget that he had built this great edifice, which he called a monastery, so that they might send up their prayers, in unending, irresistible volume, for the souls of the royal dead. He himself frequently joined the monks at matins or vespers, in a high balcony of the church. The altar is so placed that when the priest is saying Mass he stands directly over the tomb of the Emperor Charles in the pantheon below. On a balcony to the left of the altar is a group of gilded bronze statues representing in life size Charles, his queen, his daughter, and his two sisters. In a matching group on the right are the kneeling figures of Philip, his son Don Carlos, and three of his four wives. Absent only is his second wife, Mary of England, who has her tomb and memorial in Westminster Abbey.

The throne room at the Escorial is, by standards of royalty, singularly unimpressive. Philip seldom entered it, and when he did he used his father's old campaign chair for a throne. A more flamboyant room is the Hall of Battles, with a one-hundred-eighty-foot mural that depicts the victory of John of Castile over the Moors in 1431. But the finest room in the palace, aside from the church, is the library, with tall cases of leather-bound books and a ceiling adorned with symbolic paintings of the seven liberal arts. Philip was an avid collector of books, who never let an auction come up without seeking to buy its treasures for the royal collection.

Even stronger than Philip's love of books was his love of painting. The walls of the Escorial, as well as the galleries of the Prado museum, testify to his zeal in bringing great artists and great paintings to Spain. He would have preferred Michelangelo to design the building and Titian to decorate the altar, but both those

Italian giants were in their eighties and declined to make the journey to Spain, as did their junior, Veronese. Philip fell back, therefore, on Italians of lesser genius and on Spaniards. There were disappointments. Federigo Zuccaro came from Rome with the highest recommendations to paint a *Nativity* for the high altar. But when Philip inspected the painting his meticulous eye noticed that Zuccaro had depicted one of the shepherds carrying a basketful of eggs—an unlikely errand for a shepherd at midnight. With his usual courtesy the king said nothing but the painting was removed from the altar.

In the case of El Greco, the greatest Spanish painter of the time, Philip's concern for realistic detail played him false. El Greco was commissioned to paint a *Martyrdom of Saint Maurice*, but it, too, was denied a place on the altar. The king was put off by El Greco's distorted figures and lurid colors, and faulted him for placing the actual scene of the saint's bloody execution in the middle distance instead of the foreground.

Philip showed excellent taste in acquiring paintings by such artists as Titian, Tintoretto, and Veronese. Remarkably, his favorite seems to have been Hieronymus Bosch. The painting that Philip kept beside his bed was the Dutch artist's strange triptych in which panels of Paradise and Hell flank a central "Garden of Earthly Delights." A dreamlike meadow is filled with naked people engaged in wonderfully imaginative, arcane, sometimes mildly obscene but always passionless pastimes. Historians have never ceased to wonder what satisfaction or what moral the pious, ascetic king could have found in this scene of languid abandon.

The king's private apartment, where the Bosch hung during his lifetime, is the most fascinating and most revealing part of the Escorial. "For God a palace, for me a hut," Philip had instructed his architect, and his own rooms testify to the sincerity of that sentiment. They consist mainly of a small study with whitewashed walls and simple furniture, and an even smaller bedroom with a narrow bed and a door that opens directly onto the altar

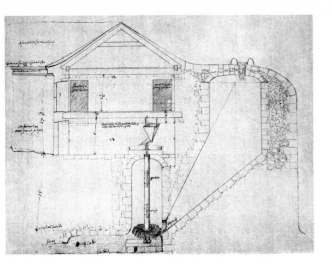

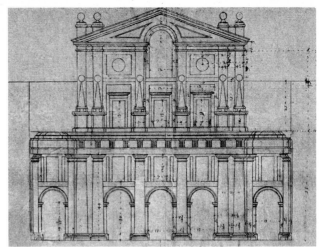

of the church. It was here in these monkish cells that the most powerful ruler in the Western world chose to spend his working and sleeping hours. It is here that we can best understand the nature of this complicated man.

The English-speaking world has never wanted to hear much good of Philip. He was the secular pillar of the Inquisition, implacable in his persecution of heretics and not loath to attend the autos-da-fé in which they were sometimes dispatched. He was the archenemy of the Reformation and of all the Protestants in Europe. He was the cruel oppressor of the Netherlands, the ultimate commander of troops that put whole Dutch villages to the sword. He was the prideful tyrant who sent the Armada against Elizabeth's England.

The people who saw Philip in his daily life knew no such monster. They were, of course, on his side of the religious wars, and what the Protestants of the northern countries looked upon as fearful vices, they perceived as virtues. They knew Philip as a king of simple tastes, deep piety, and an iron sense of duty. If he seldom smiled in public it was because he trained himself never to show emotion. If he ran his court with the strictest etiquette in Europe it was because he felt it his kingly duty to proclaim the majesty of Spain.

In the few private hours that he allowed himself, Philip was a devoted husband and father. Dynastic duty had governed the choice of each of his four wives: Princess Maria of Portugal, who died in childbirth after two years; Queen Mary of England, who never left her native country in the four years before she too died; Princess Elizabeth of Valois, who lived for eight years and left him two daughters to comfort his old age; and Princess Anne of Austria, who lived for ten years and gave him his heir, the only surviving child of four. Considering the political motivation for his marriages and their relatively short duration, it is remarkable that Philip was loved by all of them, even poor Mary, whom he saw only during a visit to England. At home in the Escorial, when he was not at his desk, he played games with his children. He

was unfailingly courteous to his humblest subjects and especially to his servants. No man can be without merit who is uniformly liked, as Philip was, by his wives, his children, and his servants.

Philip himself had once been a merry little boy with golden hair and blue eyes, but the burdens of monarchy had been loaded upon him at an early age. He was schooled for kingship by a master of the art, his imperial father Charles V. At fifteen he was given nominal command of an army in the intermittent war with France, and at 16 he was made Regent of Spain while Charles went on campaign. At 21 he made a grand tour of the Spanish possessions from which he returned in 1551. Thus he was well prepared for rule when his father, old and tired at 56, retired to a monastery and turned his throne over to Philip.

"Depend on none but yourself," Charles had counseled him, and Philip had taken the advice to heart. He could not be his father, a gregarious, boisterous man of the world, mixing freely with people of all nations and classes, dominating them by personal magnetism. But he could rule by the power of a first-rate mind and by endless hours of work. He trusted no one completely and never gave more than limited authority to anyone. If he had one strong and able counselor, such as the warlike Duke of Alba, he took care to balance him with another counselor of equal but opposite talents, such as the pacific Prince of Eboli. He made all decisions himself. He believed, as all the monarchs of the time believed, in the divine right of kings, but he also had an almost painful consciousness of the divine responsibility of kings.

The Spanish realm that he inherited from his father was the first in history on which, it may be truthfully said, the sun never set. It included not only Spain (and later Portugal) but the Netherlands, the duchy of Milan, most of the Italian peninsula south of Rome, a section of what is now France called Franche-Comté, most of the Mediterranean islands, and several enclaves on the coast of North Africa. Though he did not inherit the title of

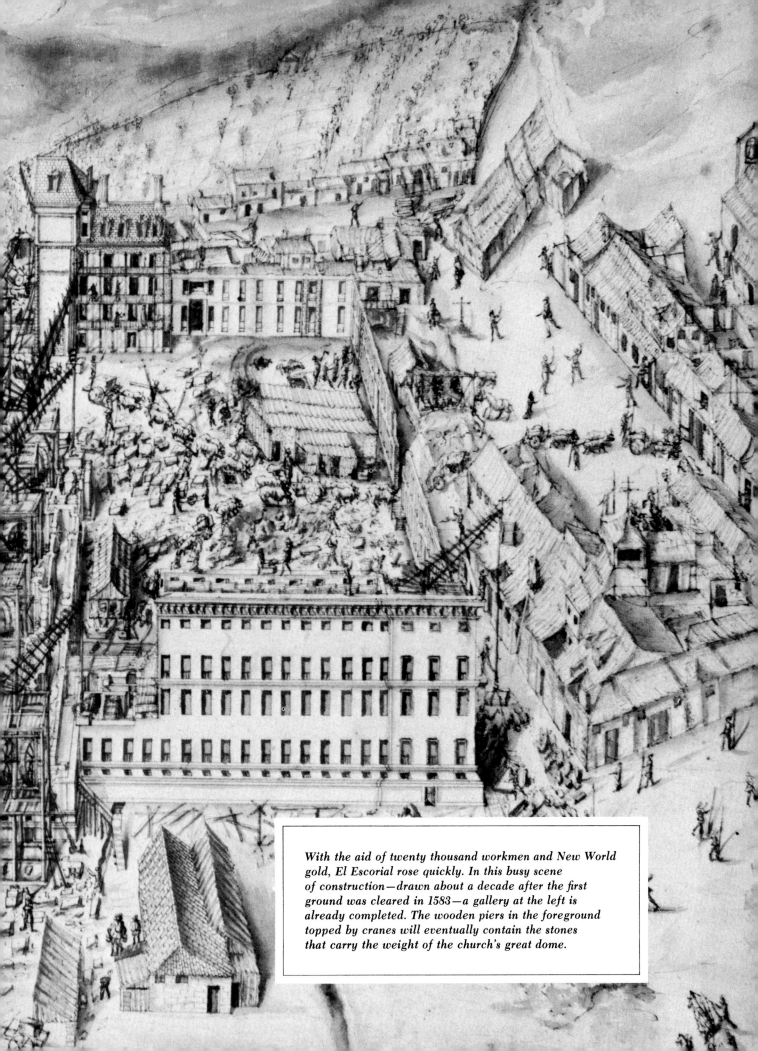

With the aid of twenty thousand workmen and New World gold, El Escorial rose quickly. In this busy scene of construction—drawn about a decade after the first ground was cleared in 1583—a gallery at the left is already completed. The wooden piers in the foreground topped by cranes will eventually contain the stones that carry the weight of the church's great dome.

*Within his splendid castle, Philip slept in this stark room. Oddly, this most dour of kings loved the dreamlike, sensual complexities of Bosch's "Garden of Earthly Delights" (detail at right), and the painting provided an incongruous decoration for his austere bedroom.*

Holy Roman Emperor, he wielded, through his uncles and cousins, considerable influence over the fractious German states that made up the so-called Empire. Overseas he ruled directly most of South America, all of Central America and part of North America, as well as a great number of islands in the Pacific and colonies on the coast of Asia.

From all these vast possessions reports and problems came to Philip's desk in the Escorial. He read the reports and dealt with the problems, though it required almost every waking hour. Some of them were of great moment: the continuing war with France, the repression of Protestant rebellion in the Netherlands, the threat of the Turks, the treatment of slaves in America. But others were merely time-consuming: the appointment of a priest in a country parish, the repair of a road, the precise punishment of a heretic. He was, it was sometimes said in contempt, "the chief clerk of the Spanish empire."

More than any monarch before his time, he ruled by paper. With only two secretaries to help him, he composed his letters with care, signing each one *"Yo, El Rey"* (I, the King). Sometimes in his later years his fourth and last wife, young Anne of Austria, would sit by him, sprinkle each letter with sand, and hand it to one of the little infantas, who would solemnly carry it across the room to be sealed by a secretary. But the paperwork piled up, and letters went long unanswered. "If death came from Spain," his viceroy for Naples once complained, "we should live to a very great age."

Philip would not be hurried. He pondered problems at exasperating length, sent them back and forth for the preparation of what we would call "position papers" and the formulation of what we would call "options." For twenty years he endured the affronts of English statesmen and the outrages of British sea captains, trying always to bring the obstreperous Elizabethans to heel by marriage or diplomacy, before resolving at last to send a naval force against them. It was at his desk in the Escorial in the years before 1588 that he planned the Armada,

ordering every detail of its construction and supply, choosing its officers, writing the orders that, in the event, doomed it to defeat. He was at his desk, too, when a dispatch brought final confirmation that the Enterprise of England was lost. The king, it was reported, barely looked up from his papers, saying, "I sent my ships to fight against men, not the winds." He thanked God that he still had the power to build another armada.

But the king was getting old, and other things were uppermost in his mind. One of these was the provision of sacred relics to gratify the faithful and give the monks visible objects of devotion. Soon after the church was finished Philip had got hold of the anklebone of its patron, Saint Lawrence, as well as the head of Saint Hermenegildo and other bits and pieces of holy men. By the time the church was consecrated the king had enriched it with relics of all twelve apostles, and the real ossuary bonanza was still to come. Fearing what might happen to Catholic relics at the hands of Protestant heretics, he sent his agents to make a sweep of German holy places. In an epic of smuggling, four packing cases of holy bones and other sacred treasures were brought out through Switzerland and Italy, passing, as the court chronicler put it, "through a thousand dangerous encounters with heretics." After an irreverent American, John Hay (later to be Secretary of State), visited the Escorial in the nineteenth century he wrote that Philip had collected in all "seven thousand four hundred and twenty-one genuine relics—whole skeletons, odd shins, teeth, toenails, and skulls of martyrs—sometimes by a miracle of special grace getting duplicate skeletons of the same saint." Hay overlooked what some considered the most precious relics of all, a piece of wood said to have come from the True Cross and a scrap of linen handkerchief believed to bear stains of the tears that Mary shed at the foot of the Cross.

Philip needed all the solace he could get from the relics and from the hours that he spent in his bedroom looking out on the altar. For in worldly affairs his reign was

*Eleven Spanish kings lie in marble sarcophagi in the pantheon, the heart of the Escorial.*

ending in disappointment and defeat. The Enterprise of England had failed. The Dutch rebels had stood off the Spanish fury to establish their own republic. The flow of gold from America, which had financed Spain in lieu of a prosperous economy, was slowing down. Though no one knew it then, the Golden Age—at its height in the reigns of Charles and Philip—was coming to an end.

Most troubling of all to Philip was the problem of the succession. The heir to the throne had been his oldest son Don Carlos, but Carlos had been from the first a willful and unstable boy. The situation between father and son was not improved when Philip arranged for Carlos to marry a pretty French princess of the boy's own age, Elizabeth of Valois, and then, for reasons of foreign policy, decided to marry her himself. Two years later Carlos, while supposedly on his way to a rendezvous with a porter's daughter, fell downstairs and broke his skull. He recovered, after one of the first trepanning operations in Europe (or, as some thought, after the bones of a long-dead holy man were dug up and placed in the bed beside him). But he was never the same again, and some years later the king was given persuasive evidence that Carlos was plotting against him with the Dutch rebels. Reluctantly Philip had his son confined in Madrid, where he died six months later, thus furnishing the king's enemies with a rumor that he had poisoned his son.

There had been four other princes, but the savage death rate in the royal family left Philip at the end with only one son, his namesake, to ensure the succession. This Philip was so unpromising a prince that during the king's long last illness, while he lay festering with sores, Philip II lamented: "God, who has given me so many kingdoms, has denied me a son capable of ruling them."

The physical and mental defects that began at this time to disable the Spanish royal family were not accidental. Philip II's grandmother, Juana, had been a certified lunatic. His two brothers had died young of epilepsy. Philip himself had always been of sickly body and melancholy spirit. Worst of all, the evil genes of the royal family had been reinforced by a deliberate policy of close inbreeding. Of Philip's own marriages, two were to first cousins, and the fourth, which produced his heir, was to a niece. (Mary Tudor was distantly related, but childless.)

Philip's half brother, Don Juan of Austria, offered, by contrast, living evidence of the merits of outbreeding. The illegitimate son of Charles by his liaison with a middle-class German girl named Barbara Blomberg, Don Juan was in everything but title the handsome, healthy model of a dashing prince. At twenty-four he became the hero of Europe as commander of the Christian forces against the Turks in the battle of Lepanto. Philip, who had given him his opportunity, had thereafter to contend with his half brother's ambition to be a king.

The long, protruding Hapsburg lower jaw is a striking, though superficial, result of the inbreeding in the royal line. The Emperor Charles had such an underbite that he could never quite close his mouth, a condition which may have led him to grow a beard and which made a problem for Titian when he painted portraits of the ruler. Philip II escaped this family affliction in its extreme form, but it returned in his descendants, as may be seen in the pitiless portraits by Velasquez. In Charles II the jaw was so grotesquely lengthened that the king could not chew food at all and had to live on a soft diet.

Philip III, who succeeded to the throne in 1598, lived up to his father's poor opinion of him. An ineffectual

*Philip housed his books and manuscripts in this 175-foot-long library.*

monarch, he preferred hunting and dancing to work and allowed the reins of government to fall into the hands of ministers. His death at forty-three, as reported by the French ambassador, François de Bassompierre, advertised the swift decline of the Spanish royal house. This Philip, according to the ambassador, was sitting beside a hot brazier. He complained of the heat, but the functionary who enjoyed the privilege of moving the brazier could not be found, so the king sat there until he suffered a fever which shortly killed him. Others reported that the king had erysipelas and would have died anyway, but Bassompierre's version appealed to such republicans as Thomas Jefferson for its reflection of the absurdity of court etiquette and the stupidity of kings.

The next king, Philip IV, who reigned from 1621 to 1665, was no better, and the last of the direct line, Charles II (the emperor had been Spain's Charles I), was feeble-minded. He reigned nevertheless for thirty-five years, passing his time by playing childish games with his patient wife or picking strawberries in the palace garden and counting them over, hour after hour. When he died, mercifully without issue, the crown passed to a French grandnephew, Philip of Anjou, who carried fewer of the malign Hapsburg genes.

None of Philip's successors spent much time at the Escorial, though in their moods of black melancholy and superstitious piety they went there to do their penances and contemplate their deaths. At last the Royal Pantheon was completed beneath the floor of the church, and the royal corpses were moved into it in 1654. In the reign of Charles II the Escorial was gutted by a fire that destroyed many of its books and paintings, but the childish king had enough grasp of his heritage to order the building restored.

The Escorial fell on hard times again a hundred years later. Early in the nineteenth century a visitor calling himself Frederic Quilliet visited the Escorial and gulled the monks into showing him their choicest treasures. In 1808, when Napoleon Bonaparte crowned his brother Joseph king of Spain, Quilliet returned with a French army and directed the soldiers as they removed the best paintings and the most valuable reliquaries for shipment to Napoleon in Paris. King Joseph himself demanded the monastery's entire library, and had thirty thousand books and forty-three hundred manuscripts moved to Madrid.

Joseph's brief, bitter reign triggered a savage civil war, throughout which troops were billeted in the Escorial. With the French defeat in 1814, the throne reverted to Ferdinand VII, a vicious, inept monarch who, despite the faults that gained him his reputation as "the worst king Spain ever had," did restore the Escorial.

Ferdinand's renovations notwithstanding, the vast building remained cold and forbidding. It attracted a great many tourists, some of whom shared the sentiments of the French critic Théophile Gautier: "I cannot help considering the Escorial to be the dullest and most dismal building imagined for the mortification of their fellow men by a gloomy monk and suspicion-haunted tyrant. . . .

"I advise those persons who have the idiocy to maintain that they are bored to go and pass three or four days at the Escorial; for there they will discover what real tedium means, and will find amusement for the rest of their lives in the thought that they might be in the Escorial, but are not."

In the middle of the nineteenth century the throne was occupied by a queen—the first in Spanish history since Isabella the Catholic. The new queen, another Isabella, made her own feminist contribution to the Escorial by beginning construction of another pantheon—this time for lesser queens and royal children.

The Hieronymite order of monks, meanwhile, was disbanded in a time of anticlerical agitation, and the eternal prayers for the Spanish kings were interrupted. But a growing respect for the country's heritage, more patriotic than religious in nature, came to the rescue of the Escorial, which is now maintained by a government agency. Within the monastery, monks of another order, the Augustinians, again send up prayers, albeit in reduced volume, for the great king who built it.

# GARDENS OF
# EARTHLY DELIGHTS

*The gazebo in Jay Gould's rose garden at Tarrytown, New York*

*"God Almighty," said Bacon, "first planted a Garden."*
*And ever since the expulsion from Eden, men have enjoyed*
*helping nature conform to their own particular ideas of*
*paradise. Naturally, the rich have always been able to bring*
*the most resources to the process, and the gardens*
*they designed—and the things they put in them—*
*are delightful indicators of both the people and their eras.*

*The Comte d'Artois ordered the face and breasts of this sphinx modeled after those of his mistress. He had several copies placed in the gardens of the Bagatelle, which he built in the Bois de Boulogne in Paris in the 1770's.*

*Living ornaments, these white peacocks are picking their way through Isola Bella, perhaps the most famous of all Italian gardens. Built in the 1600's by Count Vitaliano Borromeo, the garden is made up of ten terraces that rise, dense with baroque statuary, more than a hundred feet above Lago Maggiore.*

*This pair of stags at bay sprayed water into a small pool in the gardens of Schwetzingen, near Baden, Germany. The estate was designed in the early eighteenth century as a summer retreat for the rulers of the Palatinate.*

Topiary—sculpting shru[bs and]
trees into ornamental d[esigns,]
represents the gardener['s art]
at its most demanding. [The]
garden at left, with its
painstakingly maintaine[d]
boxwood fantasies, was [begun]
in 1689 for James Grah[am,]
of Levens Hall in Westr[orland.]

When, in the nineteenth [century,]
Thomas Brayton of Rho[de Island]
decided to give topiary [a try,]
he did so with great zes[t. His]
estate, Green Animals, [boasts]
some eighty privet beas[ts. At]
left, a gardener touches [up the]
oldest inhabitant, a gira[ffe]
that has been flourishing[there]
for more than sixty year[s.]

The ingenious boxwood [design]
at right fills one of four [squares]
of greenery that make u[p the]
twelve intricate acres o[f the]
garden of Villandry, wh[ich fronts]
a chateau built in the fi[rst]
half of the sixteenth cen[tury in]
the Loire valley by Jea[n le Breton,]
a minister of Francis I.

Stowe, the greatest of the eighteenth-century English gardens, was commissioned by Richard Temple, first Viscount Cobham, and featured a number of small temples set in stands of trees. At left is the staunchly named Temple of British Worthies, with busts of such men as Shakespeare, Bacon, Newton, and Milton. It survived the transformation of Stowe into one of England's best schools, but a temple of Bacchus made way for a chapel.

Set on a hillside, the gardens of the Villa Garzoni, at Collodi, Italy, were built at the behest of the Garzoni family, who bought a medieval castle in the mid-seventeenth century and transformed it into a sumptuous villa. The showcase of the palace is the garden, whose terraces rise to a pool watched over by an immense statue of Fame.

outline beds of coleus, geraniums, and begonias. The
stunted dome on the right-hand box bush second from
the bottom is the result of a German grenade that was
hurled at attacking Italian partisans during World War II

# 2 KINGS FOR THEIR PLEASURE

While many rulers built to display their powers, others put up monumental dwellings solely for their own pleasure—and their own private reasons. Hadrian built his Roman villa for sentimental retirement, Ludwig built three Bavarian palaces for romantic dreaming, George IV built Brighton Pavilion for partying, and Francis I built Chambord for hunting. Each of these royal homes shows what can be done with a love of architecture, an unrestrained imagination—and plenty of public money.

*Headless statues stand by a partially restored pool in the emperor Hadrian's villa, a private retreat three quarters the size of Rome.*

# Hadrian's Villa

When Hadrian became emperor in A.D. 117 he was forty-one years old. The son of a provincial Roman family settled in Spain, he had spent most of his adult years in the army. He seems to have been quite happy in a life of continual travel, moving back and forth from one military post to another. But he must have felt the basic human need to settle down somewhere, sometime, because soon after he came to the purple he began accumulating land near a town that the Romans called Tibur and the modern Italians call Tivoli. The site he chose was at the foot of the Sabine hills, where it is hot in summer but warm and pleasant the rest of the year. We do not know whether at that time he was already drawing plans for the astonishing villa he would eventually build there.

Though Hadrian's family roots were in the small town of Italica, near Seville in southern Spain, he had been schooled in Rome, probably by Greek tutors. Early in life he acquired a love of Greek culture, Greek art, Greek ideas. He also fell in with the luxury-loving young Roman aristocrats—perhaps to the alarm of family friends, for he was sent back to Spain for two years. When he returned to Rome at seventeen, it was to begin a career in the combined civil and military service of the empire under the wing of his father's cousin Trajan, an army commander under the emperors Domitian and Nerva. Hadrian was serving with a legion on the German frontier when imperial couriers arrived to tell Trajan that the Senate had appointed him emperor.

During the nineteen years of Trajan's rule Hadrian was never far from his side or at least from his guiding hand. He was with Trajan during his campaigns against the German tribes and in the Middle East. In the field Hadrian rose to command of a legion and eventually to command of the entire army of the east. Between campaigns he climbed the political ladder as praetor, provincial governor, and consul. Soon it was clear to leaders of the army and government that Hadrian was being groomed as Trajan's successor. The choice was

*Though the marble is damaged, the emperor*
*Hadrian still looks impressive in this early bust.*

made even more obvious when Plotina, the emperor's wife, arranged a marriage between Hadrian and Trajan's grandniece, Sabina. It was a diplomatic union, supported by no love on Hadrian's part and eventually by hatred on Sabina's. But between Hadrian and Plotina, the empress, there was a close bond of affection and esteem. When Trajan on his deathbed drew back from the final step of adopting Hadrian as his son and official heir, it was said that Plotina persuaded him to sign the decree of adoption or even issued it in his name.

Hadrian, the provincial, had little love for Rome, or Rome for him. The capital saw little of its new ruler. Most of his next ten years were spent on a series of journeys, first north to Gaul and Germany and England, where he spent the winter, then to Africa, Greece, and Asia Minor. Wherever he went he devoted a major part of his time and his treasury to putting up new public buildings and restoring old ones.

Hadrian's historic role, as he conceived it, was not to expand the empire but to consolidate the conquests of his predecessors. In this he was brilliantly successful. He pulled back the borders in the east to the valley of the Euphrates, a natural frontier, fortified the line of the Rhine and Danube in Germany, and built in the north of England the great wall which bears his name, to keep out the wild Picts and Scots. Throughout the vast realm where Rome held sway, men could travel in safety and live in peace—so long as they gave allegiance to Rome and paid its taxes and accepted its tokens of authority, including most fatefully the divinity of the emperors.

Hadrian had been since boyhood an athlete, a hunter, and a mountain climber. Given a strong body and unending curiosity, he never wearied of travel. In her marvelous evocation of the man in her fictional autobiography, *Memoirs of Hadrian*, Marguerite Yourcenar has him say: "In my twenty years of rule I have passed twelve without fixed abode. In succession I occupied palatial homes of Asiatic merchants, sober Greek houses, handsome villas in Roman Gaul provided with baths and

hot air heat, or mere huts and farms. My preference was still for the light tent, that architecture of canvas and cords. Life at sea was no less diversified than in lodgings on land: I had my own ship, equipped with gymnasium and library, but I was too distrustful of all fixity to attach myself to any one dwelling, even to one in motion. The pleasure bark of a Syrian millionaire, the high galleys of the fleet, the light skiff of a Greek fisherman, each served equally well. The one luxury was speed, and all that favored it, the finest horses, the best swung carriages, luggage as light as possible, clothing and accessories most fitted to the climate. But my greatest asset of all was perfect health: a forced march of twenty leagues was nothing; a night without sleep was no more than a chance to think in peace. Few men enjoy prolonged travel; it disrupts all habit and endlessly jolts each prejudice. But I was striving to have no prejudices and few habits. I welcomed the delight of a soft bed, but liked also the touch and smell of bare earth. . . . I began to know each mile of our roads, Rome's finest gift, perhaps, to the world. But best of all, and unforgettable, was the moment when a road came to an end on a mountainside, and we hoisted ourselves from crevice to crevice, from boulder to boulder, to catch the dawn from an Alpine peak, or a height of the Pyrenees."

Though he had come from the simple, rugged far-western province of Spain, Hadrian preferred the older, more cultivated lands of the Greek-speaking east. He sought out poets and philosophers, matched wits with them, and made them part of his entourage. It was in Bithynia, at the eastern edge of the empire, that he found a beautiful boy named Antinoüs, whom he kept with him for the rest of the boy's life. Some of his biographers like to believe that Hadrian regarded Antinoüs as a substitute for the son he did not have. But he never adopted the boy or did anything to train him as a successor. Nine years later, when Antinoüs drowned, mysteriously, in the Nile, it is recorded that Hadrian "wept like a woman," and shortly afterward he decreed that Antinoüs had become a

The "Island Nymphaeum," at left, served Hadrian as a quiet retreat where he could pull up a drawbridge behind him and be totally alone. The island appears at location (A) on the model opposite, a scholarly re-creation of the immense villa. Also shown are the Pecile (B), a piazza whose surrounding wall is the only major one left standing anywhere in the villa, and the Canopus (C), Hadrian's copy of a shrine on the Nile.

god. Statues of him, which were soon erected throughout the empire, show him with a soft, sensuous body and a rounded, rather sullen face—a far cry from the old Greco-Roman ideal of manhood.

In making his favorite a god Hadrian carried to absurdity the custom of conferring posthumous divinity on imperial personages. In polytheistic lands this vain whimsy was accepted with a shrug, and when an emperor died a new god merely took his place among the old gods. But to the monotheistic Jews and Christians it was a blasphemy not to be endured. Hadrian's greatest mistakes as emperor were to crush Jewish revolts with brutal force and to keep the Roman state on its fateful collision course with Christianity.

Wherever he went, meanwhile, Hadrian built. He built arches and temples and theaters and forums and aqueducts and baths. He built whole cities, as often as not named Hadrianopolis.

In the imperial train, traveling alongside all the guards and secretaries and military commanders and civil administrators, Hadrian had his personal staff of architects and masons. He was himself a trained architect. When he ordered a building to be put up or a restoration to be carried out he sometimes drew the designs himself and always took close interest in the plans drawn by his staff. An anecdote, possibly apocryphal, told by an ancient biographer concerns the emperor's own design for the Temple of Venus and Rome, which he built in the Forum. When Apollodorus of Damascus, a famous architect, was shown the plan he commented sharply that the roof was too low for the seated statues in the temple, that if the goddesses wanted to get up they would bump their heads. Hadrian, according to the story, was so incensed that he banished Apollodorus and later had him executed.

As Hadrian approached the time when he would want to settle down, he began the construction of a home for himself at Tivoli. Though called a villa, it is in fact a vast residential complex, intended to fill the needs, reflect the tastes, and call up the treasured memories of one extraordinary man. It does not have a grand overall design but consists of many separate structures and areas, all placed with relation to the sun and the vistas and the land forms rather than to each other. By the time Hadrian died, leaving it still unfinished, the estate covered seven square miles, three fourths the area of the city of Rome. At times it had taken the labor of eighteen thousand men and had used up enough brick and stucco and marble to build a provincial capital.

It is hard today to visualize the villa as it looked in Hadrian's day. It has been a ruin now for upward of fifteen hundred years, since the countryside was sacked by the Goths. During the Middle Ages its memory was so lost that peasants of the area thought it had been an ancient city, which they called Tivoli Vecchio. When the learned, urbane Renaissance pope, Pius II, rode through the ruins in 1461, he found that "the walls once covered with embroidered tapestries and hangings threaded with gold are now clothed with ivy. Briers and brambles have sprung up where purple-robed tribunes sat and queens' chambers are the lairs of serpents." It remains in much the same condition today.

Nevertheless, the popes and nobles of the Renaissance found many artistic treasures amid the ruins. Slabs of marble were stripped off to build their palaces, and statues were carted away to adorn rooms and gardens. Today there is hardly a major museum in Europe that does not boast its share of sculptures from Hadrian's villa. As late as the middle of the twentieth century tourists were free to pick up whatever scraps they could find. What remain are great structures of brickwork too large to be taken away, and a few works of art recovered by more scrupulous excavators.

One of the reasons Hadrian wanted the villa was to house the enormous quantities of pillars, statues, mosaics, and decorative objects that he brought back by the wagonload from his travels in far-off lands. But he returned from his travels with more than objects. He

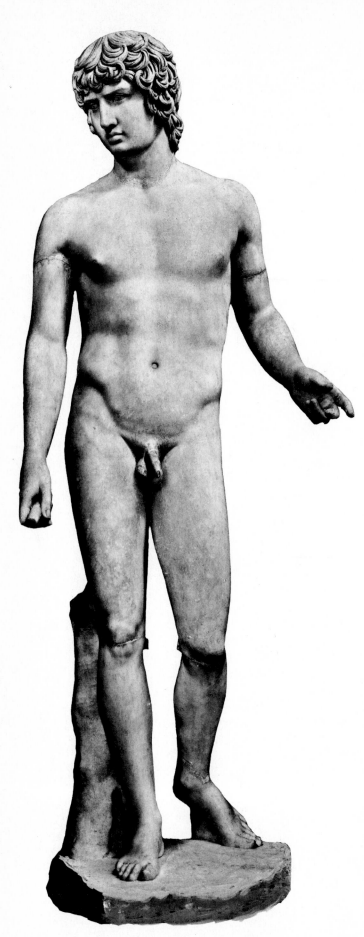

returned with the memory of buildings and places he had
liked, and these took physical form at the villa. To some
degree they were actual reproductions. More generally,
they attempted to recapture the spirit of the original,
sometimes only in certain features or on a smaller scale.
Again, Mme. Yourcenar speaks in the emperor's voice:
"The Villa was the tomb of my travels, the last encampment of the nomad, the equivalent, though in marble, of
the tents and pavilions of the princes of Asia. Almost
everything that appeals to our taste has already been
tried in the world of forms; I turned toward the realm of
color: jasper as green as the depths of the sea, porphyry
dense as flesh, basalt and somber obsidian. The crimson
of the hangings was adorned with more and more
intricate embroideries; the mosaics of the walls or pave-
ments were never too golden, too white, or too dark. Each
building-stone was the strange concretion of a will, a
memory, and sometimes a challenge. Each structure was
the chart of a dream."

One part of the villa that inspired this passage is the
Pecile, a structure that recalls the Stoa Poikile in Athens,
a painted portico adorned with scenes of Marathon and
other Greek battles. Only one section of rough brick wall,
strippd of its marble facing, still stands; but it was once a
rectangular portico enclosing a reflecting pool and gardens, where Hadrian could stroll with his intellectual
friends, as Zeno strolled in the Athenian original. Elsewhere we find a belvedere called after Plato's Academy
and a pavilion overlooking a valley that Hadrian named
the Vale of Tempe, for the lovely valley in Thessaly.

The villa was alive with water—water spurting from
fountains, playing over the gardens, cascading down
flights of steps, bubbling up in nooks and grottoes,
swirling gently through a moat that ran around the
interior walls of the dining room to cool it in summer.
Brought by an aqueduct from the river Anni, the water
was used to supply kitchens, gardens, fountains, and
baths. Finally it was used to sluice out the latrines before
flowing back to the river.

Enough remains of the baths to suggest that they were a smaller but more luxurious version of the great public baths built in Rome and other cities throughout the empire. The central feature of such an establishment was a large building containing a hot room (*calidarium*), warm room (*tepidarium*), and cold room (*frigidarium*). A bather would be anointed with oil (since the Romans had no soap) and then scraped by slaves using strigils, which were metal instruments with dull curved blades. Thus cleansed of sweat and grime, he would commonly spend some time in the hot room and a shorter time in the steam room, which was directly over the furnaces, and then finish off with a plunge in the pool of the cold room. Included within the baths were courtyards for gymnastics, ball games, wrestling, and other forms of exercise, as well as arcades for strolling and even libraries for reading.

The most photogenic area in the estate today, because it has been partially restored, with some columns and statues put in place, is the Canopus. The original, from which it takes its name, was a sanctuary of the Egyptian god Serapis, which stood at the head of a canal near Alexandria. During his travels Hadrian had been enchanted by the little waterway with its festive boats and flowery banks and its typically Egyptian atmosphere of sexually charged religion. Hadrian had been there with Antinoüs, and later, not far from there, Antinoüs had drowned. The place held poignant memories that Hadrian tried to recall at Tibur with a long marble pool, colonnaded walks, sculptures of gods and nymphs and Nile-green crocodiles, and a temple-like fountain house at the end.

The secret heart of the villa, however, is not there but in a curious circular enclosure, adjoining the palace complex of living quarters and public rooms. Enclosed within high walls but open to the sky, this retreat consists of a circular marble colonnade which surrounds a moat, which in turn surrounds a marble island, reached by a drawbridge. On the island are the remains of nine little rooms surrounding an atrium with a tiny garden and fountain. Soon after they were excavated in the eighteenth century, someone labeled them a maritime theater, apparently in the belief that aquatic shows might have been staged there. Later archaeologists speculated that this was the place where Hadrian came to be alone: one little room was for music, another for poetry, another for painting, and so forth. To Eleanor Clark, in *Rome and a Villa*, the island was the setting of a game: "Hadrian is playing Robinson Crusoe, as everyone does in childhood and longs to do forever after; the island is the oldest, most necessary image, older than the Dying God; that is the true romantic impossible, to be separated from the rubs and nudges and impurities of society by the primordial, deathly medium of water; the perfect assertion of self and the regions of the dead are alike surrounded by water. Of course it is a game; in reality Crusoe goes crazy; but the poetry is true, and the form in this case charming."

All these are guesses, but the feeling persists that this little island was the sanctum sanctorum of the imperial villa. Hadrian was an old man by Roman measure when he finally settled down at his villa, and his health was broken. Arteriosclerosis made his limbs heavy with dropsy and caused his nose to gush blood and brought on fits of sudden anger. But he still had the power of mind to perform for Rome perhaps his greatest service. An absolute ruler, with superb judgment of men and no children of his own, he addressed himself to the problem of choosing a successor. His choice fell on a senator of integrity and high ideals whom history knows as Antoninus Pius. Looking still further ahead, Hadrian then persuaded Antoninus to adopt as his own potential successors two outstanding youths, of whom one survived to become the emperor Marcus Aurelius. Under these noble-spirited emperors the Hadrianic peace was extended for another fifty years, giving Rome a last golden age before the return to despotic rule and the beginning of the barbarian invasions.

# THE PALACE THAT BECAME A CITY

*A bust of Diocletian from a frieze in his mausoleum*

A century and a half after the time of Hadrian, the Roman emperor Diocletian conceived the idea of a mammoth self-contained country estate on the bay of Split in what is now Yugoslavia. Diocletian loved building—his baths in Rome covered more than thirty acres—and while he struggled with the titanic problems of an empire on the verge of collapse, thousands of workmen descended on a tiny, barren fishing village and began clearing land for a walled enclosure some seven hundred feet long and six hundred wide. Octagonal battle towers rose to protect the walls, and within them two colonnaded streets intersected to divide the enclave into four wards, each larger than the village the palace had usurped. One of these was dominated by the ruler's mausoleum, a circular affair encrusted with a double tier of columns that did nothing but support their own weight, a bit of showy uselessness one critic thought particularly appropriate since "Diocletian came to Rome when the rose of the world was overblown, and style forgotten."

By A.D. 305, when Diocletian abdicated his power after a twenty-one-year reign to go into voluntary retirement, his palace was ready for him. There, clad in the finest fabrics and gems the empire could supply, he received an occasional guest, who had to kneel and kiss the hem of his robe, for Diocletian had decreed himself a god. One of these visitors, an old lieutenant of the emperor's, came begging him to return to power and put an end to the civil wars that had begun to tear apart the world beyond the opulent calm of the palace. Diocletian replied that if his guest could only see the fine cabbages he was growing in his garden, he would not dream of asking him to leave his sanctuary.

Diocletian died in 313 or 316, but his palace survived in a curious way. In the centuries following the emperor's death, Split became a city whose inhabitants lived in the original chambers of the palace. Christians held their services in the old pagan temples, medieval warrens went up on a foundation of Roman baths, and Venetian conquerors built homes there from Roman stone. Today, as Split approaches its seventeen-hundredth year of continuous inhabitation, the town has spilled far beyond the old walls. But much of the palace remains: taxis pick up their fares in the shadow of the battle towers, and tourists lift their drinks beneath café umbrellas scattered in between Diocletian's colonnades.

*The south front of Diocletian's palace still stoo*

*...tact when an English engraver did this view of Split in 1764.*

*The "genius of undying fame" greets King Ludwig II in this nineteenth-century painting.*

# Ludwig II's Castles

*A fairy-tale princess searching for the ultimate dream castle would do well to look in the vicinity of Munich. There she could have her choice of three fanciful palaces built late in the nineteenth century by Ludwig II, the "mad king" of Bavaria. Author Mary Cable visited all of them to write the following essay, which is adapted from an article in* Horizon *magazine.*

They called him the Crazy King! Well, I will tell you something," the guide on the tourist bus confided into a loudspeaker. "The Crazy King was *not crazy at all!*"

We were parked alongside a souvenir-and-postcard stall on the grounds of Schloss Linderhof, the sumptuous hunting lodge built some eighty years ago in the Bavarian Alps by King Ludwig II. Warm May weather had brought out sightseers, including a good many Bavarian peasants, and the atmosphere was festive, almost carnival. Souvenirs and post cards were selling briskly and so, at the outdoor restaurant nearby, were beer and wurst.

The guide was a glum and discouraged-looking man, but now that he began to speak of Ludwig, a note of enthusiasm came into his voice. "He was against war, he was against Prussia, and he loved art—so they said he was crazy! He was also very religious—so religious that he could not marry anyone because he was secretly in love with his cousin, the Empress Elizabeth of Austria." Here the guide paused and, with something like royal disdain, looked at the apathetic tourist faces before him. "Now we get out of the bus and we go through the castle. He hated crowds, the great king. He was a real Bavarian, he liked to go away to the mountains. In Munich they said he was so extravagant he must be crazy—but today the State of Bavaria can afford to keep up its other old castles because of the admission fees at Linderhof, Neuschwanstein, and Herrenchiemsee. So who's crazy? Don't touch anything and don't walk on the parquet."

The Bavarians, who love fairy tales, cherish this one—a potpourri of truth, fantasy, and speculation about King Ludwig. Although the real Ludwig, a stout, unhappy man, died at the age of forty in 1886, shortly after being taken in hand by psychiatrists, a fairy-tale Ludwig still survives: a tall, blue-eyed youth with dark wavy hair who did exactly what he pleased—which was to build castles. The three strange, resplendent castles he built, each grandly and remotely placed and glittering with riches, are so impractical as to be of use only to a fugitive from reality. Ludwig never intended them to be used in the ordinary sense: he had no queen and no children, never held any state dinners, balls, or receptions, and, since he never invited anyone to spend the night, needed but one bedroom to a castle (two in Herrenchiemsee, the extra one intended for the mystical convenience of the long-dead Louis XIV of France). Today all the royal apartments look nearly as pristine as they must have looked in the 1880's. There are no scratches, no worn carpets, no fragile springs. The rich colors of the draperies—violet, crimson, emerald, sky-blue, and lapis-lazuli—have scarcely faded. Here and there the fabric is disintegrating, but only from time and the weight of gold embroidery, not from the touch of human fingers. These are enchanted castles, not meant for flesh and blood.

Ludwig does not seem to have had any creative talents himself, and he never sought any training in architecture or design. But he was adept at writing "approved" or "not approved" on the sketches of the many architects and designers who worked for him, and he supervised his castle-building down to the last doorknob, so that the overall result reflects Ludwig and no one else. Everywhere are enigmatic clues to his personality: What sort of man, one wonders, would feel that he needed a throne of cast-zinc peacock feathers? Or a couch with mirrors at head and foot, so that he could see himself *ad infinitum*? Or a golden rococo sleigh drawn by six plumed horses in which to ride by moonlight all alone?

Ludwig was eighteen in 1864 when, upon the death of his father, Maximilian, he succeeded to the throne of Bavaria. The young king was six feet three and strikingly handsome, and the Bavarians, catching one of their first good views of him as he walked through the streets of Munich behind his father's coffin, were delighted with him. They clamored to see him more often, and the more they clamored, the more elusive he became. He feared crowds, disdained persons of common birth, and was happiest when by himself or watching a play or an opera (before long he began to combine these pleasures by having theatrical performances put on for him alone). He had seen *Lohengrin* for the first time when he was fifteen and apparently had jumped to the conclusion that a man who could bring heroes to life must necessarily be a hero, too, for one of his first acts as king was to seek out Richard Wagner—who was hard to find because he was hiding from creditors—and send for him, pay his debts, and provide him with a house in Munich, a castle on Lake Starnberg, and a comfortable income.

Ludwig himself does not seem to have been musical: after five years of piano lessons, his tutor had said there was no point in going on, because His Royal Highness the Crown Prince had "neither talent for music nor does he like it." It was not for music that he idolized Wagner but for the Wagnerian themes, and if the composer had set other stories to music, he would probably never have met the king of Bavaria. Ludwig's mind was drenched in fantasy, and his human relationships were significant to him only insofar as they helped make fantasy seem real. His obsession was to shut out the world of nineteenth-century Germany, where monarchs were bothered by niggling financial ministers, where a Prussian bully, Count Bismarck, was destroying Bavarian sovereignty, and where (even worse) no one talked in poetry and rooms were apt to be stuffed with Biedermeier furniture. To Ludwig, a royal Miniver Cheevy, almost any other century looked better.

At about this time Ludwig became engaged to his first cousin once removed, Sophie, a pretty, docile Wittelsbach princess whose elder sister, Elizabeth, was the empress of Austria. Ludwig called Sophie "Elsa," himself "Hein-

rich." "My dear Elsa!" he wrote to her, "the God of my life, as you know, is Richard Wagner." "My Beloved Elsa! . . . How happy I am to have seen Him again and talked to Him after nine long months." "W. comes to me today at 1 o'clock and we shall have a couple of beautiful hours of cosy talk together; think of Us!"

A wedding coach was ordered, painted with scenes of the life of Louis XIV plus a scene of a theater during a performance of a Wagner opera; Sophie was measured for a crown; an elaborate apartment, connected by a secret staircase with Ludwig's, was prepared for her in the Munich Residenz. And during the blessdly long time that these things took, Ludwig went off incognito to Paris in the company of his chief groom. Twice the wedding date was postponed; the bride's father was forced to make indignant inquiries; and at last Ludwig wrote Sophie as honest a letter as was possible for him: "Now I have had time to test myself, and think the whole matter over, and I see that my true and faithful brotherly love is now, and always will be, deeply rooted in my soul; but I also see that there is not the love which is necessary for a matrimonial union." In his diary Ludwig noted: "Sophie written off. The gloomy picture fades. . . . Now I live again after this torturing nightmare."

Having closed the doors to a normal life, he was free to hurry down the secret passageways of his own fantastic world. Forthwith he plunged himself into the real passion of his life—building and decorating. His trip to France, where he had seen the Paris Exposition of 1867 as well as Versailles and other royal palaces, seems to have set his imagination flying off in all directions, and the architects' offices of Munich began to burn lights late into the night. Plans were drawn up for a facsimile of Versailles, for a medieval fortress with a Singers' Hall in it like the one in *Tannhäuser*, and for a Moorish-Byzantine palace. The royal apartments in the Munich Residenz were enlarged and decorated lavishly in a late-late-rococo style, and an enormous winter garden, under a vaulted glass roof, was added to the top floor of the Residenz, complete with

*Most romantic of palaces, Ludwig's Neuschwanstein
rises from a crag in the Bavarian Alps and
commands a view of the clear, cold lake of Alpsee.*

*Linderhof had twelve royal rooms, filled with such dazzling clutter as this peacock throne. The birds are made of zinc, with glass and enamel plumage.*

palm trees, fountains, a pond and a running stream, a blue silk tent, a bamboo hut, a stalactite grotto, and an Oriental kiosk. There were swans (stuffed) and peacocks (real), and a small barque for rowing about; and in the background, a painting of the Himalayas. (A sturdy soprano who had come to the palace ostensibly to discuss a forthcoming opera, but who had hopes of bringing the aloof young man around to more personal subjects, once climbed aboard the barque, upset it, and screamed for help; Ludwig rang for footmen and bade his damp visitor good night.)

Schloss Linderhof, begun in 1869, started out to be a little garden chalet like Marly, at Versailles, but when it was completed, ten years later, it was pure Ludwigian. The chief of the architects and decorators was Christian Jank, a Munich stage designer—and certainly Linderhof looks more like a stage set than a place to live. Everything, down to the last toothbrush holder, was designed for the exact place where it still stands. Each room is so like the next that one comes away with a blurred impression of dazzle and splendor, in which only a few bits stand out clearly—the life-sized porcelain peacock, the upright Aeolian piano strewn with gold rococo squiggles, or the canopy above the king's worktable, lined with ermine from the coronation robe of Ludwig's cousin Otto of Greece (this is the sole example anywhere in Ludwig's décor of thrift, or making do, and one wonders if he minded the secondhand ermine). Some of the paintings are on tapestry, to imitate Gobelin, and the subjects are mythological or allegorical—no German sagas here. Pastel portraits of Marie Antoinette, of Louis XIV, XV, and XVI, of Madame du Barry, Madame de Pompadour, and other court figures bear identical bland, custardy expressions; the abstract idea of absolute monarchy interested Ludwig, not nuances of personality.

By the time Linderhof was ready for Ludwig to live in, his manner of life was further than ever removed from reality. He arose at six or seven in the evening and had breakfast, dined at two hours past midnight, supped and retired at dawn. He liked to take his meals alone, but the table was usually set for three or four. Who were the unseen guests? Louis XIV was one, perhaps; a servant once came upon Ludwig saluting and talking to a statue of Louis XIV that stands in the main hallway of Linderhof. Often the ghostly dinner would take place at Ludwig's *Tischlein-deck-dich*, a table copied from one at Versailles that could pop into view, fully spread, by means of machinery that boosted it through the floor. The kitchen had always to be ready for sudden changes in the royal appetite. Ludwig liked kingly-looking food—peacock, for instance, stuffed with forcemeat and truffles and served up with its head and tail feathers. He expected dishes like this to be on hand when he wanted them and thought nothing of advancing or retarding dinner without consideration of the cooks' nerves. Sometimes he would suddenly decide to dine perched amid the branches of a large lime tree in the garden; or in a mountain hut; or at the Schachen, a hunting lodge designed in a curious blend of Swiss chalet and Turkish kiosk; or in one of several outbuildings that he constructed on the Linderhof grounds—the Moorish kiosk, Hunding's Hut, or the Grotto.

Hunding's Hut (destroyed in 1945) was a replica in-the-round of a stage set for the first act of *Die Walküre*. In the middle was a living ash tree, pierced by a replica of Siegfried's sword. For the rest, there were a lot of antlers and bearskins, and when the king was in a jovial mood, he and a few favored courtiers would lie about dressed as early Teutons and drink mead out of horns. Game was their principal food; silver jugs in the shape of deer held cream for the coffee—which would doubtless have surprised Siegfried—and the salt and pepper shakers were shaped like little owls.

When the Teutonic mood was not upon him, Ludwig had a penchant for the Oriental. In 1867, at the Paris Exposition, he had bought a Moorish kiosk, the property of a bankrupt millionaire from Bohemia, and this was eventually set up at Linderhof. The kiosk was not partic-

ularly Moorish, having been conceived and built in Berlin of pressed zinc plaques. But Ludwig was enchanted with it and installed a throne in the shape of a huge zinc peacock, its tail feathers enameled and set with glittering Bohemian glass. Next to swans, peacocks were the favorite bird of the king, and he cherished a desire to be drawn about by peacocks harnessed to a small gilded car, as he had heard was done in ancient Persia; he even wrote to the incumbent Shah of Persia, asking for a shipment of sturdy peacocks along with training instructions. No peacocks arrived, but he enjoyed lolling on his peacock throne and drinking a *bowle* made by soaking violet roots in champagne, accompanied by petits fours and candied violets.

But of all the phantasmagoria at Linderhof, the Grotto is the strangest. The inspiration for the Grotto came partly from the Blue Grotto in Capri and partly from the Venus Grotto, where Tannhäuser drank the cup of oblivion. It is several hundred feet long, fifty feet high, and appears to be cut out of rock. Actually, it is made of brick and iron clothed in canvas and cement to make them look like rocks and stalagmites. It also contains a lake, which the king sometimes swam in and sometimes rowed about on in a gilded, shell-shaped boat. A waterfall gurgles noisily down from the bogus rocks, and in Ludwig's day artificial waves could be whipped up on the lake's surface by means of a small machine. Dim, varicolored lights and a luminous rainbow were provided by the first electricity plant in Bavaria, erected on an adjacent slope, and twenty-five dynamos (then very recently invented). Back of the lake, a huge painting depicts Act I of *Tannhäuser* and swarms of cherubs and fairies. The whole place must have seemed very recherché to the king, but to a modern eye it is reminiscent of the Coney Island fun house.

But if the Grotto is ridiculous, Ludwig was occasionally capable of the sublime. And if he ever achieved a triumph of creative imagination, it was in choosing the site for the castle of Neuschwanstein. It stands among monumental gray crags, with snowy Alps above, a green plain below, and the lovely little jade-green lakes of Schwansee and Alpsee not far away. One wonders if, in building it, Ludwig did not set out to outdo his father, for the windows of this castle look down on Hohenschwangau, which in comparison is only the restored fortress of a petty lord. The architects of Neuschwanstein worked from sketches made by the same scene designer who worked on Linderhof, and probably no professional architect would have arrived at such a never-never look for solid stone- and brickwork. During the construction, Ludwig was often on hand to supervise the workmen personally; but the royal apartments took so long to build and decorate that in all he was able to occupy them only for less than half a year.

Unhappily, the castle interior is less felicitous than its exterior. Romanesque, Early Gothic, Late Gothic, Tudor, Moorish, and Byzantine architecture and decorations are chucked together with a heavy hand, and everywhere are those outsized insipid paintings that could only be nineteenth century. Tristan and Isolde, Lohengrin and Elsa, Walther and Eva, and other heroes and heroines of Middle High German poetry command the walls, looking noble, vacuous, and stiff as pokers. Never was so much love celebrated with so little reference to sex. In a painting showing Tannhäuser on the Venusberg, which dominates the king's study, Venus is as naked as, but no more sensual than, a billiard ball, while Tannhäuser, fully clothed, sits at her feet and looks as if he were thinking out a chess problem. Then there are the usual Ludwigian touches: a bathroom full of artificial stalactites, a porcelain vase in the shape of a full-sized swan, and a carved oak bed-canopy in Late Gothic style that is a perfect forest of turrets, ogives, and pinnacles. Ludwig always gave most attention to the royal bedroom, which he regarded as a symbol of monarchy. Louis XIV had received courtiers, ministers, and sundry callers in bed, and Ludwig may have intended to copy him, but as he grew older he rarely received anyone.

The last room added to Neuschwanstein was a throne

room, which, like so much else in Ludwig's castles, was of
no use at all. The theme is Byzantine, for more and more
Ludwig was drawn to the Byzantine concept of royalty as
near-deity. The throne itself, which was to be of ivory
and pure gold, never materialized; above the empty
space reserved for it are murals—painted to resemble
mosaic—depicting six canonized kings of Christendom
and, above them, the risen Christ with Saint John and the
Virgin, so that the room seems something like a church.
This is the most theatrical-looking of all Ludwig's rooms,
perhaps because the paintings are faked mosaics and the
pillars, supposed to look like porphyry and lapis lazuli,
are too red and too blue and are obviously only plaster.
By the time Ludwig planned the throne room his sight
was weakening, and, being a very vain man, he would
not wear glasses.

Ludwig's third *Schloss*, Herrenchiemsee, inspired by
and partly copied from Versailles, stands on a small
island in the Chiemsee, one of the largest of the Bavarian
Alpine lakes. The cornerstone was laid in 1878 and
building continued, to the tune of twenty million marks,
until 1885, when the state treasury put a stop to it,
leaving some twenty rooms finished and sumptuously
decorated and the rest of the palace no more than bare
bricks and plaster. These royal rooms, lighted by thousands of white candles in more than a hundred crystal,
ivory, or porcelain chandeliers, are an extraordinary
sight, a sight that Ludwig is said to have seen only once,
when he walked from room to room all alone. By day,
when Ludwig never saw the palace, it looks gaudy and
overdone and reminds one all too plainly how difficult it
is for a man to escape his century. The great entrance hall
is meticulously copied after the Ambassadors' Staircase at
Versailles; yet the unsubtle colors of the ubiquitous heroic
paintings, the staring-white stucco, and the disastrous
idea of adding a glass roof (suggesting Waterloo Station)
mark it inexorably as a work of the late nineteenth
century. Dissatisfied with the empty appearance of Louis
XIV's Hall of Mirrors, Ludwig supplied his version with

A triumph of pretension, Herrenchiemsee castle tried to out-Versailles Versailles. Ludwig's version of the Sun King's palace, erected on an island in the Chiemsee in Bavaria, was the costliest of all his buildings and had a hall of mirrors longer and more opulent than the one in the original. Ludwig claimed he conceived this monster not as a home but as a shrine to absolutism—and spent only nine nights there.

47 banquettes, 12 taborets, 52 candelabras, 8 orange trees in specially designed tubs, 4 vases, 16 busts of classical emperors, and 33 chandeliers. The painted figures that swarm across the ceiling have been provided here and there with stucco legs and arms, which make them look as if they were wildly trying to struggle free of the ceiling. This whimsy of Bavarian eighteenth-century rococo would have dismayed a seventeenth-century Frenchman and imparts a slightly berserk appearance to this Hall of Mirrors.

Ludwig slept in his costly palace exactly nine nights, from September 7 to 16, 1885. He himself said that he had intended it less as a dwelling than a temple, a shrine dedicated to the Sun King, Louis XIV, and to the idea of absolutism. The most important and most expensive room in the palace is the bedroom for the symbolic use of Louis XIV, modeled after the royal bedroom at Versailles but larger and far more elaborate. He gave Louis a gilt bowl and pitcher big enough for a giant, hangings of dark red velvet that took twenty women seven years to encrust with gold embroidery, a parquet floor intricately inlaid with rosewood, and a tapestry-painting showing Louis XIV with his ancestor Saint Louis and—unobtrusively standing in the background—his spiritual descendant, Ludwig.

Ludwig's own bedroom is comparatively modest. The draperies are blue, the color Ludwig preferred in all his bedrooms, and there is a giant blue globe at the foot of the bed to serve as a night light. Here, as in every bedroom he planned for himself, is a curious juxtaposition of religious and amorous symbols. At the head of the bed is an embroidery depicting Louis XIV triumphing over Vice, while at the foot is a carved relief of Venus set between fully modeled figures of Cupid and Psyche.

Although Herrenchiemsee was not nearly finished, Ludwig set about planning more castles. There was to be a Byzantine palace, a robber-baron aerie on a higher and less accessible crag than Neuschwanstein, and a walled Chinese palace where the court was to adopt the dress and ceremonial of mandarins. There was one rather large stumbling block: money. The king's credit was no longer good anywhere, and he owed ten million marks. When a moneylender came forward with the offer of a four-hundred-thousand-mark loan in return for a title, Ludwig, though he eventually gave in, at first refused indignantly: Did they suppose the king had no honor? His advisers pleaded with him. Where else, they asked, could the money be found? "Steal it!" cried Ludwig.

Early in the morning of Thursday, June 10, 1886, a delegation of ministers of state, accompanied by a noted psychiatrist, Dr. Bernhard von Gudden, and several skilled male nurses, arrived at the gatehouse of Neuschwanstein. They brought with them a parliamentary order to place the king under medical care. There was a clause in the Bavarian constitution stating that a king incapable of carrying out his proper duties could be relieved of them and replaced by a regency. In addition to his unreasoning demands for money and his paralyzing effect on the orderly processes of government (when papers required the royal signature, ministers often had to meet the king in some remote mountain rendezvous where, in the middle of the night, Ludwig would arrive by coach-and-six, hurriedly sign the papers with his now illegible "Ludwig," and whirl away again), there was a stack of evidence obtained from his servants: that they must approach the king on their bellies, that he had them physically chastised and bound, that he talked to trees and embraced a certain pillar at Linderhof each time he passed it, and that he complained of terrible pressure in his head, sometimes so severe that he had to come to meals wearing an ice pack.

The members of the commission from Munich had not brought military support with them, and, to their annoyance, they found that the king's loyal guard would not let them into Neuschwanstein. There was nothing for them to do but withdraw to the nearest village and wonder what to do next. They had not long to wonder: within the hour a company of gendarmes arrived from

*Schloss Linderhof, Ludwig's opulent Alpine retreat*

the king with orders to arrest them. In vain they showed the captain of gendarmes a paper stating that Prince Luitpold, the king's uncle, was already regent; finally they consented to the indignity of being locked up in the Neuschwanstein gatehouse. The king now issued a series of five orders that at last shook the faith of his supporters. The orders were (1) skin the members of the commission alive, (2) scalp them, cut off their tongues and hands, and flog them to death, (3) blind them, (4) place them in heavy chains, and (5) fling them into a deep dungeon to starve to death. Afterward the captain of gendarmes admitted that if the royal order had simply directed him to shoot all members of the commission, he would unhesitatingly have carried it out. As it was, he and his assistants debated for several hours before deciding to try to get instructions from the government in Munich.

Before all the red tape had been cut and Dr. Gudden was finally free to try to take charge of his patient, two more days had passed, and Ludwig was drinking heavily, threatening suicide, and calling for the keys to the highest tower of Neuschwanstein. Dr. Gudden stationed the male nurses on the tower stairway and then had the keys sent to Ludwig. Ludwig immediately made for the tower, was taken, and then driven in a locked carriage to the small *Schloss* of Berg, on Lake Starnberg.

The last of Ludwig's pathetic story will never be known for certain. The day after the arrival at Berg, Ludwig, who was behaving in a fairly quiet and docile manner, consented to go for an evening walk along the lakeside with Dr. Gudden. Neither was ever seen alive again. The body of Dr. Gudden was found in shallow water; he had drowned, and there were bruises and marks of strangulation on his neck. The body of the king was found farther out in the lake, in water less than four feet deep. He had been an excellent swimmer, so whether he had drowned himself or had suffered a heart attack and collapsed in the water will always be a mystery. A wooden cross, often garlanded with fresh flowers, marks the place where he died.

*"The God of my life," wrote Ludwig, "is Richard Wagner,"
an adoration suggested in this nineteenth-century
composite portrait showing the king superimposed on
the composer's profile. Ludwig's Wagnerian obsession
culminated in the Grotto at Linderhof, an enclosed
pool lit by the first dynamos in Bavaria and complete
with swan boat, canvas stalagmites, and a teeming
wall painting showing the first act of Tannhäuser.*

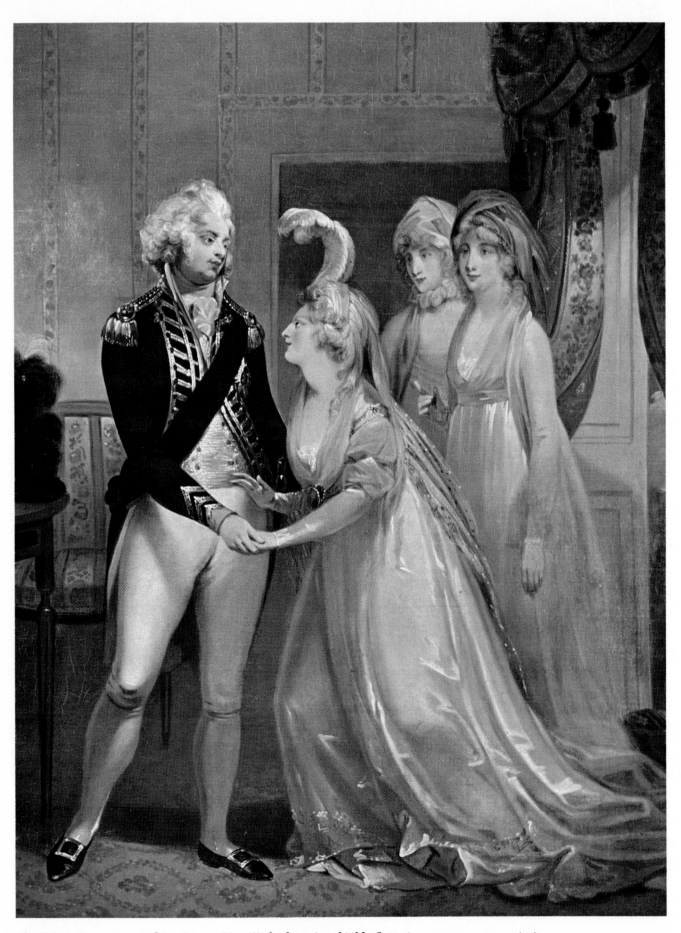

*The Prince Regent greets his mistress, Mrs. Fitzherbert, in a highly flattering contemporary painting.*

# George IV's Brighton Pavilion

*What led the Prince Regent, in the early years of the nineteenth century, to build an Oriental palace on the southern coast of England? The most revealing answer to that intriguing historical puzzle lies in the following essay by J. H. Plumb, the distinguished historian and author of* The First Four Georges. *It is adapted from an article that appeared in* Horizon *magazine.*

Today Brighton is Britain's Miami—brash, extravagant, a curious mixture of vulgarity and elegance, sophistication and naiveté, where literary lions, juvenile delinquents, successful *nouveaux riches*, and proletarian Cockneys out on a spree jostle in a lively, garish world that possesses one of the most remarkable architectural settings of any seaside resort in Europe. Throughout the length and breadth of Brighton there are squares, terraces, crescents of exquisitely classical proportions, rivaled in England only by Bath and in Europe only by Nancy. There is no whimsy about these buildings; the only exoticism is an occasional decoration in the neoclassical style of the late eighteenth and early nineteenth century. And then, lying in the very heart of this formal beauty, close to the seashore but set back from it, is the fantasy of the Brighton Pavilion—with its domes and minarets, its fretwork tracery and lacelike embattlements; and underneath this Oriental masquerade, the fine proportions of Henry Holland's classical villa, the first Pavilion, can still be discerned, as Georgian and as classical as any house in Brighton. It was built by the Prince Regent (1762-1830), the eldest son of George III, and like the prince the Pavilion grew more monstrous, more extraordinary, more dreamlike with the years. But first, why is the Pavilion in Brighton?

Two hundred fifty years ago Brighton scarcely existed—a few fishermen's hovels, a shingle beach, and right to the shore, smooth undulating grasslands that rose within a mile or so to the sharp escarpment of the Downs. It was excellent country for the horse, for riding it, racing it, or driving it. And that, later, was one of the reasons for Brighton's popularity, for many of the prince's friends were crazed about horses as only the English aristocracy can be. But Brighton first grew to fame and fashion through the salesmanship of a successful doctor. He sold sea water. Its virtues, said Dr. Russell, whether applied externally or internally, were boundless. A cold dip, it seemed, proved peculiarly efficacious to that feminine frailty of the age of elegance—the vapors—so long as it was taken at hideously inappropriate times: Fanny Burney, the novelist, bathed in November before dawn, a very good time, the doctors thought. Also, as might be expected, sea bathing or sea drinking encouraged fertility in young matrons, "better even," said its advocates, "than the mud of the river Nile."

The Prince Regent's first visit to Brighton—a short one—took place in 1783 at the invitation of his uncle, the Duke of Cumberland, whom the prince's father, George III, regarded with such horror that he had forbidden his son to visit him. As soon as the prince was twenty-one, with his own establishment, and free to please himself, he had accepted Cumberland's invitation with alacrity. The visit proved hugely successful, for Brighton seemed to offer all that the prince needed. He found Brighton gay, intimate, discreet. It was still too far from London for crowds to gather there: his own set could, and did, take over the place.

So Brighton became the prince's playground. He and his friends were fond of vulgar and noisy practical jokes on their neighbors. Who could stop them in Brighton? They raced their horses and drove their phaetons in mad competition across the wide lawns that bordered the sea. No one was likely to complain. They sat at their telescopes and watched old Martha Gunn, the ladies' bathing attendant, known popularly as "Queen of the Dippers," help their favorite girls into the sea: after all, the girls were there for adventure, too. Occasionally the men even sat in the ice-cold water themselves when they thought their health demanded it. They gambled endlessly, gazed at plays, danced, listened with respect to

the prince's fine baritone as he regaled them with ballads, drank furiously, ate gigantically, and wenched interminably. And they dressed. The prince possessed a handsome, florid face, a splendid, if slightly plump, figure, and first-class legs, of which he was inordinately proud. He was even prouder of his taste in clothes, formed and guided by his friend Beau Brummell, who had revolutionized the Englishman's dress by insisting on subdued colors, perfect cut, and exquisite linen as the marks of elegance. Only in the evening, on full-dress occasions, were princes and nobles permitted to dress like peacocks. But clothes and the wearing of them were a matter for daily concern and long discussion.

Princes and their friends, after settling on a place like a cloud of butterflies, often gorge themselves on its nectar and then flutter away to stimulate their appetites in fresh pastures. This time, however, fate riveted the prince to Brighton. He fell in love with a dangerously unusual widow—Mrs. Fitzherbert. Mrs. Fitzherbert was a Roman Catholic—pious, virtuous, very comely. She neither welcomed the prince's attentions nor responded to his ardor. She preferred to be left alone. The prince's siege grew hectic: he swore, he cajoled, he promised; presents rained on her, letters pursued her, finally marriage trapped her. Conducted in utmost secrecy, it was, of course, illegal. No prince of the British royal family could marry without the sovereign's consent; no consent could have been forthcoming from George III for a marriage to a Roman Catholic widow. On the prince's part the ceremony was meaningless folly; on hers, the necessary

religious sanction to her bedding with the prince. In Mrs. Fitzherbert's eyes, and in the eyes of her church and of her fellow believers, the prince was her husband. In English law, she could be nothing but his mistress. The prince, of course, flaunted his conquest but strenuously denied, even to a friend as close as Charles James Fox, the method by which he had achieved it. Nevertheless, rumors reverberated, and George III, never a man of easy temper, regarded his son with so prejudiced an eye that he left him to stew in his debts. During his frantic courtship, the prince, according to Lord Holland, had rolled in grief on Charles James Fox's floor, crying by the hour and "swearing that he would abandon the country, forgo the crown, sell his jewels, and scrape together a competence to fly with her to America." Instead, once wed, he drove off in ostentatious austerity to Brighton and installed Mrs. Fitzherbert conveniently near a rented farmhouse that he had begun to regard as his own.

The prince could not live in any building without letting his imagination begin to work on it. Already his palace in London—Carlton House—had been more responsible than any other extravagance for his monumental debts. So in the intervals of his amorous delights, and when he was too tired for the crude practical jokes in which he took such schoolboyish delight, he paced about his farmhouse. In his mind's eye, he knocked down walls and threw out bow windows, transforming the modest construction into a charming marine pavilion, suitable for a prince wallowing in marital bliss. Within eighteen months, one hundred fifty workmen under the direction

The Royal Pavilion, an Oriental fantasy erected
on the Brighton coast by the future king George IV,
had taken on its final, fantastic form by 1822.

Financial pressures forced the Prince Regent into
marrying the boisterous, clumsy Princess Caroline of
Brunswick. But George detested his royal mate—
the contemporary cartoon at right shows him abusing
her—and remained infatuated with his mistress,
Mrs. Fitzherbert, to whom he paid the substantial
annuity shown in the receipt at lower right.

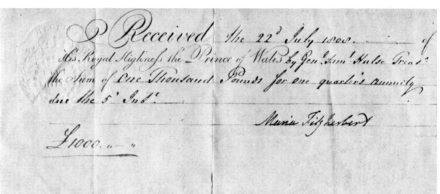

of the prince's architect, Henry Holland, had turned
dream into reality. Holland's structure possessed the
simplicity and elegance that Georgian architects
achieved so effortlessly. Its central feature was a circular
salon that was flanked by two wings with bow windows.
The building veered toward austerity, and the only
whimsy it contained was the prince's bedroom, where a
vast mirror enabled the prince, and presumably Mrs.
Fitzherbert, to lie in bed and watch not only the sea but
their friends strolling up and down the Steine, as the wide
grass lawn of Brighton was called—a quaint, but no
doubt restful, pastime.

The prince's Brighton friends were an odd bunch:
Beau Brummell, for example, lived for clothes and spent
the entire day dressing, parading, undressing, and
parading again —as fastidious and as pure in his private
life as in the cut of his coat. Others, like Lord Barrymore,
never washed; his own and his brother's fame rested
partly on their practical jokes—propping up coffins in
doorways, then ringing the doorbell, was a favorite—and
partly on their wild extravagance, due mainly to excessive gambling and lavish theatricals. And then there was
Letty Lade: anyone who was particularly foulmouthed
the prince would describe as swearing "like Letty Lade."
She had lost her virtue to "Sixteen-string Jack," a high-
wayman hanged at Tyburn in 1774, enjoyed for a short
time the bed of the prince's brother, the Duke of York,
and finally married Sir John Lade, who finished life as a
public coachman on the London-Brighton run.

Many of the prince's friends were obsessed and
ingrown characters. Great wealth and absolute social
security combined to create a hothouse atmosphere in
which human characters could flower like monstrous
orchids—vivid, splotched, nightmarish, haunting. Brighton was for them a paradise, where for months on end
they could forget the real world of lawyers, tradesmen,
stewards, politicians, and above all, the threats and later
the horrors of war.

The prince and Mrs. Fitzherbert had begun their life
in Brighton determined to live sparely. That resolution
quickly vanished, and his debts mounted: by 1795 to well
over half a million pounds. Furthermore, there was no
immediate heir to the throne. All his brothers either lived
in sin or, like himself, had contracted marriages that no
one would recognize: although George III had plenty of
bastard grandchildren, the direct succession of his house
seemed to be in jeopardy. And the prince's love for Mrs.
Fitzherbert had withered to habit, and habit itself had
grown brittle.

The solution to his financial difficulties was to marry a
German princess, breed an heir, and allow a grateful
country to discharge his debts and increase his income.
The alternative was a personal crisis of monumental
proportions that would almost certainly entail a sharp
contraction in his style of living. He was far too middle-
aged to face that. So he married. He loathed his strange
bride and got through the marriage ceremony only by
fortifying himself with brandy. His wife was dotty: a
hoydenish, blowsy, free-speaking German wench who
dressed in outrageous taste, swore like a hostler, and smelt

like a farmyard. Or so the prince and his friends said—at
least it gave an excuse for the vile way he treated her. He
managed, however, to get his princess pregnant and, duty
done and the daughter born, he turned the princess out of
his house but not out of his life. She careered around
Europe in vulgar ostentation, as much to embarrass the
prince as to enjoy herself. Certainly the prince's legal
marriage was the most disastrous act of his life.

Once he had extricated himself from this horror, he
naturally wished to re-create the years with Mrs. Fitzherbert, which now glowed in his imagination. Her pride
bruised, she showed her former indifference, which once
again fanned the prince's ardor to fever heat. There was
nothing like denial to raise the prince's passion. After a
becoming interval, Mrs. Fitzherbert sent a priest off to
Rome for advice. It was apt: return to your husband. She
did, and both returned to Brighton.

Not only did Mrs. Fitzherbert make the prince
supremely happy—the next eight years, she was to say,
were the happiest in his life—she also made him creative.
Again he began to play about with the Pavilion. In 1802
the gift of some Chinese wallpaper, received no doubt
because he had created a Chinese room at Carlton House
in 1801, gave him the idea of making not only a Chinese
gallery at the Pavilion but a room with walls of painted
glass, which gave one the impression of being inside a
Chinese lantern. For the next few years, shortage of
money and the need to complete the stables (they cost
£54,000—no horses, nor grooms for that matter, had ever
been more splendidly housed) limited the prince's ambitions, but the Pavilion was enlarged a little and the
interior decoration made more and more what the
English thought to be Chinese. But the prince was not
satisfied, and he decided to reconstruct the Pavilion, to
turn it from a princely cottage into a miniature palace,
small in size, yet rich, fabulous, Oriental in decoration.
Not a Chinese pagoda: the prince was moving away from
Chinese toward what he conceived to be an Indian style.
Already at Sezincote in Gloucestershire a nabob, returned

with a huge fortune from India, had built himself an
Oriental palace; fortunately for him, his brother—S. P.
Cockerell—was an excellent architect who took his task
very seriously and carefully used water-color drawings of
actual Indian buildings. The result was strange but
pleasing. William Porden, who built the stables at Brighton, had worked for Cockerell, and he used this exceptionally original style of decoration at Brighton This
entranced the prince; in 1805 he commissioned Hum-
phrey Repton to plan an Aladdin-like transformation of
his classical marine villa into an Indian palace. The
prince praised the drawings but did not build. Once
more, he was broke. And possibly he had doubts about
Repton's scheme, which conformed very strictly to
Indian models. Highly disciplined and rather dry in tone,
it lacked, perhaps, the personal accent for which the
prince's imagination was searching.

He hesitated for another six years until, indeed, the
final madness of his father made him king in all but
name. Then he got hold of a regal income and began to
build as no English king had ever built before. The
encouragement he gave to John Nash, the surveyor-
general whom he personally appointed in 1815, made the
regent as responsible as anyone for the most beautiful
domestic architecture London possesses—the great
terraces of Regent's Park. Nash's Pavilion at Brighton,
however, owed as much to the effects of time and
experience on the prince's character as to Nash's architectural genius. It was the final expresssion of his life. Every
detail in decoration, furnishing, and color was personally
supervised by the regent and, if need be, changed time
and time again. To understand the strange fantasy that
came to life by Brighton's seashore, it is necessary to
understand how time had changed the prince.

By 1815 his youth had passed; Mrs. Fitzherbert had
been rejected a second time. Indeed, another reason for
his delay in reconstructing the Pavilion was the change in
direction of his amorous life, which kept him away from
Brighton for a year or two. Gross in body, somewhat

wandering in mind, prone to invalidism, the prince was driven farther into his private dream world by the antics of his wife and the hatred of his subjects. At the visit of the crowned heads of the European alliance to London in 1815, his wife had returned to London and insisted on undertaking what she considered to be her rightful duties. The regent was outraged and, this time supported by his mother, refused to countenance what he considered infamous behavior. The radical politicians denounced the prince, and the mob pelted him when he appeared in public, so that he became afraid to go out of doors. He knew himself to be a figure of contempt, and could banish age and a sense of decay only by shutting himself in a private world: a world of eating, drinking, singing, building, and decorating—shared with a few dependable friends and ruled by matriarchs. The first of these was Lady Hertford, the second Lady Conyngham—two enormous, elderly women, much older than himself, who could treat him as he wished to be treated, as a loveless, foolish boy to be scolded, pampered, bullied, and always forgiven.

Yet the prince still possessed a saving grace. He needed to express himself, to create, to allow his imagination to roam. His nature, as his life showed, was deeply fissured with anxieties, frustrations, and other weaknesses that were hard to face. In fantasy he could be soothed: pretense with him easily became reality. He was a man of romantic imagination, with the impulse of an artist and the temperament of an actor. His strange nature found its most effective, if not its most satisfactory, fulfillment in building and decorating; and the two architectural fantasies of his broken old age—the final Brighton Pavilion and the restoration and rebuilding of Windsor Castle—are both in their way romantic masterpieces. Windsor, with its stupendous Round Tower, is central to the tradition created by the Gothic Revival, but Brighton, when completed, had neither past nor future. Outside, Indian and Moorish mingled with the eighteenth-century elegance of sash and bow windows to create a unique

building that baffled the understanding as much as it stimulated the imagination. The Pavilion is a dream, belonging neither to Russia nor India nor China nor Mongolia nor to Moorish Spain, but to the prince's longing for a smart originality that would astound his friends. The inside, like the outside, is a strange pastiche, at times, with its strong reds and yellows and blues, almost vulgar, yet never quite. On first viewing, it is overpowering and slightly repellent: the huge lotuslike chandeliers, the dragons writhing down the walls, the imitation blue skies, palms in cast iron, banana trees in bronze, seats pretending to be dolphins, and everywhere bamboo chairs, bamboo beds, bamboo bookcases, bamboo seats (but, of course, imitation bamboo—even bamboo in iron). The Pavilion shocks as few other buildings do; it creates immediately the atmosphere of a life, the true setting for the man who made it. It is easy to imagine these rooms grossly overheated, to see again the vast kitchen teeming with gargantuan piles of food and noisy with sweating cooks and scullions, orchestrated by Carême, one of the greatest of French chefs, to provide excitement for the palates of the twenty or so old roués, and their wives or mistresses, who sat with the prince in his Banqueting Room. This room and the Music Room are the two most extravagant and extraordinary rooms not only in the Pavilion but in Great Britain.

The Banqueting Room is dominated by its central chandelier—a vast structure in 1818—immensely modern because it was lit by gas, not candles. It weighs a ton and consists of a bronze-leaved plantain tree from which hangs a large silver dragon holding in his claws an enormous glass bowl; around its rim are six smaller dragons with lotus flowers in their mouths. The cost was £5,613 (approximately $70,000 in present-day American money). The prince took advantage of all the technical achievements of his time: the Pavilion is the first house to use cast-iron pillars both for structure and decoration. He loved light as well as heat, so, besides this huge chandelier, there are four other enormous water lilies and eight

The Prince Regent was compulsive about the smallest details of his Pavilion. He oversaw all the furnishings and changed them again and again until he got them to his liking. His care is visible in the capital of the pillar shown at far left and the ormolu-crested mirrors next to it. After George's death much of his meticulously chosen furniture was dispersed. Recently, however, private families and institutions have donated to the palace selected examples of period furniture that echo the prince's taste, among them this couch in the form of an Egyptian riverboat and a chair that at one time belonged to an uncle of George's old archenemy, Napoleon.

*The Pavilion swarmed with chinoiserie, including, clockwise beginning above: a wall painting; stained glass windows; a simulated bamboo cabinet; and a dragon from which a chandelier once hung.*

83

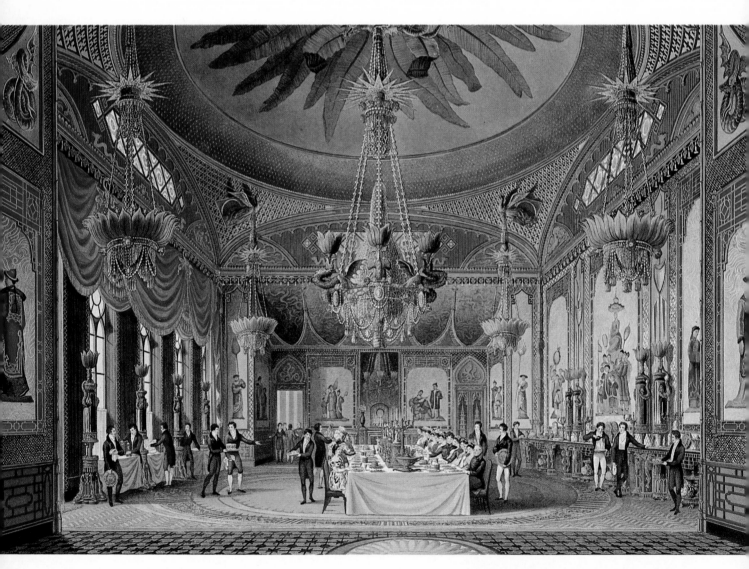

*The prince satisfied his appetite in the Banqueting Room, the largest and most ornate salon in the palace. In this aquatint by John Nash—the architect who completed the Pavilion—George is among the diners on the right side of the table, reaching for his wine.*

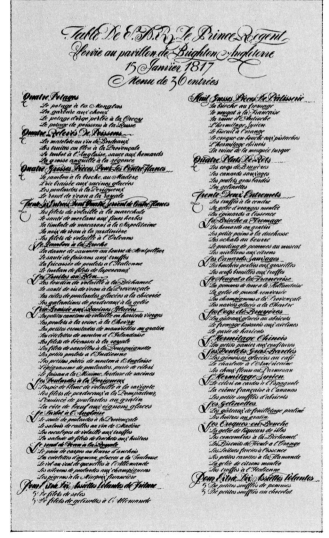

ten-foot-high standard lamps—a pedestal of gilded dolphins, a huge, deep-blue Spode vase topped by a lotus flower of tinted glass (cost: more than five thousand pounds). The room itself is painted with Chinese scenes; the décor is crimson, gold, and blue. The decorative work cost more than eight thousand pounds, and the furniture nearly ten thousand. The total expense of this single room was the equivalent of about one million dollars. (The entire Pavilion cost about five hundred thousand pounds in gold, some fifteen million dollars today.)

Certainly Carême's meals were worthy of it. The richness of the dishes was matched only by their number. At a dinner of no particular importance the prince, greedier than ever, offered the guests the choice of one hundred sixteen dishes in nine courses. He adored the table, not only for the food and wine, but also because while he remained at table his audience was captive. There, among the silver and the glass and the hissing gaslight, in a room that might have been Samuel Goldwyn's idea of the Summer Palace at Peking, he told of the battles he had never fought, the women he had never possessed, and the triumphs he had never known. There he was, a huge mass of flesh, corseted, bedecked, corrupted by his life and nature, yet retaining, even in decay, an originality and something of the singularity of the artist. His outrageous stories were so vivid that his audience—softened by good food and excessive drink—could at least *pretend* without difficulty to believe them. When in top form or reckless with drink, he took to mimicry. Then he entered so wholeheartedly into the subject of his satire that his huge face and vast body seemed to transform themselves even into the lean figure and hatchet face of a Wellington or the austere, arrogant good looks of his minister, Sir Robert Peel.

When tired, at last, of the table, the prince withdrew with his guests into one of the three small drawing rooms that had been the heart of Holland's villa. Here, as in the Long Corridor, the decoration is restrained and restful, the colors soft and delicate and rare. But beyond this suite of drawing rooms lies the second wonder of the Pavilion—the Music Room. It was of this room that Princess de Lieven wrote, "I do not believe that, since the days of Heliogabalus, there has been such magnificence and such luxury. There is something effeminate in it which is disgusting. One spends the evening half-lying on cushions; the lights are dazzling; there are perfumes, music, liqueurs." (As might be expected, the prince loved perfumes, and cases of quart bottles were constantly being sent to Brighton.)

The room seems to recall Marco Polo's description of the great tent of Kublai Khan. As in that, serpents writhe headfirst down the columns which divide the great red lacquer panels painted in gold with Chinese scenes. The great convex ceilings of the recesses have roofs of beribboned bamboos. The central ceiling is a vast dome, decorated with diminishing scales. Flying dragons abound, and the central chandelier is a vast Chinese water lily. Again the cost was prodigious and the result fabulous. In this room the prince held his formal concerts at which Rossini and Kelby sang. Here, too, the prince rendered his ballads in his dramatic baritone, now a little uncertain with age and drink, yet performed with *brio*.

Some of the most beautiful though far less impressive rooms of the Pavilion are the private apartments of his brother, the Duke of Clarence, who afterward became King William IV, and those of the prince's ill-fated daughter, Princess Charlotte, who, much to the prince's grief, had died in childbirth in 1817. In these the scale is domestic, the colors delicate, and the Chinese and Oriental motifs give a gaiety and a difference to rooms that are essentially in the English Regency style. They illustrate, as the public rooms do, the prince's exceptionally fine sense of color, for he had them painted time and time again until he achieved the perfection he sought.

Although architecturally the Pavilion escaped into fantasy, it never extricated itself from the heart of Brighton. The prince had bought land and houses at outrageous prices to give himself some privacy, but his gardens remained small, the front lawns scarcely bigger than those of a large villa. After George died in 1830, King William IV took a fancy to the Pavilion. He had been bred a sailor and he loved Brighton, loved to strut up and down the pier as if it were his own quarter-deck, loved even better having his own cronies in to dinner at the Pavilion, utterly oblivious to the Oriental magnificence that surrounded him. His queen, Adelaide, as homely as her husband, sat patiently at her embroidery and worried so much about the weight of the chandeliers that the king finally ordered the one in the Banqueting Room to be taken down. The resulting gap in the ceiling did not disturb either of them.

He even liked the growing crowds of middle-class people who were coming to Brighton. He liked walking among them and talking to them; the more the merrier. But when Queen Victoria came to the throne she found the Pavilion vulgar. She hated the staring crowds, peering through the railings almost into the drawing room. So off went Victoria and her husband to Osborne on the Isle of Wight to build their own marine villa, where the furniture, instead of imitation bamboo, was real staghorn.

The Pavilion itself hung on the brink of disaster. The best bits of furniture and the finer and less ornate chimneypieces and mirrors were packed off to Buckingham Palace and Windsor Castle, leaving the rooms bare and lifeless. Not until the twentieth century did the custodians of English taste take a new look at the Pavilion and decide that it deserved restoration. Slowly and steadily the old colors were discovered and revived; attics and cellars were searched at Windsor Castle and Buckingham Palace for furniture bearing the mark of the Pavilion and the regent. Some has been given, some returned on loan by the royal family, and a few pieces that had escaped from the royal collection were bought. Now, with many of the original furnishings back in place, it can once more be appreciated as the outward expression of a strange king's character in all its extravagance, oddity, and poetry.

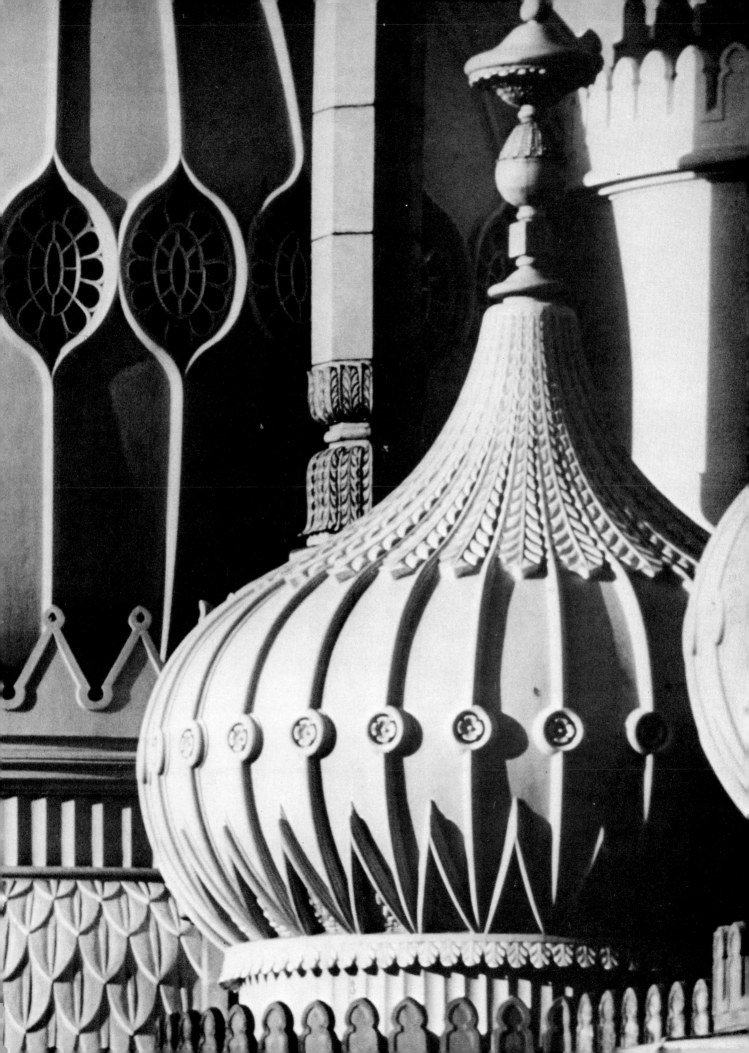

*This sixteenth-century miniature shows Francis I surrounded by his court.*

# Francis I's Chambord

*Francis's device, the royal salamander*

A visitor making his approach to the chateau of Chambord is struck, first of all, by the sight of the most extraordinary roof in Europe. It is a forest of turrrets, pinnacles, chimneys, and towers, all crowded together and rising as much as five stories above the level of the roof terrace. It looks for all the world like a fairy-tale village in the sky.

If the visitor had come on the right afternoon in the sixteenth century, he would have seen, among those rooftop pavilions, the finely dressed ladies of the French court. The roof was the viewing stand from which they watched their lords set out for the hunt in the forest behind the chateau. Chambord, in all its massive stone splendor, was the hunting lodge of that great prince of the French Renaissance, King Francis I.

Thirty years earlier, when Francis was born, there was no good reason to believe that he would one day be king of France. But his mother thought so anyway. In her journal, written long after, she recorded: "François, by God's grace King of France and my own gentle Emperor, had his first experience of this world's light at Cognac about two o'clock of the afternoon in 1494, on the twelfth day of September." His father was the Count d'Angoulême, a cousin of the reigning king.

Since the count was principally occupied with his books and his mistresses, the upbringing of the boy Francis was left in large part to his mother, Louise. She saw that he was trained in all the arts and skills—as warrior, huntsman, diplomat, poet, and gracious courtier—that a chivalric age required. He was not really handsome, with his long Valois nose, but he was tall and broad-shouldered and a natural athlete. He dressed with such elegance, moved with such grace, and spoke with such charm that few women, young or old, could resist him.

We are indebted to his talented sister Margaret, later queen of Navarre and author of a book of love tales called the *Heptameron*, for an account of the first who did. It seems that Francis, at the age of fifteen, was smitten with a pretty brown-haired girl he had seen in church. She was the sister-in-law of his butler, but she resisted all the young nobleman's appeals for favor. Francis went so far as to fall off his horse in front of her house so that he might be carried into her parlor to pursue his suit. It was all in vain. With great gallantry, considering the power that noble lords wielded over the families of those in their service, Francis gave up, allowed her to marry a young man of her choice, and ever after sent them presents.

The amorous young prince went on to establish a precocious reputation as a lady's man. By the time he was seventeen his mother was worrying that he had contracted a venereal disease (if so, it was cured), but she was more concerned about his chances for the throne. In order to further them he was married, in a ceremony of medieval splendor, to the reigning king's daughter, Claude of France, described as "very small and strangely fat," with a squint in one eye. Claude gave him children but otherwise played little part in his life.

Louis XII, who had grudgingly recognized Francis as heir presumptive in the absence of any royal princes, ruled a prosperous kingdom but a frugal court. When he was reproached for his shabby dress the king replied: "I would much rather my [people] laughed at my meanness than wept at their poverty." There were few banquets, since the king ate mostly boiled meat, and few evening festivities, since he liked to go to bed early. In that drab court young Francis shone with special brilliance. He was the leader of a coterie of high-spirited nobles who spent their days in hunting and jousting, their nights in feasting and lovemaking. Observing his heir with dismay, the king lamented: "Ah, we toil in vain—this great boy will spoil everything."

After his queen's death, the king, though old and feeble, made a last attempt to save France from his heir by taking a young bride, Mary Tudor, the daughter of Henry VII of England. Francis or his mother must have had a spy in the nuptial chamber because on the

*Some details of the chateau are (from left) the base of a cupola, a staircase ceiling, and a chimney top.*

following morning he was able to crow: "I am sure, unless someone has lied to me, that it is not possible for the King and Queen to beget children." So it turned out, and when Louis died four months later, Francis was king.

The reign began with a victory on the battlefield. Francis led an army across the Alps and down into Italy to inflict a crushing defeat on the Duke of Milan at Marignano. Francis lingered in Italy for four months, savoring his triumph, and when he returned to France he brought back more than a claim to Italian territory. He brought back an enthusiasm for the Italian Renaissance, which he had seen firsthand at the height of its brilliance. From that time on there was a steady flow of Italian painters, sculptors, and designers, along with some of their finest works, to the French court. One who came at Francis's call was the aged Leonardo da Vinci, to take up residence at the French court, where he died a few years later. From the collaboration of gifted Italians with equally gifted French craftsmen came the new and original style of the French Renaissance.

It was in the flush of this enthusiasm for the new culture that Francis decided to build the chateau of Chambord. He did not lack for grand places to live: he had not only the old palace of the Louvre in Paris but Fontainebleau, Blois, Amboise, and many others scattered conveniently about France. But to Francis's eyes they now seemed old-fashioned. For his new chateau he chose a site in the Loire valley, not for any special attractions of landscape but because it was in the center of the finest hunting country. An old castle stood on the site, but if anything was left of it after the king's builders got through, it was changed beyond recognition.

The chateau of Chambord is a standing illustration of the transition from medieval to Renaissance architecture. Its central structure is a square block with massive round towers at each corner—the typical plan of a medieval keep. But where the old castle had narrow slits just big enough to shoot through, the windows of Chambord are wide and elaborately embellished with ornamental stone-

work. The walls are thick but not for defense. They were built to support the enormous tonnage of stones that stands on the roof. Most of the towers and pinnacles of the roofscape are purely decorative, but the four conical structures at the corners contain small apartments— perhaps the first penthouses ever built. The central lantern contains the top spirals of a double staircase that extends down to the floor of the chateau.

In the afternoons and evenings, the chroniclers tell us, the nooks and crannies on the roof provided many inviting spots for romantic dalliance, a major preoccupation of the court. The twin staircases that wound about each other were almost equally amusing, because a person ascending one stair could catch only glimpses of a person descending the other. In a later century the Grande Mademoiselle of France, Louise, remembered playing peekaboo on the stairs with her father, Gaston d'Orléans, the brother of Louis XIII.

The king's day, whether at Paris or at Fontainebleau or at Chambord, began late. It was his pleasure to rise at ten o'clock, an hour that might well have astonished the other great rulers of the age. At that time of day Henry VIII of England had been up for four or five hours. Charles V of Spain did much of his work in the morning. Ivan the Terrible of Russia and Suleiman the Magnificent of Turkey were both early risers. Halfway across the world in India the Great Mogul, Baber, had been at prayers before dawn.

But not Francis. He dressed with care and sat down for a leisurely breakfast about eleven. The food was for him alone, but he liked to have about him at table his brighter courtiers, scholars, and any artists who might be at court. Often there were readings from his favorite books, which included histories of the kings of France, translations of Greek and Roman classical authors, and chivalric epics. It was no wonder that visitors were almost always impressed by Francis's wide knowledge and good conversation.

At noon Francis was ready for hunting. As described by his recent biographer, Desmond Seward, in *Prince of*

The grand design for the huge chateau of Chambord in the Loire valley began to materialize in 1526, when 1,800 workmen descended on a fever-haunted stretch of lowland. Twelve years later it was virtually complete, boasting more than 400 rooms and almost as many fireplaces. The first-floor plan is shown at right, and an early engraving of the chateau below.

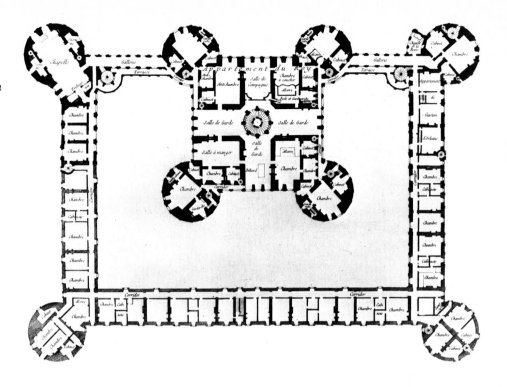

A city in itself, Chambord's intricate rooftop is a thicket of towers, chimneys, and walkways where the court liked to gather for, among other amusements, a view of the progress of the incessant hunts.

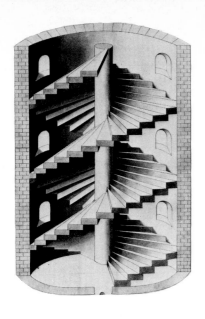

*Among the architectural marvels of Chambord is its central double staircase, ingeniously designed so that someone going up it could pass somebody descending without being seen—a device that gave flirtatious courtiers no end of amusement. The staircase, whose steps are depicted in the architectural rendering at near left, continued on through the roof to become the tower (right) that capped the chateau. Though it was a tour de force of design, the open tower in the roof made Chambord almost impossible to heat.*

*the Renaissance*, this was no casual pastime: "A massive establishment was kept. François never hunted with less than twenty-five couple of 'lime hounds' and six harbourers to find his quarry or with less than twenty-five couple of hounds and six whips to hunt it; in addition, he always had twelve skilled huntsmen at his side. There were also scores of grooms and running footmen. The Grand Huntsman's staff included a Captain of the Nets who was assisted by 100 archers. The Captain's function was to drive game into an area enclosed by nets, for the King to shoot at with a crossbow or an arquebus. The equipment for this was carried in fifty carts. . . .

"There were deer—red, fallow, and roe—and boar, besides wolves and beech martens, otters, and hares. In François's time, as nowadays, French hunting was a slow, stately ritual conducted with military pomp and music. Along the woodland rides, noblemen gravely caracoled their horses in response to melodious signals from great brass horns. At the climax, when the animal had been brought to bay, the lord who dispatched it, amid the whoops of the *hallali*, did so with a gilded sword or boar-spear, after which the mort was blown. Even then the pageant was not over. When the hunt came home at dusk, another concert of braying horn music took place in a château courtyard lit by hissing flambeaux before huntsmen drawn up in ranks like soldiers. . . . "

It was in the evening, after an elaborate dinner, that the ladies of the court came into their own. Francis had a sharp eye for beautiful women, and he liked to see them dressed in all the finery that the kingdom's best dressmakers and jewelers could provide. "A court without ladies," he liked to say, "is a garden without beautiful flowers." The ladies who enjoyed special royal favor were known as the *petite bande* and included two official mistresses, Françoise de Foix, Dame de Châteaubriant, and later Anne de Pisseleu, Duchesse d'Etampes. Queen Claude seldom appeared in this glamorous company, being quite content to keep her own dowdy court at the chateau of Blois, about ten miles to the east of Chambord.

The splendor of Francis's court was most famously put on display at a meeting with Henry VIII of England in 1520 at a village near Calais, which was still English soil. It has been known ever since as the Field of the Cloth of Gold, from the gold cloth with blue stripes that covered Francis's tent and the pavilion where the rulers met. Not to be outdone in elegance, Henry countered with a mock castle of wood and canvas, and banners painted by Holbein. Both monarchs were loaded with robes and jewels that would have taxed the strength of less robust men. "Is he as tall as I am?" Henry had inquired in advance. (About the same: six feet.) "Is he as stout?" (No.)

The meeting was a month-long splurge of feasting, jousting, and diplomatic maneuvering. Before they left, Henry challenged Francis to a wrestling match, and to Henry's great surprise, Francis threw him. Politically, the Field of the Cloth of Gold was a standoff—Francis could not persuade Henry to join his struggle against Charles V. But the two rulers did develop a genuine regard for each other, and the splendor of the occasion impressed Europe with the magnificence of both kings. It also put a strain on both royal treasuries.

Francis's finest hour, and his greatest disaster, occurred only five years later. In a battle with the forces of Charles V, king of Spain and Holy Roman Emperor, fought near Pavia in Italy, his troops broke and ran, leaving the French king and his courtiers to fight on alone. They were cut down, one by one, until only Francis, in his silver coat and long plumes, was still standing. He killed several Spanish soldiers with his sword before he was taken, alive but badly wounded, and sent off to Spain as Charles's prisoner. After more than a year in a tower of the alcazar at Madrid and at least one unsuccessful escape attempt, Francis negotiated a settlement with Charles. In return for his release and Charles's sister Eleanor for a bride, Francis promised to give up Burgundy, Flanders, and Artois, to abandon his claims to Milan and Naples,

and to send his two elder sons, Francis and Henry, to take his place in the prison. They were kept hostage there for four more years.

Work on Chambord had been suspended for lack of funds while Francis was campaigning against the emperor. After his return from Spain he finished the building but devoted more of his attention to remaking the old palace of Fontainebleau. The court came to Chambord for brief visits in the autumn when the hunting was best, but it never stayed long because the game could not withstand for many days the army of bowmen that the king always brought with him. Chambord was Francis's favorite castle—he referred to his trips there as "going home"—but he spent only twenty-seven nights there in the course of five separate visits.

It was probably just as well that the royal party did not stay longer. When Chambord was being built Francis had diverted the river Cosson to flow past the chateau and to fill the wide moat—almost a lake—which served as a reflecting pond for the building. Between the stagnant moat and the surrounding swamps, Chambord was proved in later years to be an extremely unhealthy place. In the eighteenth century, when Stanislas Leszczynski, the exiled king of Poland, was given the chateau as a home by his son-in-law, Louis XV, his entourage came down with fever that Stanislas attributed to "the exhalations from the marshes." Stanislas narrowed the moat and tried to drain the swamp, but twenty years later, when the chateau was given to Maréchal Saxe for his victory at Fontenoy, conditions were not much better. "Chambord is a hospital," the old soldier grumbled. "I have more than three hundred sick, several dead, and the others have the look of exhumed corpses."

Since that time Chambord has seldom been occupied for long. Stripped of most of its furnishings during the French Revolution—when, in its dismantled state, it was used as a prison—the chateau is an empty, cheerless cavern. But the staircase and roof are still the delight of visitors young enough to play hide-and-seek.

# A SWEEP OF STAIRCASES

*Spiral staircase in a town house on Boston's Beacon Hill*

*The elegant and intricately contrived staircases in a chateau such as Chambord were an indispensable element of court splendor, since they served as the stage for the exquisite entrances and exits the nobility so loved. In fact, almost every magnificent builder has used staircases— those most fluid and difficult of architectural elements— to reflect his grandeur or at the very least his ingenuity.*

The graceful ellipses of the freestanding
spiral stairway above are one of the
salient features of merchant Nathaniel
Bussell's house in Charleston, built in 1809
for the then tremendous cost of $80,000.

The more solidly anchored stairs at left,
ingeniously planned to give the climber
a choice of turning to the left or right,
were designed by the English architect Robert
Adam in 1777 at the behest of David Kennedy,
the tenth earl of Cassilis, for the earl's
ancestral home, Culzean castle in Scotland.

Architect Levi Weeks borrowed the plan for
the swirling staircase opposite from a British
Palladian design book and built it in the
Natchez home of Yankee merchant Lyman Harding.

OVERLEAF: Stone lions guard the grand staircase of
the palace of Caserta, built by the future Charles II
of Spain after he conquered Naples in 1734.

The strength and malleability of wrought iron made it an ideal material to express elaborate whim. The Belgian architect Victor Horta designed the staircase at left for the world's first art nouveau building, the 1893 Brussels home of a Professor Tassel. Three years later August Engel, a German counterpart of Horta's, put even more sinuous loops along the staircase shown below left. Early in the nineteenth century King Ferdinand IV of the Kingdom of the Two Sicilies commissioned the delightful iron stairs opposite. Exiled in Palermo between 1806 and 1815, the king spent his time building a Chinese palace; the double stairway led from the queen's apartment down to a Turkish salon.

# 3 ARCHITECTS FOR THEMSELVES

Architects spend most of their careers building for clients. As one of their number (Richard Morris Hunt) said to his son, "If they want you to build a house upside down standing on its chimney, it is up to you to do it." But the great day usually comes when an architect has the perfect client: himself. On these pages we look at some of the houses that architects built to please themselves.

*Philip Johnson stands in his sculpture gallery, his favorite of the five buildings in his famous New Canaan, Connecticut, compound.*

# Frank Lloyd Wright's Taliesins

To Frank Lloyd Wright, home was more than a place to hang his wide-brimmed hat and his flowing black cape. It was his office, his studio, and his pulpit. It was a standing advertisement of his genius. It was headquarters and dwelling place, not only for his family but also for a devoted band of architectural students, usually numbering from twenty to forty, who came to learn from the master.

Wright built the first of two such homes among the green hills of southern Wisconsin, the land of his birth. The second was built a quarter century later in the harsh, bare desert of Arizona. He named each Taliesin, after a legendary Welsh poet. The first Taliesin was the scene of repeated turmoil in Wright's tempestuous married life—and of one fearful tragedy. Taliesin West was the sunny stage on which he played out with immense enjoyment his role as the greatest architect of America and, as his admirers fervently believed, of the world. When he died there in 1959, a few months short of ninety-two, he stood at the professional peak of a life that had begun only two years after the Civil War.

Frank Lloyd Wright's early years were such as to fill a boy's mind with all sorts of dreams and ambitions, but not to give him much sense of security. His father, William Cary Wright, was at various times a lawyer, a preacher, a lecturer, and a music master—a man whose considerable gifts in all those fields never yielded more than a shaky financial footing for his family. The father was a forty-one-year-old widower with grown children when he married Frank's mother, Anna Lloyd Jones, then twenty-four. Frank, their eldest child, was born in Richland Center, Wisconsin, but within two years the family began a series of moves that took them to Iowa, then to Rhode Island, and then to Massachusetts, where the senior Wright became a Baptist minister. Finally, when Frank was ten, they returned to Wisconsin.

In Madison, William Cary Wright started a music conservatory, but within a few years that too failed. Unable to earn a living, and convinced that his native gifts had been crushed by the obligations of family life, he took out his bitterness on his wife until at last she said: "Very well, Mr. Wright, leave us." Frank was eighteen when his father packed a bag, took his violin, and walked out the door, never to be seen again by his wife or children.

In Wisconsin, where his father had found only frustration, Frank Lloyd Wright found security among the solid Welsh farmers and teachers and ministers of his mother's family. The hills and meadows where he spent his summers in farm work nourished a conviction that was basic to his later professional work: that a building should not, as so many architects of the past and of his own time thought, be a freestanding reflection of man's own vertical image; but rather that it should be an expression of man's close connection with nature, seeming almost to grow out of the earth.

His mother had always wanted Frank to become an architect. Even before he was born, in some superstitious hope of prenatal influence, she claimed to have spent time looking at pictures of English cathedrals. When he was still in long Fauntleroy curls she bought him, out of her savings, an expensive set of blocks designed by the German educational pioneer Friedrich Froebel to help children learn forms and spatial relationships. In later years Wright gave credit to those blocks as a major influence on his architectural career. It is not too far-fetched to discern their reflection in the sweeping horizontal masses, one piled upon another, that distinguish some of his finest work, including notably the Robie house in Chicago and Fallingwater, the Kaufmann house in Pennsylvania.

Burdened by an obligation to support his mother, Wright spared only two years, after his father's departure, for the study of engineering at the University of Wisconsin and part-time work in a contractor's office. At nineteen he left Madison for Chicago and soon found his way to the office of Louis Sullivan, at that time the most innovative architect practicing in the United States.

*Wright built Taliesen North, right, his home and studio in Spring Green, Wisconsin, in 1911. He rebuilt the house twice after fires leveled it, and he summered there until his death in 1959. The airy, comfortable chamber below served as both living and dining room. Wright himself designed the colorful rug in 1957, but died before it could be completed and installed.*

Master and apprentice took to each other at once. They shared a contempt for almost everything that had been built so far in the United States, a contempt specifically for Gothic churches and Georgian houses and everything that borrowed its character from other lands or times. They felt, as Wright had thought as a boy, that a building should derive its inspiration from its own environment, without resort to preordained forms or to frills of ornamentation.

In the first flush of early success Wright, who had scarcely even dated girls in his youth, married Catherine Tobin, the daughter of a well-to-do businessman. For their home he designed and built in Oak Park, a suburb of Chicago, a house that prefigured, in its overhanging roof and its curved brick wall, something of what would be the Wright style. Within the next decade the house was filled by six children. For twenty years Wright seemed quite content to be a fond, conventional suburban husband and father.

At the Sullivan firm Wright was handed many of the commissions for residential buildings, which did not interest the older architect. But when Sullivan found that Wright was also taking private commissions outside the firm, their relationship came to an angry end. In 1893 Wright set up his own studio and, although he ever after referred to Sullivan as *lieber Meister*, they did not speak for twenty years. The prairie houses that Wright went on to design, in the last years of the nineteenth century, look modern even today. They are long and low, hugging the earth and exuding the warm feeling of privacy and shelter that mark Wright's work. Inside, the bedrooms and service rooms are generally tucked away in corners and under eaves, to clear space for one high, spacious living room that almost always has, as its centerpiece, a massive stone fireplace.

Admirers of the so-called modern or Bauhaus or International style, which did not reach America from Europe until thirty years later, are often astonished to see how many "modern" features were used by Wright in his

prairie houses. These included ribbon and corner windows, a utility core of kitchen and bathroom and heating facilities, slab floors with radiant heating, split levels, cathedral ceilings, built-in lighting (when the incandescent bulb was new), and carports (before the Model T).

Already Wright was assuming the airs and prerogatives of genius. He let his hair grow longer and began to wear the flowing capes that later became a trademark. Clients were charmed by his initial gracious attention to their wants, but sometimes nonplused by his refusal to consider changes in the designs he handed them. If they objected that doors were too low to pass through without stooping or that windows were too high to look out of, Wright seemed to feel that such mundane considerations should give way to the beauty of form and line. There seems to be no basis for stories that he required one client to buy ten more acres to set off the house or that he advised one lady to wear dresses with horizontal stripes in order to complement her new residence. But there is no doubt that some clients were put off by his air of infallibility and his bearing of a modern Michelangelo.

Like his father before him—but rather because of success than of failure—Wright began to chafe under the duties and distractions of family life. Soon he was seeing less of his wife and more of one of his wealthy, sophisticated clients, Mrs. Edwin H. Cheney. In 1909 he took the same course his father had taken by walking out on his family. Mrs. Cheney, meanwhile, left her husband and two children to go with Wright to Europe. Because

*"Taliesin West is a look over the rim of the world," boasted Wright of his Scottsdale, Arizona, winter home. The building, which Wright began in 1938 and continued to refine for the rest of his life, reflects his conviction that a structure should meld with its environment. He built the low walls from the volcanic rock of the desert on which they stand. Redwood trusses supported the canvas roof, and everywhere he made the building open to desert wind and sun.*

111

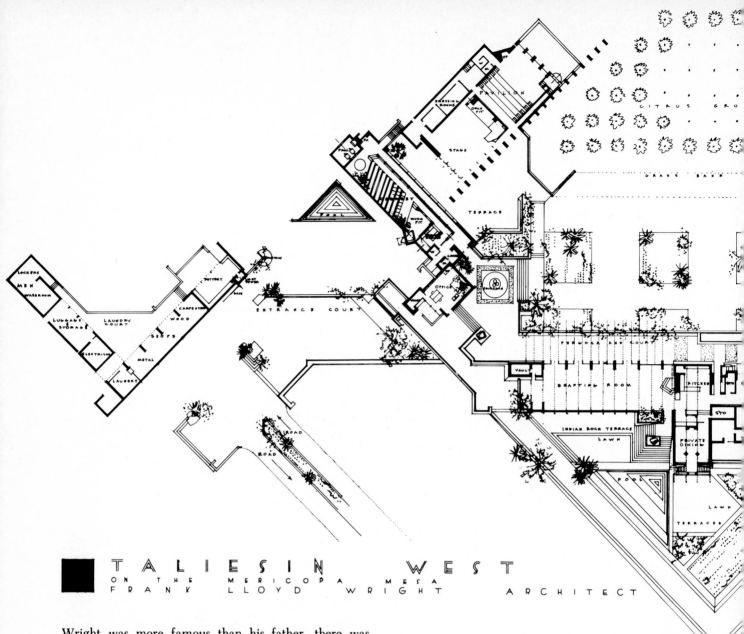

**TALIESIN WEST**
ON THE MERICOPA MESA
FRANK LLOYD WRIGHT ARCHITECT

Wright was more famous than his father, there was scandal in the papers and denunciation in the pulpits. For whatever reasons of anger or guilt, Wright did not let the furor die down but kept it alive by issuing a long and florid apologia for his conduct, explaining the horrors of loveless marriage, the claims of true romance, and the immunity of genius from the fetters of bourgeois morality. Needless to say, the editors and preachers of the country were stirred to further expressions of outrage.

Wright and Mrs. Cheney, still unmarried as the stubborn Mrs. Wright refused to be divorced, returned not to Chicago but to Wisconsin. At a place called Spring Green, on land that had been in his mother's family, he began construction of the first Taliesin. "No house," he said, "should be *on* a hill, it should be *of* the hill." Taliesin (which means, literally, "shining brow" in Welsh) was therefore built beneath the brow of a hill. It had the long, low lines of his prairie houses, with ribbon windows that opened it up to the rolling Wisconsin landscape. When the furor over his private life died down, Wright began to get commissions for larger build-

ings, including the Midway Gardens, an entertainment complex in Chicago. As his reputation continued to grow, architectural students began coming to Taliesin to learn from the master. Mrs. Cheney was seeing her children again, and all seemed serene.

Then, one day in 1914, Wright's second family life went up in one horrifying blaze. He was lunching with his oldest son in Chicago when word came that a demented servant had set fire to Taliesin. Within two minutes' time seven people had died, including Mrs. Cheney, her two children, and four apprentices and workmen. To some unforgiving guardians of the public morals, it looked as if Wright were being punished for his sins, and they said so. Again Wright replied with a long, grandiloquent defense of his private life.

After months of mourning Wright recovered from the blow and in 1915 began work on one of his greatest

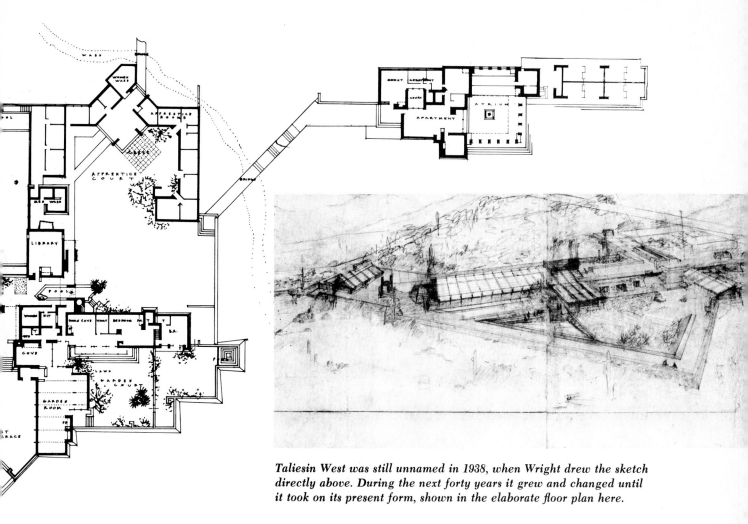

*Taliesin West was still unnamed in 1938, when Wright drew the sketch directly above. During the next forty years it grew and changed until it took on its present form, shown in the elaborate floor plan here.*

projects, the Imperial Hotel in Tokyo. More ornate than most of his work, it combined his own style with Japanese elements and more than a touch of ancient Mayan. To make it proof against earthquakes he built it on piles, in several independent sections. He had his reward within two years of its completion when the Tokyo earthquake of 1923 shook down many of the city's biggest buildings. Wright received from Baron Okura, the chairman of the board of the hotel corporation, a telegram saying, "HOTEL STANDS UNDAMAGED AS MONUMENT OF YOUR GENIUS."

Wright was now recognized, though more fully abroad than at home, as one of the world's leading architects. However, his personal troubles were not over. In the time of his sorrow, after the Taliesin fire, he had received a letter of sympathy from a lady named Miriam Noel. They met, and presently she became the mistress of a rebuilt Taliesin. Miriam was a lady of Continental polish and the traces of great beauty, though of somewhat shaky mind. Their relationship was stormy, but in 1923, after his first wife had finally given him a divorce, he made Miriam Noel his second. Within months the marriage

collapsed, and Miriam went off to Los Angeles while Wright found a more understanding companion in Olga Milanoff Hinzenberg, a Montenegrin educated in Czarist Russia.

For the next years the pair were hounded by an avenging Miriam. Sometimes she would burst into Taliesin with lawyers, police, and the press at her heels. In the quaint legal terminology of the day Wright was charged with everything from lewd and lascivious conduct to alienation of affection. As a final indignity he was arrested and jailed overnight under the Mann Act, a federal antiprostitution statute that forbade anyone to transport a female across state lines for immoral purposes. Not until 1928, after Miriam had finally accepted most of Wright's property in return for a divorce, were Wright and Olgivanna, as he called her, free to marry.

Then began the final, peaceful, and amazingly fruitful last period of Wright's life. In his sixties he designed such notable buildings as the Johnson Wax headquarters in Racine and produced plans for a model "Broadacre City" of freestanding houses. In his seventies he designed the

Catherine Wright      Mamah B. Cheney      Miriam Wright      Olga Wright

striking Unitarian church at Madison and the buildings of Florida Southern College. In his eighties he built the Guggenheim Museum in New York and drew plans for a mile-high skyscraper for Chicago.

In the time of his financial distress Wright had turned Taliesin into a foundation and had begun taking architectural students for a fee. But Taliesin was cold in the winter and costly to heat, and besides, Wright had discovered the Arizona desert. In 1938 he bought a tract of barren land west of Phoenix in what is known, not without irony, as Paradise Valley. That fall he led his family and followers, like some nomadic tribe, in the first of many seasonal migrations from Wisconsin to Arizona.

There in the desert Wright and his apprentices began to build with their own hands the winter encampment of Taliesin West. Because he had no one to please but himself, Taliesin West became perhaps the purest embodiment of Wright's mature architectural genius. The walls of the house were built of rocks, in all shades of brown and green and blue and red, gathered from the surrounding desert and embedded in rough concrete. Many of the windows were apertures covered by canvas flaps that could be pulled up to let the wind blow through. Across the tops of the walls, and projecting beyond them, were laid thick redwood rafters. Under the rafters, by way of roof, were hung sheets of canvas that suffused the rooms below with soft white light.

The layout of Taliesin West follows no formal plan but is governed by the contours of the land, by the vistas to be had in every direction, and by Wright's sure feeling for line and space. Interior walls may be curved, dented, or unfinished but are seldom straight. Some of the rooms have the feeling of caves, others of tents. It is easy to get lost, hard to know where one room ends and another begins.

The outside lines of the buildings are broken with terraces, steps, and arcades. The grounds are strewn with large boulders, planted with cactus, and dotted with pools of water. Sunlight is used as an element of architecture,

with careful calculation of the shadow cast by every step or beam or wall. To some visitors the whole establishment looks as if it had been formed by nature. Others are reminded of an ancient Indian ruin.

In this desert capital Wright enjoyed the authority and respect of a feudal prince. In the morning his followers labored with their hands on building walls or molding landscape. In the afternoon they worked on their own architectural projects or helped the master with his designs. On Saturday and Sunday evenings they gathered for talk, games, and music in the great living room with its stone fireplace, a piano and harp, and mounds of colored pillows.

In this congenial atmosphere Wright's most extravagant remarks were received as the judgments of an oracle. Here he tried out and polished up the pronouncements he later made to the press: on a distinguished peer, Le Corbusier ("Only a painter, and not a very good one"); on women's hats ("Throw them away"); on Pittsburgh ("Destroy it and start over"); on the public's negative reaction to architectural innovation ("We go on living in boxes of stone and brick while the modern world is crying to be born again in the discovery that concrete and steel can sleep together"). The twinkle that accompanied these judgments disappeared, of course, in the printed reports.

It is often charged that Wright exploited his apprentices, using them chiefly as manual laborers and scorning their architectural efforts. Sometimes he would look at a drawing on which an apprentice had spent many hours and slash a crayon across it. But, as one of them said, "I always had three coats of lacquer on a finished drawing, so it wiped right off."

Among his followers who stayed, there was never any expression of doubt that Wright was the greatest living architect. Indeed to him and to them, that seemed a limited accolade. A biographer, Finis Farr, describes an occasion when someone spoke of a historian who called Wright the greatest architect since the Renaissance: "The

*The charismatic Wright carried his creative faculties miraculously unimpaired through a personal life as turbulent and well-publicized as that of any movie star. When he upset twenty years of tranquil upper-middle-class life with his first wife, Catherine, to run away with a client, Mrs. Edwin Cheney, he triggered an outpouring of shrill disgust in the local press. After the tragic death of Mrs. Cheney, Wright suffered a brief, stormy marriage to the high-strung Miriam Noel. During his later years—still the very picture of the self-possessed boulevardier—he found a measure of peace with his third and last wife, Olga.*

apprentices promptly began to analyze this statement like literary critics puzzling over a passage of James Joyce. They asked each other, 'Who of the Renaissance could the historian have had in mind as greater than Mr. Wright? Was it Michelangelo? Bramante? Raphael? Brunelleschi of the Chapter House at Florence?' In the end their only agreement was that the writer must have been singularly ignorant not to know that the entire Renaissance had failed to produce anyone who could surpass the master of Taliesin. In the midst of this sat Frank Lloyd Wright, flashing his penetrating glance from face to face, and holding his white head high. While the discussion continued, it was observed that Wright, who had never been known to keep silence in the presence of anything with which he disagreed, did not interrupt the apprentices with so much as a murmur of deprecation."

Certain prices had to be paid for living in such a superlative work of art as Taliesin West. On warm days, in early spring or late fall, it was hot under the canvas, and in midwinter, with no glass in the windows, it could be cruelly cold. The sudden, drenching rains of the desert were a problem. A visitor who arrived during a desert cloudburst found the master huddling inside the huge fireplace to escape the water dropping into the living room from the canvas roof. But Wright was never one to let a few practical problems interfere with his lofty conception of a building as a work of art.

Since his death in 1959 the Taliesin fellowship has carried on as a learning center under the direction of his widow. It is still a shrine for students who recognize Wright as the greatest architect America has produced. But some changes have been made. The establishment is air-conditioned now, at some cost to its free and airy feeling. Birds no longer fly through the open windows. And the lovely canvas tenting, which had to be renewed every few years, has been replaced by a roof of Plexiglas.

Plexiglas!

# A MOSAIC GROTTO

Juan O'Gorman, the Mexican architect and artist, is best known for the spectacular library that he designed for the University of Mexico. All four sides of the ten-story structure are covered with mosaics depicting in bright colors the history of Mexico from its Indian origins through the Spanish conquest to the present day.

No less remarkable was the house that O'Gorman built for himself on a volcanic rock formation in the Pedregal of San Angel, a park in Mexico City. The living room was a grotto hollowed out beneath an overhanging ledge of lava. The rest of the house was built of the same rock, with rough walls, curves, and irregular crenelations that might almost have been formed by nature. Inside and out, surfaces were covered with mosaics made from bits of colored stone. Some of them depicted Aztec warriors, Mayan serpents, jaguars, condors, and abstract symbols taken from the ancient Indian cultures of Mesoamerica. Other mosaics mimicked the animal life and the lush vegetation of the surrounding country. Year by year, as the trees and vines and the cactus grew over and around it, the house came to seem almost as much a part of the natural landsape as the lava flow on which it was built. Some ten years ago O'Gorman sold his house to a developer who, having promised to preserve it in its original form, promptly made what the architect glumly called "significant changes."

*O'Gorman appears four times—five, counting the hand holding the paintbrush—in this 1950 self-portrait.*

*O'Gorman and his wife relax under the skylights in the lava-rock living room of their house, which O'Gorman called "the most complete and satisfying work I have done in architecture." This is the only known color photograph of the brightly decorated home.*

O'Gorman stands in a window of his home beneath a
serpent, one of the many stylized native animals
the architect incorporated into his mosaic designs.

More fauna of the region, including birds and various
animals, decorated the upper terrace of the house.

A detail of exterior mosaic shows
a gaping mouth containing a window.

The bird atop the upper terrace was
both decoration and windbreak.

A rough-hewn stone cantilevered
staircase led to the second floor.

# THE PRAIRIE CHICKEN

Hunched against the northers
that regularly scour the Oklahoma
prairie, architect Herbert Greene's
own house looks, he insists,
like a mother hen protecting her
young. Others have compared it
to a praying mantis or an armadillo.
To Greene, however, it is clearly
a reflection of the characteristics
of the land on which it sits.
"From prairies to barns, from birds
to buffaloes and from wagons
to planes . . . all this is embodied
in the design by its very
geometry, texture, and color."
Born in upstate New York
in 1929, Greene left the East
when he learned that schools
there placed little emphasis on
fitting architecture into its
environment—a concept he had
embraced after learning of it from
Frank Lloyd Wright. Greene
found the attitudes he wanted at
the University of Oklahoma, where
he studied what would become
his lifelong interest: "to discover
how architectural form . . . can
be evocative of happenings,
architectural or otherwise, that
have had their histories on or
near the site of the building."
When Greene built his house
at Norman in 1962, he used shingle,
corrugated metal, and wood planks
to make the idiosyncratic building
upon whose weathered, bristling
surfaces, he feels, can be read
something of the history and
atmosphere of his adopted state.

*Herbert Greene in 1973*

*Greene's 1962 house squats on the Oklahoma prairie.*

121

# Philip Johnson's Glass House

At the time when Philip Johnson built his glass house in New Canaan, Connecticut, in 1949, he was a follower of Ludwig Mies van der Rohe, whose architectural philosophy was expressed in the phrase "Less is more." Johnson carried that principle to its logical conclusion by building a house that is as close as anyone can get to nothing at all.

The house stands in a clearing on Johnson's estate, surrounded at some distance by oak and maple woods. A visitor approaching in certain light conditions may hardly see that it is there. What he sees instead is the reflection of the trees and the carefully landscaped grounds in the walls of the house.

Structurally, the house is a rectangular glass box with the thinnest of steel columns painted black supporting the roof, and with no interior partitions. Standing near one end of the interior space and extending through the roof is a brick cylinder, which contains a bathroom, service facilities, and a fireplace. Otherwise, the interior is broken only by two rows of cabinets, which define the living, dining, cooking, and sleeping areas.

The "living room" is as carefully arranged as an art gallery. There are two big Mies (it is a long-standing convention among architects to refer to Ludwig Mies van der Rohe by the first part of his surname) chairs of steel and leather with a matching stool, a glass coffee table, a steel-and-rosewood couch upholstered in brown leather, two almost life-size ladies in papier-mâché by the sculptor Elie Nadelman, and a single painting, *The Death of Phocion,* by Nicolas Poussin, on an easel by the fireplace. A visitor who carelessly put her handbag on the couch was quickly admonished by a friend to pick it up, since the house had been conceived as a still life.

It is certainly not a house for untidy people or for anyone who values comfort over aesthetic satisfaction. It is definitely not a house for children. In fact, as the architectural critic Paul Goldberger once pointed out, it is probably not a house for anyone but Philip Johnson.

The son of a wealthy Cleveland lawyer, Johnson claims to have become enamored of architecture early. In 1919, when he went to France as a thirteen-year-old with his mother, he was stunned by his first glimpse of Chartres Cathedral. "There was a funeral going on," he said; "I was so moved I don't know why *I* wasn't dead."

But in fact he had little to do with architecture during his seven years as an undergraduate at Harvard; he majored in philosophy and took a minor in Greek. However, in 1929, the year before his own graduation, he went to his sister's commencement at Wellesley and there met a professor named Alfred Barr, whose revolutionary course on modern art embodied the ideas that were to go into the foundation of New York City's Museum of Modern Art the next year. Johnson and Barr took to each other immediately, and they talked for hours. That, said Johnson, "was the start of everything."

Impressed by his energy and intelligence, Barr chose Johnson to form the fledgling museum's department of architecture. This turned out to be an extraordinarily good arrangement for the museum, for not only was Johnson brilliant; he had also recently inherited a large chunk of Alcoa stock, and he paid his own salary, his secretary's, and the museum librarian's. He and Barr studied the work of such great European modernists as Mies, Walter Gropius, and Charles-Edouard Le Corbusier and, like those men, turned their backs on nineteenth-century eclecticism and neoclassicism. Rather than a reliance on antique architectural elements, they advocated a purity of design in which a building's form reflected its function. This so-called structural integrity made use of such new materials as reinforced concrete and large sheets of glass, and stressed the volume of open spaces rather than the mass of heavy, ornate walls and columns. Barr himself gave the movement its name: the International Style. Johnson learned his new subject quickly, and together he and Barr played a major part in introducing modern architecture to America.

Then in 1934 Johnson suddenly quit the museum to make an abortive foray into right-wing politics. "People

As the plan at left indicates, Johnson
carefully sited his famous Connecticut
home to take the best advantage
of the view of the surrounding woods—and
of their reflection in the eighteen-foot
panels of glass that are the walls
of the house. Johnson calls the effect "the
most beautiful wallpaper in the world."
Mies designed the furniture, and Elie
Nadelman did the sculpture visible in both
the interior and exterior views at right.

were starving, which seemed very stupid in a country as rich as this one. I felt that since I was privileged enough not to have to earn my living, I should do *something*." Johnson and Alan Blackburn, the museum's executive director, volunteered their services to Huey Long. "We went down to see what he was up to. We didn't have any sort of idea of what we could do, and Huey didn't want any part of us, so we came home." Johnson's radical politicking culminated with a stint as the Berlin correspondent for *Social Justice*, Father Charles E. Coughlin's magazine, during the summer of 1939.

In 1940, having tired of his increasingly unpopular public stand, Johnson returned to architecture, this time to the practice rather than the theory. He passed easily through graduate school at Harvard, and for his thesis he built a house in Cambridge based on the principles of Mies, an austere wooden rectangle with a glass wall. One of his friends, visiting there, remembered the occasion as the first time he saw somebody walk into a glass wall. Johnson watched the man sink semiconscious to the floor. "Damn fool," he muttered.

That luckless guest would almost certainly have killed himself in the all-glass house Johnson built a few years later in New Canaan, which made the architect famous almost immediately. "I think," said art historian Vincent Scully, "its's one of the most important buildings in America. The glass house is a real archetype—a fundamental piece of architecture—and as such it is full of suggestions for the future." Even today, after such greater triumphs as New York's bronze and glass Seagram Building, which Johnson designed with Mies, most people remember him best for that house.

This persistence of memory irritates Johnson considerably; though he enjoys his house, the impatient, blunt-spoken, enthusiastic man found he had little interest in a project once he had completed it. When his friend Lee Radziwill asked him about the house in a recent interview, he replied, "All architects [feel] . . . the next building is the only interesting one. I want to be remem-

Sculpture gallery

*Pavilion*

Johnson's compound grew to its final
size over the course of twenty-one years.
He added the guesthouse in 1954, the
pavilion in 1962, the art gallery in
1965, and the sculpture gallery in 1970.
Together they constitute what friends have
called "the only truly modern estate in
the country." Johnson dismisses that:
"It's not an estate. . . . It has nothing to do
with Victorian estates. It's a little
group of buildings, five elements—no
barns or stables or anything like that."

Underground art gallery

Guesthouse

Glass house

127

bered for . . . the peculiar, strong statements that I have been able to make now, that I couldn't make when I was young. So the Glass House, the early work, makes me rather ill . . . . When things are once built, they should be put in moth balls."

Johnson, in fact, moved quickly to put his house in moth balls. Unlike the European masters, who saw themselves as revolutionary form-givers, Johnson had a thorough knowledge of architectural history and a personal predilection for elegance. In another age he might well have been a follower of Bernini instead of Mies. As it was, he began moving away from the dogma that form follows function. To a startled audience at Harvard in 1954, he said: "I would rather sleep in Chartres Cathedral, with the nearest john two blocks away, than in a Harvard house with back-to-back bathrooms."

The other structures that Johnson built on his New Canaan estate reflect his changing tastes. Across the lawn from his glass house, in obvious counterpoint, stands a second house that appears to be a solid, windowless bunker. It is the guesthouse, and actually it has three circular windows, like large portholes, on the side facing away from the main house. Its bedroom is designed to give, in his own words, "a feeling of cuddle," in contrast to the severe elegance of the glass house interiors.

By 1961 Johnson had deviated far enough from the International Style to declare, "Structural honesty seems to me one of the great bugaboos that we should free ourselves from very quickly." He backed up this statement by building, on the shore of a small artificial pond, a pavilion of white precast concrete columns, classical in appearance but on a miniature scale. A man cannot enter it standing straight up without bumping his head. Nothing could have been more surely calculated to outrage devout followers of the modern style than something so ornamental and so totally useless.

"I built it," said Johnson, "mainly to thumb my nose at modern architecture that had to have a use. I was thinking about the quarters the Duke of Mantua made

for his dwarfs, in the sixteenth century. Also about an island house, like the one you see in Böcklin's *Island of the Dead*. Also about tree houses and doll houses—the appeal of the small."

Johnson has also put the sort of painstaking care generally associated with Renaissance princes into the grounds of his thirty-two-acre New Canaan estate (he prefers the word *compound*). For instance, having noticed that the trunks of oaks turn dark after a rain while maples remain light, he has rearranged the forest surrounding his home to achieve the most pleasing mixture of post-storm shades.

The most recent structures on Johnson's estate are a gallery of paintings, built entirely underground, and a sculpture gallery of white-painted brick with a roof of mirrored glass. The sculpture is arranged on five levels of a single open space and is viewed from landings of a twisting staircase in the center. Johnson considers it the finest room he has ever done.

Johnson insists that while a building must function effectively, the larger purpose of architecture is "the creation of beautiful spaces." The structures he has built at New Canaan were built for the pleasure and amusement of a man who had both the talent and the means to build them. But any notion that he is a dilettante is dispelled by the volume of distinguished buildings he has turned out in the last twenty years. They include— besides the Seagram Building—such skyscrapers as Pennzoil Place in Houston and the Investors Diversified Services Center in Minneapolis, the New York State Theater at Lincoln Center, art museums for Washington, Fort Worth, Utica, Corpus Christi, and Lincoln, Nebraska, many college buildings, several churches, a nuclear reactor in Israel, and the fanciful Water Garden in the center of Fort Worth.

As for Johnson's personal project, the glass house, it is already obsolescent, a victim of the high cost of fuel oil. And Johnson admits wryly that no one has ever asked him to build another like it.

# Richard Foster's Revolving House

One of the problems troubling builders through the ages has been which way to have the house or palace face. For some it has been a choice between the mountain view and the valley view; for others, a choice between sunrise and sunset. Mr. and Mrs. Gerard Lambert of the Listerine fortune built a house at Palm Beach that has one part on one side of the coastal highway and one part on the other, with connecting quarters under the road; it was designed that way because he preferred the ocean view while his wife preferred the view of Lake Worth.

All these fastidious people could have solved their problems more simply if they had been able to avail themselves of the services of an architect named Richard Foster. When Foster bought a six-acre tract of land in Wilton, Connecticut, he found that he had three hundred sixty degrees of beautiful vistas and that siting the house to take advantage of one of them would mean playing down the others. He drafted four sets of plans and discarded them all before hitting on his simple but totally original solution: a revolving house.

The house that Foster completed in 1968 is circular, with pie-shaped rooms and glass walls, and turns three hundred sixty degrees on a pedestal. From any room the Fosters can, if they choose, face the sunrise in the morning, the southern skies at noon, the sunset in the evening, and the Big Dipper at night.

The full weight of the house rests on a three-ton ball bearing of the type originally designed for the gun turrets of battleships. Yet it is powered by a motor of only one and a half horsepower and costs no more to operate than an electric refrigerator. When moving at top speed the house makes a complete revolution in forty-eight minutes, at the lowest speed in four hours. While the movement is not fast enough to be dizzying, or even perceptible, the change of view from the same window sometimes has a disorienting effect on cocktail guests.

The chief problem in building the house was to connect the utilities, which rise through a central

*The architect stands on the spiral staircase that leads to the circular dwelling's front door.*

*Foster's house turns majestically in a Connecticut dusk.*

131

*With the house in motion, the landscape
wheels sedately past the living-room window.*

*Sole entrance is in the shingle-covered
concrete stationary core supporting the house.*

*This floor plan of the 39,000-square-foot house shows how the nine rooms radiate off the circular hallway.*

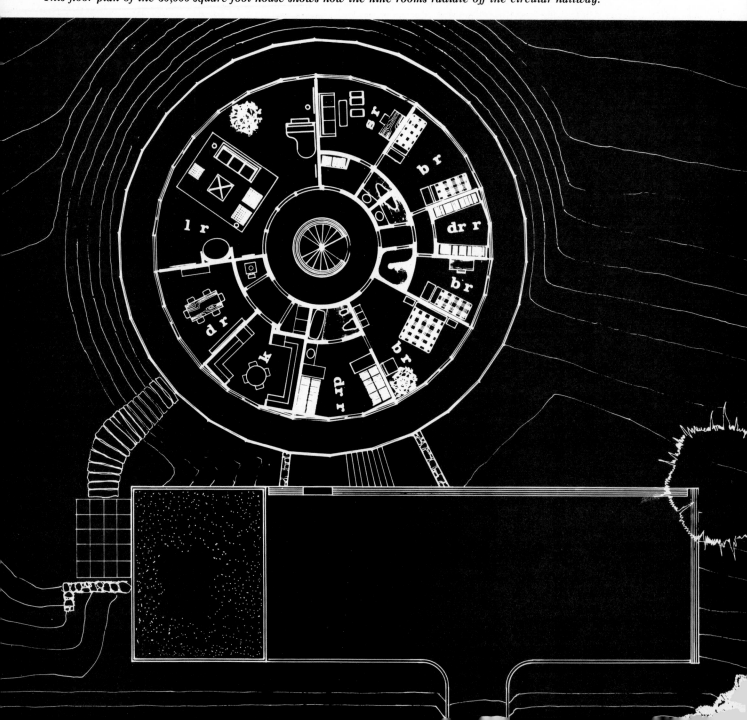

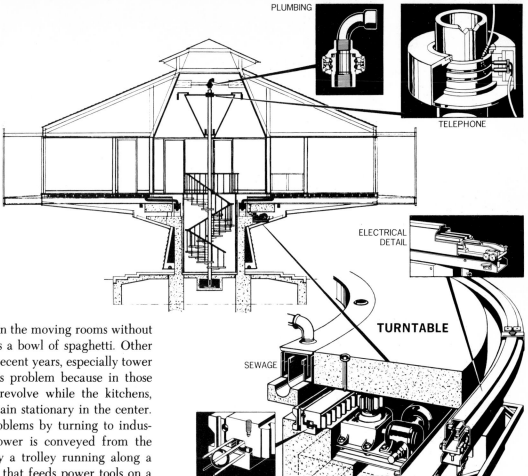

concrete core, to the outlets in the moving rooms without their becoming as tangled as a bowl of spaghetti. Other revolving structures built in recent years, especially tower restaurants, do not have this problem because in those cases only the outer shells revolve while the kitchens, bathrooms, and so forth remain stationary in the center. Foster solved his unique problems by turning to industrial technology. Electric power is conveyed from the core to the moving areas by a trolley running along a track—the same mechanism that feeds power tools on a factory assembly line. Water is delivered through the kind of swivel joint used in drilling for oil or loading tankers. Fuel tanks for the oil furnace are located under the roof. Though its manufacturers claim the main bearing will be good for eighty-seven years, Foster has included four jack points in the attic stretching down between partitions so that the whole house can be lifted and the huge mechanism replaced. Until that time, the house is solidly anchored: it can stand against 125-mile-per-hour winds and take a vertical load of five million pounds.

For all its innovations, the house is easier to care for than any traditional Cape Cod shingle; Foster was careful to specify that virtually all the materials used in its construction be maintenance-free. With the exception of the oak planking in the hall, the floors are made of hexagonal glazed ceramic tiles, and the terrace is resin-topped fiber glass—the same durable and impervious substance used to weatherproof the decks of ships.

In addition to its dramatic appearance and ingenious construction, the house has many advantages. It is great fun for children, who like to press the buttons marked "Forward," "Backward," and "Stop." When kept on a regular schedule, it does away with the necessity of looking at one's watch to know what time it is: if one is facing the pond it must be three o'clock. And at night the circular house on its pedestal offers a spectacular sight, seeming to hover like some sort of space ship. When reports of UFO's emanate from Wilton, it is likely that some stranger has just sighted the Foster house.

*These cross-sections reveal the complex engineering problems posed by the building— and Foster's ingenious solutions, which include a telephone linkage system of a type commonly used in swiveling radarscopes, an elaborate airtight sewage-disposal trough, and the bearing on which the structure turns.*

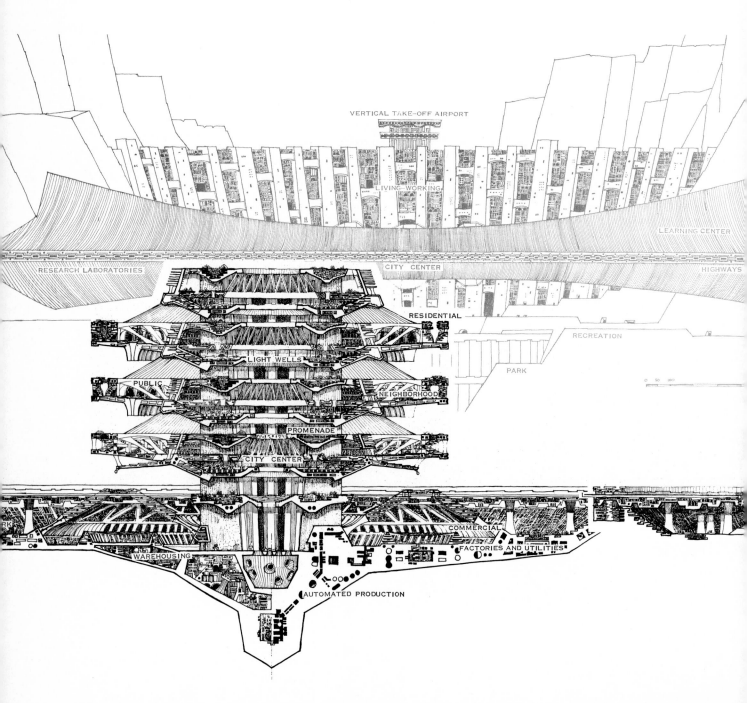

VERTICAL TAKE-OFF AIRPORT

LIVING-WORKING

LEARNING CENTER

RESEARCH LABORATORIES

CITY CENTER

HIGHWAYS

RESIDENTIAL

LIGHT WELLS

RECREATION

PUBLIC

PARK

NEIGHBORHOOD

PROMENADE

CITY CENTER

COMMERCIAL

WAREHOUSING

FACTORIES AND UTILITIES

AUTOMATED PRODUCTION

# Paolo Soleri's Arcosanti

*Soleri sits before a model of one of his cities.*

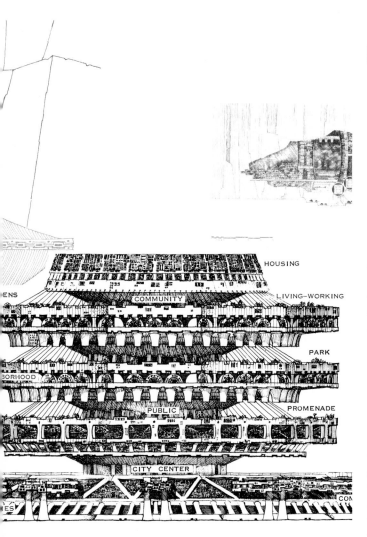

*Typical of Soleri's visions, Babel 11B is a hyperstructure capable of housing half a million people. Baffling as such concepts are, Soleri says his so-called arcologies are "Model T's" and will be regarded as merely "the beginning of progress."*

One of the great visionaries of the architectural world is Paolo Soleri, who came to the United States from Italy thirty-one years ago. Soleri's fame does not rest on the structures he has actually built, for these are few in number: a striking glass-domed house, a ceramics factory on the Amalfi coast, and the so-called earth colony where he and his followers lived in Arizona. His impact on the world of design has been made almost entirely through his intricate, detailed drawings for the city of the future—in which he fully intends to live. These drawings, rendered with the skill of a Piranesi, have astonished and mesmerized visitors to museum shows around the country.

Soleri envisions a future in which thousands of people such as he live in huge megastructures standing by themselves in the countryside. Inside the metal-and-concrete walls of such constructions are offices, factories, schools, stores, theaters, and every other facility of the complete city. On their outside skins are garden apartments for the residents, who would have no need to leave their megastructure except to enjoy the world outside. The concept is Soleri's solution to the problem of how to house the growing population of the world while still preserving the natural character of the earth's surface.

Soleri calls his structures arcologies, a word made up from *architecture* and *ecology*. They come in various models: one is a mile-high tower with concave sides; another is a right-side-up pyramid set on top of an upside-down pyramid; another serves a double purpose as a power dam; another floats upon the sea. Each of them is a self-contained metropolis housing from three thousand to more than half a million people and so condensed as to take up only two or three per cent as much space as a present-day city of the same population. Some viewers find them utopian, others find them monstrous. They are certainly unforgettable.

Considering how he thinks people should live, it is somewhat surprising to see what Soleri first built for himself—a one-story dwelling hollowed partly out of the

*Believing that "violence against nature is violence against man," Soleri built his first earth house, right, to blend with its desert environment. The dwelling has glass walls at each end and a roof covered with plants.*

*Hung with the ceramic bells that Soleri sells, the dramatic room opposite—one of several buildings in his Scottsdale, Arizona, complex—serves both as a workshop and a gathering place for the architect's followers.*

Arizona desert near Scottsdale and built of native materials. Nearby is a studio (shown on the opposite page) where Soleri and his students divided their time between working on architectural plans and manufacturing ceramic wind bells for sale. These early buildings, with their sculptural concrete columns and translucent glass panels, have the atmosphere of romantic modern caves offering refuge from the desert sun. They seem a far cry from the towering self-contained cities that took shape on Soleri's drawing boards.

When he first came to the United States, Soleri spent a few months in Frank Lloyd Wright's nearby Taliesin West. They did not get along, partly, it would seem, because Soleri would not work on the master's designs and was therefore assigned to manual labor. Actually, Wright might well have liked Soleri's early buildings. But he would surely have been horrified by the arcologies, which represent the antithesis of his own futuristic Broadacre City, with its stretches of single-family houses. Perhaps the most important thing that Soleri copied from Wright was the plan of a colony made up of students who come to learn from the master and work on the actual construction of his projects. Soleri calls his own fellowship the Cosanti Foundation and, like Wright, charges students a fee for a combined course of study and manual labor. Each applicant is told to be prepared for "the possible drudgery of the task at hand, since if those tasks are not carried on, the whole effort becomes a game among irresponsible people."

For the past seven years Soleri and his followers have been building the first arcology. Arcosanti, as he calls it, is not a project on the scale of the megastructures he has drawn on paper, but it is a smaller version of the same thing, designed to house five thousand people when it is finished. It will occupy fourteen acres of an eight-hundred-sixty-acre tract on a high, dry mesa seventy miles north of the original earth colony. Soleri and his students are building it largely by hand, using the desert sand to make concrete panels for the walls.

The buildings now under construction stand in what will be the forecourt of the arcology. They include a housing unit for students, a foundry for the manufacture of the bells that help to finance the project, a studio, and a visitor center with restaurant and exhibition hall. A significant element in this group will be a cloister dedicated to the memory of Pierre Teilhard de Chardin, the French religious mystic of the early twentieth century. It was Teilhard de Chardin's belief that in the evolution of human consciousness the individual mind had taken on an added dimension as part of an organic superconsciousness shared by all humankind. Soleri thinks of his arcologies as reflecting in concrete the conception of the individual as part of an encompassing structure of civilization.

Behind the cluster of buildings in the forecourt will rise the main structure of Arcosanti in the form of a great arc, twenty-five stories tall, with apartments on the outside and all the other elements of a city within. On a slope to the south of the forecourt will be a matching arc of greenhouses, designed for the dual purpose of growing food and trapping the sun's rays. Solar batteries will heat the rooms and the water, run the elevators and machinery, and supply all other needs, making Arcosanti independent of outside energy. Except perhaps for going somewhere else, automobiles will not be needed.

With a constantly changing work force of sixty or seventy untrained apprentices, the project is proceeding slowly. To a visitor it seems rather like setting out to build a Gothic cathedral in one's back yard with the help of the neighbors. But Soleri at fifty-nine is undiscouraged. During most of the years since he moved into the Arizona desert he has lived in makeshift quarters, the original earth house having proved too small for his growing family. At the present time he is living in a unit of one of the small completed buildings. But just beyond it he is building a future home for himself and five thousand fellow spirits and, he would like to think, a model for the human race.

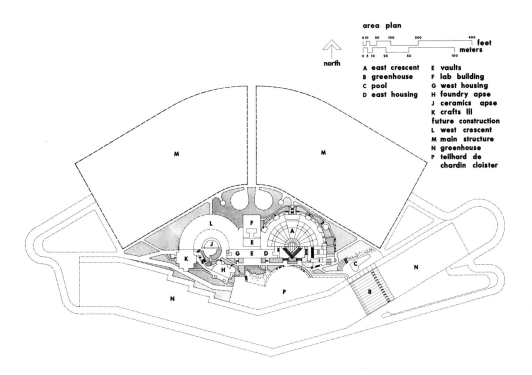

area plan

0 10  50  100        200              400
|_|__|___|_____|_____|  feet
                                     meters
0 5 10  25      50              100

A east crescent     E vaults
B greenhouse        F lab building
C pool              G west housing
D east housing      H foundry apse
                    J ceramics apse
                    K crafts III
                    future construction
                    L west crescent
                    M main structure
                    N greenhouse
                    P teilhard de
                      chardin cloister

north

*Although Soleri has designed cities for hundreds of thousands of people, Arcosanti, his prototype arcology, will house about five thousand. The model opposite and the diagram above show the completed city, including a five-acre greenhouse which will supply the inhabitants with food and heat.*
*The twenty-five-story main structure has yet to be built, but the nucleus of the city—shown in the photograph below—is well under way, having been constructed almost entirely by Soleri's disciples, who pay him tuition for the privilege.*

# John Soane's Museum House

B y the 1830's, in the latter years of his career, Sir John Soane had emerged as the dean of the British architectural establishment. His style was basically neoclassic, derived from Greek and Roman models, but he could never resist the temptation to add romantic, Gothic, Norman, Tudor, and rustic touches. He was at his best when tight purses imposed a restraint on his exuberant tastes. He left his mark most grandly on the Bank of England, whose piecemeal reconstruction he supervised for forty-five years, from 1788 to 1833. But his finest monument is the house that he designed for himself at No. 13 Lincoln's Inn Fields, in London's East End.

Wedged in between two other town houses, the façade of No. 13 is recognized today as a small masterpiece of neoclassic design, executed in off-white Portland stone. But the chief interest of the house lies in what Sir John did with the rooms behind the façade and what he put inside them. No. 13 is the best surviving example of what scholarly gentlemen of a hundred fifty years ago called a cabinet of curiosities.

Even in the United States every proper Victorian family had an Aunt Lizzie who loaded her mantel with a clutter of bric-a-brac and filled her living room with homely objets d'art that evoked romantic visions of ages past or her own sentimental memories of her visit to the Centennial Exposition. Just imagine what Aunt Lizzie might have done if she had possessed a good classical education, the experience of travel in Europe, ample means, the talent of an architect, and a house built especially to house and show off her treasures. All these advantages Sir John Soane had.

A water color that hangs in the house shows Soane with his wife at breakfast in a handsome, sunny library lined with cabinets of books. In old age he was very tall and thin and dressed entirely in black. "It can scarcely be said," wrote one of his assistants, "that he had any front face. In profile his countenance was extensive; but looking at it 'edgeways' it would have been 'to any thick

*Soane, shown in Thomas Lawrence's portrait, filled his house with relics, as in the domed well opposite.*

*Statue of George III*

*Sarcophagus of Seti I*

*Roman copy of Ephesian Diana*

*Roman cinerary urn*

*As this stylized 1827 cross-section of Soane's house suggests, his collection grew like a coral reef, each tiny increment add*

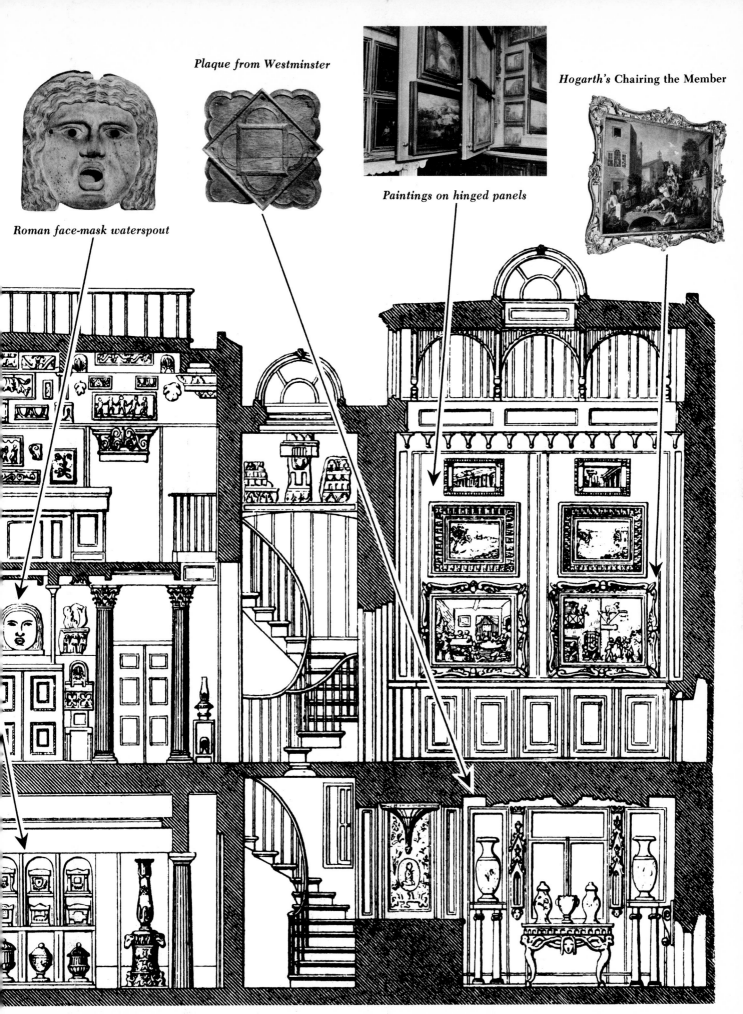

Roman face-mask waterspout

Plaque from Westminster

Paintings on hinged panels

Hogarth's Chairing the Member

*the ultimate, baffling whole—of which the eight treasures shown above are, in their diversity, perfectly representative.*

sight' something of the invisible. A brown wig carried the elevation of his head to the almost unattainable height; so that his physiognomy was suggestive of the picture which is presented on the back of a spoon held vertically." He must have looked right at home in his somewhat spooky abode.

The most striking part of the house is a central well rising through all three floors to the roof. The walls are covered with treasures of classical art, including busts, vases, broken bits of sculpture, fragments of Greek and Roman friezes, capitals, and architraves. A colored lithograph shows the vault as Sir John first adorned it in 1813, bathed in a dim, romantic light from a skylight. Sir John went on adding pieces and making changes for the rest of his life. As frozen for posterity at the time of his death, the house contains as its centerpiece the elaborately carved sarcophagus of the Egyptian pharaoh Seti I, removed from the Valley of the Kings in 1817.

Sir John mixed together authentic classical works of art with plaster casts of such famous statues as the Apollo of the Belvedere in a manner that would be the despair of any modern museum director. His interest was not in showing off individual pieces but in evoking the feeling of ancient times and far-off places. It reflects the same romantic passion for the classical past that caused British antiquarians to dig in the ruins of Pompeii and Keats to write his "Ode on a Grecian Urn."

Two of the more remarkable rooms in the house are among the smallest. Spanning the center of the tiny Breakfast Parlor—designed in 1812—is a canopy studded with mirrors and opening at the top to a lantern, which admits direct downward light. The north and south walls are bathed in natural sunlight coming from skylights hidden between the canopy and real ceiling. The proud architect wrote of the Breakfast Parlor that "the design and decoration of this limited space, present a succession of those fanciful effects which constitute the poetry of architecture."

Soane again used limited space imaginatively in the Picture Room—added in 1824—where his own architectural drawings are displayed as well as works by other artists, most notably William Hogarth. They hang on layers of hinged panels that open inward to reveal more pictures behind. By Soane's own calculations, he managed to compress into a space twelve by fifteen feet enough pictures to fill a gallery forty-five feet long.

A layer of hinged doors on the southern side of the Picture Room opens to reveal—at basement level—the Monk's Parlor, contrived with the help of medieval sculpture and artifacts to represent a cell in a ruined monastery. It opens onto the shadowy Monk's Courtyard, constructed from pieces of stonework that Soane saved from his restoration of the old palace of Westminster. Soane was by nature a gloomy man, especially in his last years, when his wife had died and his sons had disappointed his hopes for them. But even his fascination with the macabre was of the sentimental nineteenth-century sort. The creepy atmosphere of the Monk's Yard is broken by a dog's tomb inscribed "Alas Poor Fanny."

Tucked away in nooks and crannies of this magpie's nest are such items as a vase commemorating the Battle of Trafalgar, first-rate paintings by Joshua Reynolds and J. M. W. Turner and Thomas Lawrence, a Roman lion's-head waterspout, fifty-two rare volumes of the architectural drawings of Robert and James Adam, a silver watch that may have belonged to Christopher Wren, some dried cats, a bust of Soane himself, an equestrian statue of George III, and a jewel supposedly found in the baggage of Charles I after the Battle of Naseby.

All these curiosities, so lovingly gathered, so carefully arranged, so constantly enjoyed, were bequeathed to the nation when Sir John died. Seti's sarcophagus has lost its blue lining; the plaster casts have yellowed; the mirrors so cleverly installed in the Breakfast Parlor have grown silvery and dim. Aging aside, the house and its contents stand, by act of Parliament, exactly as their owner left them, a unique revelation of the mind and taste of a cultivated English gentleman.

# AMATEURS BY
# THEIR OWN HANDS

*Home-made castle in Loveland, Ohio, fashioned of rock from a nearby river*

*The fervent amateurs on these pages, though not as moneyed as the other magnificent builders, did not let lack of resources check them. Ohioan Harry Andrews, for instance, built the castle above by hand, stone by stone. Without professional help, he and others like him used virtually anything they could find to create lasting visions that are eccentric, charming, joyful—and occasionally beautiful.*

146

Ferdinand Cheval was forty-three years old when, going on his postman's rounds in Hauterives, France, in 1921, he tripped over a stone. "It had such a strange shape," he said, "that I picked it up and took it away with me." The next day he came back, gathered some "even more beautiful stones," and was launched into a project that took him "ten thousand days, thirty-three years of work." Over that time, Cheval built in his back yard a monument to himself that, he believed, represented "the rebirth of all the ancient architectures of primitive times." With his beautiful stones—and chips of mosaic, fragments of broken glass, pieces of discarded furniture—the driven postman built a fantasy of beetling towers swarming with mythological and Biblical figures, leering animals, and stone plants. He had never touched a trowel before, but he taught himself masonry and invented a home-brewed variation on reinforced concrete. His creation finished, he found the authorities would not let him be buried in it. He went back to his foraging and, in a final effort, built a tomb for himself in the local cemetery.

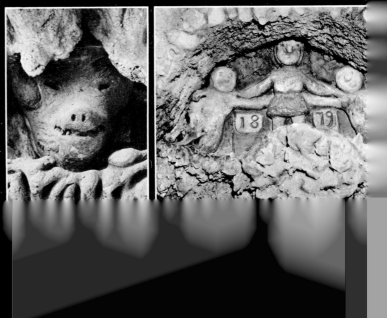

Chris Roberts's strongly sculptural
Madonna, *left*, is one of the
dozens of vessels that make up
the colorful houseboat community
of Waldo Point in Sausalito,
California. Since the late
1960's the authorities of wealthy
Marin County have been trying
to dislodge the houseboaters
and make room for high-rises and
similar income-producing dross.
But the Waldo Point residents
are fighters, and have made a
strong stand. Roberts himself won
an early skirmish; after a long
trial the court, finding itself
unable to have the Madonna
destroyed, instead officially
declared it to be a work of art.

George Plumb, a British Columbia
carpenter, sought to immortalize
himself by building the house at
top right entirely out of bottles.
He began work in 1963, and as
late as 1978 was still building,
having used over 180,000 liquor,
medicine, soda, and beer bottles.

"You know," Bryce Luther Gulley
once said, "not only do houses
look alike, but people are beginning
to look alike." Gulley himself had
little reason to worry about
becoming a stereotype. In 1927
this middle-aged shoe salesman,
having promised to build a castle
for his daughter, moved to Phoenix
and got to work. Starting with
wood salvaged from an abandoned
boxcar, he built eighteen rooms
and decorated the exterior with
fanciful mock-medieval trappings.
After he died in 1945 his daughter,
who had yet to see her castle,
moved into it and never left.

When Baldasare Forestiere emigrated from Sicily in the early 1900's
he found the Fresno, California, landscape so harsh and unwelcoming
that he decided to live underneath it. Burrowing with hand tools—
and leaving openings beneath which his well-loved fruit trees
could grow—Forestiere eventually carved out some ninety rooms.
When he died in 1946 he was working on a five-thousand-square-
foot room that was to be an underground restaurant. The
entire forty-year project, he said, cost him around three hundred dollars.

Perhaps no homemade edifice
is more exotic than the lacy
towers that rise from the ravaged
Los Angeles district of Watts.
They are the creation of Simon
Rodia, an Italian tilesetter
who built them, he said, because
he "wanted to do something for
the United States because there
are nice people in this country."
Starting in 1921, Rodia began
bending steel rods to form his
delicate towers and covering them
with cement inlaid with mosaic
tile, bits of glass, and sometimes
whole bottles. As the spires grew
skyward—one of them reached a
few inches shy of a hundred
feet—Rodia circled them with
concentric rings, each serving as
a scaffold on which he could
continue his work. Surrounding
the property on which the towers
went up he built a cement wall,
also richly inlaid with mosaics.
On weekends and evenings he took
the trolley out to Long Beach,
where he gathered shells and other
jetsam (see inlays at right) to
incorporate into his gleaming,
intricate, spidery obsession. Often
he strung lights and worked long
into the night. "I did it all by
myself," he said once. "If I hire a
man, he don't know what to do.
A million times, I don't know what
to do myself." In 1954 Rodia, then
seventy-nine years old, finished
his thirty-three-year task. He
turned his property over to a
neighbor and disappeared. Five
years later a reporter found the

# 4 INSPIRED WOMEN

"If Fenway Court is to be built at all, it will be built as I wish and not as you wish." So said Mrs. Jack Gardner to the building inspector in Boston. With determination of that sort the ladies in this chapter set out to make their architectural dreams come true. All of them got what they wanted except the duchess of Marlborough. While the duke fought England's wars, Sarah fought the queen, the architect, and the workmen in a fourteen-year battle over building a "wild, unmercifull Hous."

*Two women vied for possession of Chenonceaux—*
*this fairyland-like chateau in the Loire Valley.*

*This frank, though somewhat surreal portrait is of Diane de Poitiers, mistress of Chenonceaux.*

# Diane de Poitiers's Chenonceaux

The chateau of Chenonceaux stands on massive piles sunk in the waters of the little river Cher, a tributary of the Loire, some one hundred twenty-five miles southwest of Paris. From the south side of the building, which hugs the northern bank, a newer wing stretches out over five graceful stone arches to reach the southern bank. From any direction Chenonceaux is a chateau of surpassing beauty, but the best view is to be had from the river, and the best way to see it is to float down toward it in the morning sun, when its reflection shimmers in the gently rippling waters of the Cher. It gives us an idea of what the world might look like if its design had been entrusted to French ladies of taste.

Chenonceaux is best known as the prize of a famous rivalry between two ladies of the sixteenth century, Diane de Poitiers, the mistress of Henry II, and Catherine de Médicis, his queen. But the first lady to put her mark on the building was neither of these. It was Catherine Bohier, the wife of a royal collector of taxes in the reign of Henry's father, Francis I (the builder of Chambord, see page 88). The estate of Chenonceaux and the small castle that stood on it had been owned for generations by an old but improvident family named Marques. For years Bohier had watched their declining fortunes with all the patient cunning of a cat watching a careless mouse. Each time they needed money to pay their debts, Bohier had bought a piece of their property, until finally he owned the whole estate.

To clear the way for a chateau the old castle was torn down except for one tower that still stands by the entrance. Since Bohier was absent much of the time on foreign campaigns with his royal master, it was Catherine, his wife, who superintended the erection of the chateau. It is a square block of gray stone, set off by slim, graceful towers at each corner. The walls, inside and out, are lightened with a profusion of balconies, reliefs, projections, and squinches, carried out by local craftsmen with a fine sense of the line between exuberance and flamboyance. Some observers discern a woman's touch in the placement of kitchens and pantries within the supporting piles and in the arrangement of suites with connecting doors.

The Bohiers, like the Marqueses before them, learned the dangers of owning too attractive an estate. When the tax collector died, the court announced that he was in debt for arrears to the king, and Chenonceaux was taken in payment. Thus it was a royal property when Henry came to the throne in 1547.

At the court of his father, the embodiment of Renaissance charm and gallantry, Henry had been an unprepossessing prince. He was only seven when his father had the misfortune to be captured in battle by his archrival, Charles V, Holy Roman Emperor and king of Spain. As a condition of his release, he had to turn over his two sons, Francis and Henry, as hostages. For four years the boys were shut up in a Spanish fortress before Charles accepted a ransom and let them go. So long as the older brother lived, the father cared little about his shy and graceless younger son, but when the dauphin suddenly died, Francis decided that something must be done to make Henry shape up as a Valois king. For this task he turned to a lady of his court, Diane de Poitiers.

Diane, the daughter of a noble family, had been married at fifteen to one of the king's henchmen, Louis de Brézé, the Grand Seneschal (administrative officer) of Normandy. Though Brézé was forty years older than she and a hunchback, Diane spent sixteen years as his faithful wife in their gloomy castle of Anet. When he died she was only thirty-one and had made such an impression on Francis that he welcomed her into the *petite bande* of lovely ladies with whom he liked to surround himself.

Henry, as the new dauphin, was seventeen when Diane took him under her tutelage, and she was twenty years older. But by all contemporary accounts she had the gift of eternal youth. While most of the court ladies were still abed, Diane rose early to hunt with the men. In an age when perfume was commonly used as a substitute for washing, she bathed each morning in cold spring

*The intertwined initials at left—which one could interpret as either H-D or H-C—graced the wall of Diane's bedroom at Chenonceaux. After Henry's death, Catherine barred Diane but used her architect, Philibert Delorme, to design the interior of the five-arched bridge across the Cher, seen opposite.*

water. She wore no makeup and dressed at all times in black and white. One of her conceits was that she was Diana, the cool, silvery moon goddess.

In short order Diane not only carried out her instructions to make a man of Henry, but brought out in him qualities of mind and spirit that no one knew he possessed. "This lady," the Venetian ambassador reported to his government, "has undertaken to teach, to correct, to counsel the Dauphin, and to incite him to all actions worthy of him." The results were soon apparent: "The most Serene Dauphin . . . is of a very proper presence." Diane, beginning as Henry's tutor and surrogate mother, became not only his mistress but his closest adviser.

At the age of fourteen, Henry had been joined in a political marriage to Catherine de Médicis, a member of the famous Florentine family and niece of Pope Clement VII. Catherine had a good mind and a loving disposition, but she was plain of face and early ran to flesh. One of Diane's services to France was to urge Henry to carry out his marital duties often enough to ensure a supply of princes. As the children were born, they were taken from Catherine, at Henry's wish, and given to Diane to raise.

Ambitious and acquisitive, Diane was not content with any of the royal dwellings, which included the palace of Fontainebleau as well as the chateaux of Blois, Amboise, and Chambord. She had her eye on Chenonceaux, and as soon as Francis died she asked Henry for it. As always, he refused her nothing.

Diane made no changes in the building itself, but with the help of the leading architect-designer of the time, Philibert Delorme, she redid the interiors to her own taste. Doors, beds, fireplaces were carved with the intertwined initials H and D. It was Diane also who built an elaborate formal garden on a two-acre terrace above the river, and who threw a wooden bridge across the river itself. Diane spared no expense and her lover paid the bills. It was at about this time that François Rabelais, who had a ribald joke for every occasion, heard that Henry had levied a new tax on church bells. "The king," he

gibed, "is hanging all the bells of his realm around the neck of his mare."

Diane filled the chateau with works of art, including some of the many paintings and sculptures for which she herself was the model. Though well into her forties, she posed in the nude for Benvenuto Cellini as the Nymph of Fontainebleau and for Jean Goujon as Diana the Huntress. Many of the paintings, including one by Primaticcio, portray her as the chaste moon goddess, but others depict her in a more playful mood, bathing with another lady of the court.

Diane's tenancy of Chenonceaux lasted only as long as Henry's life. The king's end came suddenly in 1559 during a jousting match in Paris when his opponent drove a lance through his helmet and into his brain. Henry was carried into the Palais des Tournelles and, although he was not yet dead, Diane was barred at the door by order of the queen. As soon as he died, Catherine exerted her power to take Chenonceaux for her own. Diane was awarded the chateau of Chaumont in return, but she chose instead to return to her husband's chateau of Anet, where she lived the remaining seven years of her life.

Now, as the mother of the new sixteen-year-old king, Francis II, Catherine came into her own. Released from the long years of childbearing and royal neglect, she proved herself a true Medici, with a fine taste in art and literature and a gift for magnificence. At Chenonceaux she added a second formal garden and replaced Diane's simple bridge with a stone structure containing two long galleries, one above the other, that became the scene of splendid receptions and balls. Guests observed with amusement that wherever the H-D monogram had been carved Catherine had had the sides of the D's altered to make it into H-C for Henry and Catherine.

The first of Catherine's great fetes at Chenonceaux was given in 1560 to mark the accession of Francis II and his wife, Mary Stuart, Queen of Scots, who became thereby queen of France as well. These two royal children had been betrothed when the girl was six and the boy five, in

*Before Henry's death, which put an abrupt end to Diane's tenure at Chenonceaux, she enjoyed posing as the lithe huntress— her fanciful self-image—for paintings and statues like the one at right. Subsequently, she was ousted by the dowdy Catherine, who appears in the tapestry at left with her husband and a court dwarf.*

the interests of promoting an alliance between the two countries. Mary had been sent to France and raised among the French princes and princesses, under the tutelage of Diane de Poitiers. She was still only seventeen when she and the young king were entertained at Chenonceaux by the queen mother, Catherine. The party was stage-managed by Francesco Primaticcio, the Italian painter who had been brought to the French court as superintendent of royal buildings—and sometimes on the side as superintendent of revels. For the occasion he not only decorated the grounds with statues, columns, obelisks, and fountains, but dictated the costumes of the royal guests and ordered thirty cannon for noisemakers.

If Francis and Mary had had a son, he would have united the kingdoms of France and Scotland. But that prospect disappeared when Francis, a sickly prince throughout his life, died after only a year on the throne. Mary, who had loved France and French ways, returned sadly to Scotland to take the path of duty that led to long years of virtual imprisonment in England (see page 168) and finally to the headsman's block.

After Francis's death two more of Catherine's sons ascended the throne of France. Charles IX died of tuberculosis at 24, to be succeeded by Henry III. It was during the latter's reign that Catherine gave the greatest party of all at Chenonceaux to welcome her fourth son, the duke of Alençon, back from a minor military victory over the Huguenots. King Henry came in the costume of a woman, as he usually did at fancy-dress parties, with his cheeks rouged, his hair powdered violet, his doublet open and his neck hung with pearls. The ladies of the court were dressed in the manner of brides on their wedding nights, with their hair falling loose and nothing above their waists except transparent veils. It was an orgy that cost 100,000 francs at the time, and went far to empty the royal treasury.

Henry III was killed after fifteen years of rule by an assassin's dagger, and since Catherine had died in the same year, Chenonceaux passed to Henry's widow,

Louise of Lorraine, who plunged the chateau into mourning. Her bedroom, her bed, her carpets, her drapes were all of black. She herself wore only white. The walls were painted with coffins and gravediggers' tools, "all in festoons and held in place by widows' girdles."

After this macabre period Chenonceaux had one more brief moment of romance, around the end of the sixteenth century, when it was occupied by Gabrielle d'Estrées, the glamorous mistress of Henry IV. But after that it passed into the hands of the parsimonious dukes of Vendôme, who would not spend enough to keep it up. In the reign of Louis XIV his perceptive cousin the Grande Mademoiselle found the chateau still "extremely beautiful . . . absolutely enchanting," and added: "The only thing it lacks is a master willing to pay for painting and gilding the galleries as they deserve."

In the eighteenth century Chenonceaux was sold to a financier named Dupin, whose wife entertained such luminaries of the Enlightenment as Voltaire and Diderot and staged a production of Rousseau's opera *Le Devin du village* in the second-story gallery over the bridge. During the French Revolution the chateau narrowly escaped destruction by a mob. A farsighted local abbé managed to save the building by pleading, "Come now, citizens, do you not know that Chenonceaux is a bridge? You have only one bridge between Montrichard and Bléré, and you talk of destroying it. You are the enemies of public welfare."

In the nineteenth century Chenonceaux passed into the hands of a Madame Pelouze, an enthusiastic antiquarian who devoted most of her fortune to removing the embellishments of Catherine de Médicis and restoring the older part of the chateau to the purity of the original Bohier design. In 1913 Chenonceaux was acquired by the Menier family of chocolate manufacturers. Since then it has been open to the public as a designated historic monument. On summer evenings visitors are treated to a *son et lumière* spectacle which celebrates the history of Chenonceaux as the Chateau of Love.

OVERLEAF: *With its old keep, far left, capped by sixteenth-century Italianate embellishments, and its cleanly designed gallery, Chenonceaux remains one of the most superb examples of French Renaissance architecture.*

# "Building Bess's" Hardwick Hall

*"Building Bess" of Hardwick around 1590*

The redoubtable lady who built Hardwick Hall was seventy when she finished her masterpiece. She knew that she had built the finest house in Elizabethan England and she did not want anyone to forget it. On each side of each of the six towers, in stone letters three feet high, she signed the house with her initials: E S for Elizabeth Shrewsbury. She was then the dowager countess of Shrewsbury, and before that she had been Lady St. Loe, and before that Lady Cavendish, and before that Mrs. Robert Barlow. But to all who knew her she was never anything but Bess of Hardwick.

Bess had come back, as the richest woman in England except the queen, to build her house at the place of her birth. She had been born, probably in 1527, in a small manor house, also called Hardwick Hall, a stone's throw from the new mansion. Her father was a country squire, owning some four hundred acres of good Derbyshire pasture and farmland. But his death at the age of forty-one, when Bess was still a baby, had brought disaster to his widow and young children. In accordance with a cruel law of the times, the entire estate was seized by the Master of Wards, to be held until the oldest boy, then a child of two, should come of age. In theory the land reverted to the Crown until the heir could render "knight service" to the king. In fact, of course, knights were no longer of use in warfare, but Henry VIII found the ancient law a convenient source of revenue. Any family that ran afoul of it, as the Hardwicks did, could be left destitute. Much of Bess's energy in later life was devoted to making sure that nothing like that would ever happen to her own descendants.

Her mother, of necessity, remarried, and little is known of Bess's early life. According to her recent biographer, David N. Durant, it is likely that she was sent to live in the London household of a distant kinswoman, Lady Zouch, and there met a boy named Robert Barlow. They were married when she was only fifteen and Master Barlow was even younger. The pattern of Bess's marital life was set when Robert died, less than two years later, of "a Chronical Distemper," leaving her with an income of something like eight pounds a year—no great sum but about three times a household servant's annual wage.

Bess stayed on in London, possibly as lady in waiting to the Countess of Dorset. Bess was a redheaded young woman of no striking beauty, to judge by later portraits, but of ready wit, a quick mind, and a natural instinct for getting ahead in the royal court. Within three years she took a great step upward in the social scale by marrying Sir William Cavendish, a wealthy widower twice her age. Cavendish was an official of the Court of Augmentation, charged with the handling of church properties seized by Henry VIII. The purpose of that aptly named body was to augment Henry's revenue. In one way or another it had clearly augmented that of Cavendish as well.

Bess was now in a position to do what she wanted most to do: buy land and build houses. To please her, Sir William put most of his fortune into buying the manor of Chatsworth and some thousands of adjoining acres in Derbyshire. There Bess began building a great stone castle of a country house which became, by the time she was finished, one of the showplaces of England. The project was to keep her busy, off and on as funds became available, for the next twenty-five years, and to draw upon the fortunes of three successive husbands.

When Cavendish died in 1557 Bess was a woman of about thirty, with six growing children. She inherited all of her husband's estate, together with one serious encumbrance: a claim by the Lord Treasurer that Cavendish had helped himself to five thousand pounds that had to be returned to the government. Fortunately, Bess had won the favor of the princess Elizabeth, who in 1558 succeeded her sister Mary on the throne. Bess returned to court as lady in waiting to the new queen. In time she was able to settle the Lord Treasurer's claim for a thousand pounds and to find another rich husband, Sir William St. Loe, Captain of the Queen's Guard and Chief Butler of England.

It was not easy to find a safe path through the rivalries

*Husband No. 2:*
*Sir William Cavendish*

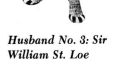

*Husband No. 3: Sir*
*William St. Loe*

*Husband No. 4: George Talbot,*
*sixth earl of Shrewsbury*

165

*Hardwick's curious staircase, with low risers and vestigial banister, meanders through the entire house.*

and intrigues of Elizabeth's court. During her marriage to St. Loe, Bess made one misstep when she involved herself in the secret marriage of Catherine Grey, the daughter of her old patroness, Lady Dorset. Catherine Grey was of the blood royal, and Elizabeth did not approve of the marriage. Bess paid for her meddling by spending thirty-one weeks in the Tower. It was a fairly comfortable confinement, in which she had her own servant and her own kitchen, and it did no lasting damage to her standing at court. Evidently, the queen recognized in Bess a kindred spirit, high-spirited, bold, and ruthless. It was not many years later that she said of Bess, "There is no Lady in this land that I better love and like."

Bess had only a few years to get on with the building of Chatsworth before St. Loe died, leaving her another sizable fortune. In search of a fourth husband she returned once more to the best of marriage markets, the royal court. This time fate, or the queen, presented her with George Talbot, sixth earl of Shrewsbury, a great favorite of Elizabeth and one of the richest men in England.

One thing that must have commended the earl to Bess was that he owned no fewer than eight principal houses, all doubtless in need of her attention. But there was another matter that caused her concern: the earl was a widower with children of his own, who would normally inherit his entire estate. The problem was neatly solved. In the marriage agreement between Bess and Shrewsbury it was stipulated that *his* son Gilbert should marry *her* daughter Mary, and that *her* son Henry should marry *his* daughter Grace. Although the youngest of the children involved was only eight at the time, the marriages were duly performed and a great part of the Shrewsbury fortune was ensured to the dynasty that Bess was determined to found.

Any prospects Bess and the earl may have entertained for a happy married life, as distinct from a dynastic merger, were not improved by the fact that within two years they were saddled with a permanent house guest.

This was Mary Queen of Scots, who had been forced to abdicate her throne and had sought asylum in England. Since the Catholic Mary was next in line to Elizabeth's own throne, the queen wanted her kept under close surveillance. It is a mark of the esteem in which Elizabeth held both Lord and Lady Shrewsbury that she asked them to receive Mary and her retinue at the earl's Tutbury Castle. For the next sixteen years, while Elizabeth worried about what to do with her Scottish cousin, Shrewsbury was Mary's host and in effect her jailer. Mary was a difficult charge, constantly complaining about her treatment, making plans for escape, and lending herself to plots against Elizabeth. But when she was not in a rage or in tears, she exerted her famous charm. She and Bess shared a love of embroidery and spent many afternoons together with their needles. Later there were rumors of an affair between Shrewsbury and Mary, but the record shows only the earl's continuous complaints to the Lord Treasurer that Mary was costing him more money than the Crown was paying for her upkeep.

The expense of keeping his royal prisoner was nothing, however, beside the inroads that were being made on the earl's fortune by his countess. Bess was busy during this period marrying off to suitably noble mates those of her Cavendish children who were not already married to the earl's heirs, setting them up with dowries and estates befitting their rank. At the same time, she was earning her nickname, "Building Bess," by finishing Chatsworth and greatly enlarging her old family manor at Hardwick. The earl complained to friends that she was always singing "her old song" for more money. Ten years before, in desperation, he had signed a deed giving to her sons William and Charles all the property Bess had brought to the marriage in return for an end to further demands. But this had only made him poorer, and as he saw his vast fortune dwindling away the earl turned bitterly against Bess. He wrote her a letter making his feelings toward her all too clear: "The faults and offences which you have committed against me which no good wife would do, are

admonitions sufficient for all men to be advised within their marriage.... Your fair words...though they appear beautiful... are mixed with a hidden poison."

Bess left for Chatsworth, and the earl would not have her back. The domestic discord of the Shrewsburys became such a worry to the queen that a royal commission, composed of the Lord Chancellor and two chief justices, was set up to hear the conflicting claims. To the earl's dismay, it concluded in general that his losses were only what he had brought upon himself by his marriage agreement and the deed of gift. However, hopes "that her Majestie hath reconciled the great Erle and his wief" were not fulfilled immediately. The queen and her advisers turned their attention to more pressing state problems, among them Mary's execution in February, 1587, supervised by Shrewsbury, in his position as Earl Marshal. Just two months later, for reasons that are still unclear, the queen managed to bring about an uneasy truce between Bess and the earl.

Perhaps the earl's great mistake in his marriage to Bess was that, in comparison with her other husbands, he had lived too long. Bess was impatient to get on with a much greater building project, a new Hardwick Hall, which waited upon her sole possession of her fortune. The way was cleared when the earl finally died, complaining to the end, in 1590.

Bess was in her sixties but filled with a fierce determination to build her final monument. Even before the earl was dead she had her surveyors at work on the chosen site, just a hundred yards from her birthplace. From her years of building she knew all the best designers and masons and plasterers and decorators in England. And now that she was the richest woman in the kingdom next to the queen, she did not have to build piecemeal.

Some of the credit for the design of Hardwick Hall should probably go to Robert Smythson, who designed many Elizabethan houses, including Longleat and Wollaton, and had helped Bess with Chatsworth. But Bess herself was quite capable of sitting down at a drawing

*Though she prized them, Bess saw tapestries
as a sort of glorified wallpaper rather
than works of art in their own right.
Among the scores of hangings she put
up at Hardwick are the ones at left
depicting the Virtues and the panels
telling the story of Adam and Eve
on the walls of her bedchamber, below.*

*More glass than stone, the west front of Hardwick Hall rises to parapets that still bear the huge, triumphant initials of Bess, the house's creator.*

board and making her own architectural sketches. By the summer of 1591 a force of at least fifty men began work. Most of the materials—stone and lumber, sand and lime—came from Bess's own lands; lead and iron came from her own mines.

The old lady was in a hurry. Because there was no time for seasoning the wood, the timbers went into the construction green, with the result that when they dried they sagged, leaving the floors uneven to this day. Local legend says that during one cold spell, when the masons complained that their mortar froze in the mixing, Bess bethought herself that alcohol would not freeze; she had them mix the mortar with beer instead of water.

Hardwick Hall was begun just two years after the defeat of the Spanish Armada. When it was completed nine years later, with banners flying from the towers and bugles sounding in the courtyard, the building expressed the spirit of Elizabethan England at its triumphant peak. With three stories, each taller than the one below, and six towers rising above the roof, Hardwick looks rather like a castle. But the walls are merely frames for the great tiered windows, each set with many small, diamond-shaped panes. Some early visitor, perhaps seeing the west front shimmering in the sunset, coined the jingle "Hardwick Hall/More glass than wall."

Inside, the first striking feature is the staircase, which is not confined to the usual stairwell but stretches through the house, broadening and narrowing and turning corners as it rises to the great rooms of state on the third floor. It was up these stairs that a procession of waiters marched each day, bringing Bess her dinner.

On the third floor are two splended rooms, each hung with fine Brussels tapestries. In the Long Gallery, which stretches the length of the eastern side, Bess did not hesitate to treat the tapestries as wall coverings, hanging over them portraits of herself and three of her husbands, Mary Queen of Scots, and Queen Elizabeth. The other set of tapestries, depicting the story of Ulysses, hangs in the High Great Chamber, which Sacheverell Sitwell called "the most beautiful room, not in England alone, but in the whole of Europe." This was Bess's favorite room, where she liked to walk from end to end as the sun or rain beat upon the tall windows.

Bess's joy and despair in these last years was her granddaughter Arbella Stuart, the child of a marriage that Bess had arranged between her daughter Elizabeth and the earl of Lennox. Through her Stuart blood Arbella was the queen's cousin twice removed, and had she been a boy would probably have been designated the heir to the throne. As it was, the queen might still have preferred her over another cousin, the king of Scotland. But during a stay at court Arbella had managed to offend the queen, and later she made matters worse by attempting to marry without either Bess's or the queen's approval. Bess seemed always to be involved in some way with possible successors to the jealous queen. She had gone to the Tower for meddling in the affairs of Catherine Grey. She had played hostess, at the queen's bidding, to Mary Queen of Scots. Now her granddaughter had incurred the queen's anger. The trouble passed and Bess remained in royal favor, but she had lost any hope of being the grandmother of royalty.

Bess lived on, content with her life's work but keeping busy with small construction projects, perhaps half believing what others said, that as long as Building Bess kept on building she would never die. She did die at last, probably in her eightieth year, on a winter day in 1608 and was buried in a vault she had built at All Saints Cathedral in Derby. She had founded her dynasty: among her descendants have been dukes of Devonshire, Portland, Kingston, and Newcastle. The descendants of her son William, who inherited most of her lands, chose to make Chatsworth their home, and one of them rebuilt it so extensively that hardly a trace of Bess's first spectacular project remains. Because they owned Hardwick but did not use it, that great mansion stands today almost as Bess built it. Now maintained by the National Trust, it is the finest of all Elizabethan houses.

# A FAMILY OBSESSION

Bess left Hardwick as a monument to her taste and energy, but Chatsworth, her earlier creation, owes its present form to several descendants who were infected by her own compulsive zest for building. The first was William Cavendish, the fourth earl and first duke of Devonshire, and he inherited the building in 1684. Finding it in shaky condition, he decided to rebuild the south front. That done, he felt that the other fronts did not look well with the new one. And so, with no real knowledge of the scope of the task that lay before him, he embarked on what would be a twenty-year career of rebuilding first one part and then another. He started out with a thirty-thousand-pound fine hanging over his head as the result of a curious peccadillo (he tweaked the nose of a political opponent). But even when that was waived, his lifelong infatuation with horse racing kept him in perpetual financial scrapes. Nevertheless, with an inspired mixture of sleazy financial maneuverings and appeals to the loyalty of his master masons, he managed to keep the work going forward despite threats, lawsuits, and court actions. When the duke died in 1707, the long, frustrating, piecemeal chore was done; the old Elizabethan core had been entirely hidden and the house magnificently transformed. This left the second duke free to concentrate on the interior. A

*Chatsworth's façade covers an Elizabethan skeleton.*

tireless collector, he assembled
an impressive marshaling of the
European masters of sixteenth-
and seventeenth-century painting, as
well as a distinguished collection
of coins and of gems from classical
antiquity and the Renaissance.

The fourth duke inherited the
first's urge to build and transform.
He married into one of the richest
families in England, thereby acquiring
almost limitless funds, and spent
a fair chunk of them bending nature
to better suit his grand house.
He hired Capability Brown, England's
greatest landscape architect. Brown
studied the manor's gloomy Derwent
Valley surroundings and worked out
ways to sculpt them into a series
of dramatic vistas. Stables
and kitchens disappeared from the
west front of the house, to be
replaced, at a cost of forty
thousand golden guineas, with
formal gardens and a façade that,
in the opinion of the usually testy
and critical Horace Walpole,
was "as delicate as wrought plate."

The sixth duke was interested
neither in painting nor in building,
but in sculpture; he occasionally
bought a picture by Landseer,
but for the most part he preferred
to spend his money on bronzes and
marbles, among them Canova's
*Endymion* and Tadolini's *Ganymede*.
After the sixth duke's time only
a relatively few objects have been
added to the manor's collection,
and some items have been sold at
Christie's, victims of modern
Britain's staggering death duties.
But what remains still represents
a truly unparalleled private collection
that, along with the grandeur of
the house and grounds, draws
hundreds of thousands of visitors
annually, all of them in debt to
the family's mania for constantly
improving their Elizabethan home.

*The muralist Louis Laguerre decorated the walls of the manor's*
*Painted Hall with scenes from the life of Gaius Julius*
*Caesar; the ceiling shows the gods receiving Caesar in heaven.*

# Sarah Winchester's Ghostproof Mansion

*A waxwork of camera-shy Sarah Winchester*

Of all the reasons people have had for building houses, perhaps the most bizarre was that of Sarah Winchester, the owner of a big, rambling, crazily constructed mansion in San Jose, California. The whole purpose of her lifelong building project—or so the legend goes—was to keep out ghosts.

Mrs. Winchester was the widow of William Wirt Winchester, son of Oliver Winchester, who made a fortune from the Winchester repeating rifle. When she was a young woman in New Haven, Connecticut, in the 1870's her baby daughter and her husband died in quick succession. In her grief Sarah consulted a spiritualist who, it is said, told her that she was being afflicted by ghosts of the people killed by the Winchester rifle.

These angry spirits constituted a large company, including some of the roughest and meanest characters in American history—murderers and bandits, cattle rustlers and bank robbers. Also among the victims of "the gun that won the West" were a great many Indians and not a few Army troopers, probably including some of General George Custer's command at the Little Bighorn.

In order to escape this terrifying company of spirits Sarah Winchester was advised to acquire a new home far from New Haven. To confuse the spirits she should keep adding new rooms to it. And of course she should make it as ghostproof as possible.

In 1884 she bought a nine-room house in San Jose and promptly began a building program that lasted until her death in 1922. Twenty or thirty carpenters, masons, and plasterers were kept working in shifts around the clock, seven days a week including Christmas, so that construction would never cease. Sarah Winchester built about seven hundred fifty rooms, most of which were torn down and replaced. When she died at the age of eighty-five the room count stood at one hundred sixty.

Those who believe that Sarah Winchester's purpose was to outwit the haunts find in the mansion many examples of her ingenuity. Since ghosts commonly gain access to a house through a chimney, some of the

176

*Amid the wild architectural clutter of the roof hangs the bell, which sounded only between midnight and 2:00 A.M. to summon and dismiss the spirits.*

Staircases played a special role in confounding evil ghosts and soothing friendly ones. The facing stairs below left have seven and eleven steps respectively—spiritually significant numbers—while the one at bottom right rises inanely to the ceiling. The two-inch-high steps in the staircases directly below may also have served a supernatural function or, more prosaically, may simply have made it easier for the house's arthritic mistress to climb them.

seventeen chimneys are dummies, without flues. A staircase leads only to a ceiling, against which an ascending ghost would bump its head. A doorway eight feet tall is followed immediately by one only five feet tall. A balcony three feet wide narrows sharply to a width of three inches. Doors open onto blank walls or onto the outside air, two stories up. One door has a bar eighteen inches above the sill to trip unwary spirits. A staircase has seven turns and forty-four steps to ascend nine feet, since each riser is only two or three inches tall. Some inside windows are barred, while outside windows are unbarred. All these sly devices, according to legend, were devised by Mrs. Winchester to foil or injure the avenging spirits.

But they do not explain all the curious aspects of the mansion. Some fanciers of the occult theorize that Sarah Winchester was as concerned to propitiate friendly ghosts as she was to foil the unfriendly ones. Someday she would have to confront the victims of the Winchester rifle in the other world, and she would need strong protectors. Therefore, it was said, she had a séance room where she communed with friendly spirits each night, asking their advice on her building plans. For their convenience she installed clocks which struck only two hours in each twenty-four—midnight, when ghosts arrive, and 2:00 A.M., when they depart.

There are, as always, skeptics. They suggest that Sarah Winchester was simply an untrained architect who drew her own plans and made many mistakes. They cite evidence of her loyal servants and the few others who knew her that she was a sane and kindly, if eccentric, woman who chose to live as a recluse and found her pleasure in continual building.

Whatever the truth may be, the house is as odd and spooky as a Coney Island fun house. The present owners, who operate it as a tourist attraction, run guided tours for visitors, who might otherwise get lost for hours among the false doors and dead-end corridors. There is no use looking for ghosts, however. None has been seen since Sarah Winchester went to join the spirits in 1922.

*The séance room at the center of the house had thirteen hooks for the robes Sarah wore while communing with spirits.*

*With a ghost in pursuit, the diminutive Sarah could dart through the full-size door of the pair at right, then run out through the five-foot one next to it, leaving the spirit to knock its head. For all its handsome millwork, the door below opens only onto a two-story drop through a skylight, while the cupboard next to it yields up a wafer of storage space only half an inch deep.*

*The chimney at left, another foil for spirits, stops just shy of the roof.*

*The beautiful Sarah, first duchess of Marlborough, by Sir Godfrey Kneller*

# Sarah Churchill's Blenheim Palace

S arah, Duchess of Marlborough, was at home in London on August 13, 1704, when her husband's aide-de-camp came pounding up the Dover road with a scrap of paper that is now one of England's national treasures. John Churchill, duke of Marlborough, had written his message on the back of a tavern bill before dismounting from his horse after the battle of Blenheim. It read: "I have not time to say more, but to beg you will give my duty to the Queen, and let her know her army has had a glorious victory. M. Tallard and two other generals are in my coach, and I am following the rest. The bearer, Colonel Parke, will give her an account of what has passed. I shall do it in a day or two by another more at large."

The duchess sent Colonel Parke galloping on to Windsor to tell Queen Anne. In a few days the second note arrived. In this, Marlborough, the most reticent of men, allowed himself a rare sentence of self-congratulation: "I cannot end my letter without being soe vain as to tell my dearest soull that within the memory of man there has been noe Victory soe great as this."

All Europe agreed. Throughout England bells and bonfires celebrated the news. In France, by royal proclamation, it was made unlawful for anyone to speak of the French defeat. The historic importance of the event was that on the field of Blenheim Marlborough and his Austrian allies, under Prince Eugene of Savoy, had ended the grand plan of Louis XIV to unite France and Spain for the domination of Europe.

The queen and the duchess rode together in the royal coach behind eight horses to give thanks at the unfinished St. Paul's Cathedral. They had been close friends since girlhood—the plain, pious queen, who could never think of much to talk about beyond the weather, and the striking, spirited duchess, who had something sharp to say about almost everything. It was a relationship rarely found between monarch and subject. By Anne's whim, Sarah always addressed her in private as "Mrs. Morley," while she called Sarah "Mrs. Freeman." The queen's

*This statue of Queen Anne stands at Blenheim.*

*Blenheim's architect, Sir John Vanbrugh, saw the palace as a monument not only to Marlborough's genius, but to his own as well. The impossibly massive baroque house inspired a sardonic contemporary to pen the following epitaph for its author: "Under this stone, reader, survey/ Dear Sir John Vanbrugh's house of clay./ Lie heavy on him, earth, for he/ Laid many a heavy load on thee."*

consort, Prince George, and the duke of Marlborough had to go along with this girlish fancy, becoming "Mr. Morley" and "Mr. Freeman" in the ladies' conversation.

As they rode back from St. Paul's, having thanked God for the duke's victory, the two old friends had something else to think about: how could the queen find fitting expression for the nation's thanks to the duke himself? At length, the queen decided to bestow on her most illustrious subject the manor of Woodstock, a Crown property in Oxfordshire, and to erect on it a palace befitting the magnitude of the duke's victory. Presumably, the Treasury would pay the cost, or maybe the queen herself, although in later years no one could find any paper in which she said as much.

The choice of John Vanbrugh as architect seems to have been almost as casual. The assignment, Sarah thought, might more properly have gone to Sir Christopher Wren, the Queen's Surveyor and the most renowned English architect of the age. Vanbrugh was a man of Flemish descent who had turned to architecture from playwriting and had just recently designed a few buildings of note, including a London opera house and the earl of Carlisle's new country seat, Castle Howard. Besides, he was a congenial member of the Kit-Cat Club, a London social club to which Marlborough, Carlisle, and other Whig magnificoes belonged.

Vanbrugh made a wooden model of a monumental palace—he called it a castle—which pleased both the queen and the duke. Sarah, on the other hand, was put off by the grandness of the design, by the cost (one hundred thousand pounds by Wren's estimate), and by Vanbrugh himself. "As soon as I knew him," she wrote later, "and saw the maddnesse of the whole Design I opposed it all that was possible for me to doe."

Had Vanbrugh realized then what a formidable opponent he was up against, he might have taken her objections to heart. But, as he said, "I am not one of those who drop their Spirits on every Rebuff: if I had, I had been under ground long ago." With the queen and the duke

behind him, Vanbrugh plunged into the job of clearing the seven acres of the Woodstock estate that would be covered by the palace. On June 18, 1705, the foundation stone was laid, with great festivity. Vanbrugh wrote to the duke that the number of workmen would soon rise to a thousand; by August it was "near fifteen hundred."

In this first summer of work Vanbrugh assembled most of the talented assistants and specialists who were to share the credit for Blenheim. His deputy as architect and overall boss was Nicholas Hawskmoor, later to rank with Vanbrugh himself as one of England's leading architects. Representing the Board of Works as a controller of the project was Henry Joynes, who was twenty-one in that first year of construction but soon became the indispensable working manager on the site. Of the many fine craftsmen on the job the most notable were two master masons, the Edward Strongs, father and son, who had just completed the main part of their work on St. Paul's and were now entrusted with the most important of the stonework. For purely decorative stonework, including statues, Vanbrugh would later call upon the talented carver, Grinling Gibbons. The gardens, an enterprise on the scale of the palace itself, were the responsibility of Henry Wise, the queen's own landscape gardener.

The greatest problem to the builders in that first year was the stone. The strongest impression one has of Blenheim Palace as it stands today is that of an enormous pile of stone—"a great quarry of stones above ground" as the earl of Shrewsbury said when it was finished. That first impression is reinforced by the realization that all those walls, for reasons best known to the architect, are seven feet thick. At first the masons hoped to use the native granite of the estate, but during the winter after the first building season it tended to "fflye in the ffrost." Better sources were found on neighboring estates, but they were insufficient and, before the project was through, it was drawing upon twenty-two quarries, scattered over a hundred square miles.

In the building season, which lasted from spring to fall,

the duke could never be at the site because that was also the battle season, and the war on the Continent was not over. But he always had time for the letters, plans, and accounts that flowed in a steady stream to his field headquarters. He liked Vanbrugh and, unlike the duchess, he was not troubled by the cost or the grandiosity of the enterprise. Marlborough drew in his own mind a curious distinction between himself, as a man of moderation, and his genius, which was in the nature of a national treasure. His illustrious descendant and biographer, Winston Churchill, understood his point of view: "Marlborough had set his heart upon this mighty house. . . . It was as a monument, not as a dwelling, that he so earnestly desired it . . . . As the Pharaohs built their Pyramids so he sought a physical monument which would certainly stand, if only as a ruin, for thousands of years. About his achievements he preserved a complete silence, offering neither explanations nor excuses for any of his deeds. His answer was to be this great house." The duke was anxious only that the construction of the palace be carried on with the same dispatch and energy that he employed to move his armies across Europe. "The great fault I find," he wrote to Sarah in the fall of 1706, "is that I shall never live to see it finished."

Only for love of her husband did Sarah visit the "sea of mud" at Woodstock. There she saw a vast scene of confusion in which "nothing had been finished, nearly everything had been begun." Why, she wanted to know, was Vanbrugh not finishing up the main house first instead of using his army of workmen on the wings of the palace and the kitchen gardens? And why were they scattered all over the landscape, building mounds and filling hollows and moving trees? What, especially, were they doing on those old ruins?

Just across the valley from the site that Vanbrugh had chosen for Blenheim Palace stood the ruins of Woodstock Manor, which had been a royal residence since the time of Henry I some five hundred years before. It was the romantic hideaway in which Henry II dallied with

Rosamund Clifford, the "Fair Rosamund" of medieval legend, until Henry's wife, the imperious Eleanor of Aquitaine, discovered her there and, as the chroniclers tell it, "so dealt with her that she died not long after." Rosamund's Bower and Rosamund's Well were still pointed out to visitors at the time Blenheim Palace was under way. To Vanbrugh the ruins of the manor were a romantic treasure, to be used in the grand design of the estate. To Sarah they were an eyesore.

In going over the bills Sarah discovered that the architect had been using the palace labor force to make repairs on the manor house, rebuild the tower, and put up a new wall around it—at a cost of two thousand pounds. What was more, he had moved into the refurbished ruin himself for his own "agreable Lodging." Furious, Sarah brought the duke down to Woodstock to see what was going on. Vanbrugh turned on all his considerable charm and even painted a picture in oils to show how the manor would add to the view from the palace. To no avail: the manor must come down. From then on the architect resorted to subterfuge. Whenever he heard that the Marlboroughs were coming he would set workmen to tearing down some of the manor's outbuildings, which he did not care about, while out of sight they went on with the work of restoring the main house. This charade went on for four years.

If anything enraged Sarah more than Vanbrugh's work on the ruins, it was his preoccupation with the bridge. The approach road to the palace had to cross the little river Glyme, a stream, as Sarah acidly pointed out, that "anyone could jump." In response to her request, that good and sensible man, Sir Christopher Wren, had sketched up just what was needed to bridge this brook: a modest span standing just fifteen feet above the water. But here was Vanbrugh starting work on a monstrous stone pile that would look at home in the Roman Forum. In the plans for this structure that Vanbrugh called a bridge Sarah counted thirty-three rooms, meant for what purpose she could not imagine, unless they were to sit in

*This triumphal painting by John Closterman shows Marlborough trampling a French flag at the victory that gained him his house.*

*Ever loyal to her husband's memory, Sarah built this victory column on the grounds of Blenheim after his death.*

"while the coaches drove over your head." Again the duke was called in. Vanbrugh pointed out that the bridge would be the first thing an arriving visitor would see and that it ought to match the dignity of the whole estate. This time Vanbrugh prevailed.

But even these tempests were minor compared to the clouds that were gathering over the unfinished palace. "Mrs. Morley," more secure now in her queenship, was tired of being bullied by "Mrs. Freeman." The next time they drove together to St. Paul's, to celebrate yet another of the duke's victories (at Oudenaarde in 1708), there was a scene in the cathedral. The queen said that Sarah told her to hold her tongue; Sarah said she was just trying to quiet the queen lest they be overheard.

It was much more than a spat between two old friends. The queen had found a more congenial companion in Abigail Hill, and Abigail was a protégée of Robert Harley, later earl of Oxford, one of the leaders of the Tory party in Parliament. In short order the Whig supporters of the Marlboroughs were being replaced in key positions by Tories.

Even when the duke's friends had been in power the Treasury had been slow about paying the bills for Blenheim. In the second year of building, the workmen had to wait until December to be paid for their summer's work. Now, with the duke's enemies in power and the queen estranged, who would pay the bills? While Vanbrugh cajoled the men to stay on the job, Sarah kept after him to finish up the living quarters and let the rest go. But the architect could not seem to keep from making costly changes in the design, at one point tearing down the colonnade when it was halfway up in order to change the style of the columns from Doric to Corinthian.

At the duke's insistence, the work on the gardens, all planned in the formal French style, kept pace with the building of the palace. Since the gardens were to cover seventy-seven acres, the requirements for flowers and plants, shrubs and trees were prodigious. One of the first shipments in 1705 included the following quantities of

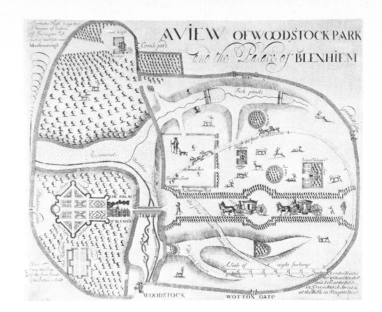

limes alone: "248 Large standard Limes at 14d each, 2219 Large Espalier standard Limes at 1s. each, and 2566 of a smaller size ditto at 6d." Another shipment included 5,600 white narcissuses, 18,500 Dutch yellow crocuses, and so on. There was a bill for £126 for "1,120 solid yards of Dung." To Sarah the duke wrote from Europe: "If possible I should wish that you might, or somebody you can rely on, taste the fruit of every tree, so that what is not good might be changed."

By 1710 the builders at Blenheim were racing against the decline of the Marlboroughs' political fortunes. Work continued through the summer. The gallery between the great hall and the saloon was finished; the pillars in the south portico were fluted; Gibbons carved the coat of arms for the pediment of the north portico; the keystone was placed in the main arch of the bridge. But in August the Marlboroughs' friend Sidney Godolphin was dismissed as Lord Treasurer and replaced by their enemy, Robert Harley. Alarmed that the duke might be held responsible for the unpaid bills, Sarah sent orders to Joynes, the manager at Blenheim, that all work was to stop at once and not a man was to be employed another day. Vanbrugh protested that at least they must cover in the work that was in progress to protect it from the winter weather. But, as he recounted later, "all I had to say was cut short by Mr. Joynes's Shewing me a Postscript my Lady Dutchess had added to her Letter, forbidding any regard to whatever I might say or do."

Joynes appealed to Sarah on behalf of the workmen: "If ye masons stop and I have no money to pay them and if turn'd off without their money, will Cause a great murmer in ye Country, beside ye afflictions to ye poor Wretches and ye DisinCouragement to all ye country people which will think they never shall be paid . . . ." Angry workmen, he said, had already broken some capitals of the columns, and he did not know what further damage they might do. Moreover, there was an election coming up, and Joynes feared that the disgruntled townsfolk would turn down the Whig candidates for

Parliament, which could only mean "a mighty Disappointment in My Lord Duke's interest."

Sarah was not impressed. She did not believe that responsible men like the Strongs, with so great a debt already owed them, would leave their work uncovered. She could not see the workmen pulling down the palace—that was "a thing to frighten children." And as for the election, it was not in the interest of the townsfolk to "disoblige the Duke of Marlborough." Sarah had a clear understanding of what the English workmen of the early eighteenth century would or would not dare to do. The workers grumbled and doubtless suffered, but they did no further damage and the district voted dutifully for the Whig candidates.

It was left to Vanbrugh to pry open the public purse strings. On a visit to the Lord Treasurer he pointed out that Blenheim was properly regarded as a monument to the queen's glory, and added on his own account: "I cannot help looking on this Building as with ye tenderness of a sort of Child of my Owne, and therefore hope you will forgive my troubling you for its Preservation."

Upon Harley's assurance that funds would be supplied as before, work began again in the spring of 1711. During that summer the private wing was all but finished. But much remained to be done when the duke was hit by the hardest blow of all. On a groundless charge by his enemies that he had misappropriated government funds at his military headquarters, the duke was dismissed as captain-general of the armies of the queen. Treasury payments for Blenheim ceased, and so did almost all work on the building for the next three years.

By this time the palace, with its massive central block, its corner towers, and its two flanking wings, was all but finished on the outside. Even those who thought that it looked big and impressive enough to contain the houses of Parliament had to admit that Vanbrugh had created a masterpiece of monumental baroque design. But the interior was still unfinished, and Sarah's patience, never in good supply, was exhausted. Behind Vanbrugh's back

she had her groundskeeper draw up a plan of the main
floor as it then stood. This plan, found by David Green
among the Blenheim papers and reproduced in his
definitive book *Blenheim Palace*, shows everywhere "no
pavement," "no Chimney piece," "not so much as
Ceiled," and "not one of ye Stair cases finished in the
whole House." With the floor plan in hand, Sarah
composed a document of more than twenty pages
detailing all the architect's faults, sins, and false promises
since the start of the project. Vanbrugh took it, quite
rightly, as his dismissal.

For herself, Sarah would gladly have left Blenheim as
it stood, an empty, unfinished "monument of ingrati-
tude." But the duke, now tired and sick, clung to his
dream of living in the place before he died. Since the
Treasury would not foot the bill, he would finish the job
at his own expense. Work resumed in 1716, with Sarah in
direct control. By the summer of 1719, fourteen years
after work had begun, Blenheim Palace, while still not
finished, was ready for the Marlboroughs to move in.

There was no festivity, no music, no dancing to mark
the occasion. The weary duke had two summers left in
which to move slowly through the vast rooms of his
personal monument, taste the fruits of his gardens, and
look upon the stone cannons and flags and drums that
Grinling Gibbons had placed on the roof to glorify his
military victories. He died in 1722, not at Blenheim but
at Windsor Lodge, his old home, where Sarah watched
over him (in Winston Churchill's words) "like a she-bear
guarding its slowly dying mate."

Sarah outlived her husband by twenty-two years. She
outlived all but one of her six children, outlived the
queen, outlived Vanbrugh, and outlived her enemy
Harley, who was sent to the Tower in 1715 by the new
king, George I, for conspiring with the Stuart pretender.
Much of her time in the years just after the duke's death
was taken up with litigation. The Strongs and many of
the other workmen, despairing of collecting their back
pay from the Crown, had sued the Marlboroughs. Sarah

fought back with a monstrous countersuit against "Every Body that Had been Concern'd" in the building of Blenheim—four hundred one persons, from Vanbrugh down to masons, carters, and laborers—charging they had conspired to cheat the Marlboroughs. The litigation continued for three years, but very little came of it.

At Blenheim there was still work to be done. Sarah erected a triumphal arch at the western entrance, carved with scenes of the duke's victories, and a column topped with the duke's statue. In the Long Gallery she installed a bust of Queen Anne. She pulled down the last remnants of the manor, leaving only Rosamund's Well. In the house itself there were one hundred eighty-seven rooms to be decorated and furnished. Blenheim, she complained, was "so vast a place that it tires one allmost to death to look after it and keep it in order." In the last years of her life, wracked by gout, she lived at one or another of her other houses and came to Blenheim only to see that the "wild, unmercifull Hous" was kept up.

Vanbrugh (now Sir John) paid a visit in 1725, as a member of a coaching party made up of the earl of Carlisle and other convivial members of the Kit-Cat Club. They were on a tour of English country houses and stopped at Blenheim. The duchess was not there, but she had heard they were coming and had sent the servants an order that under no circumstances was Sir John Vanbrugh to be allowed past the gate. Sir John repaired to the local inn while his friends made a tour of the house he regarded as his "owne Child."

Though Blenheim belonged to Sarah as long as she lived, the Marlborough title had passed first to her daughter Henrietta and then, when she died, to her daughter Anne's son, Charles Spencer, earl of Sunderland, who thus became the third duke of Marlborough. He and the eight dukes who followed him left Blenheim Palace little changed in the course of more than two centuries, though the fourth duke made radical changes in the grounds. His landscape architect was the famous Lancelot ("Capability") Brown, who tore up most of the

formal gardens which had so pleased the first duke and replaced them with "natural" groupings of lawn and shrubs. Whatever the merit of this change, Brown showed how he had won his nickname by discerning a new "capability" in the handling of water on the estate. As Sarah had predicted, Vanbrugh's monstrous bridge on the entrance drive had always looked absurdly out of proportion to the little stream it crossed. Brown dammed up the river and flooded the valley behind it, thus providing a handsome lake and giving the bridge something worth crossing. Sarah would have been gratified to learn that the waters now rose over the lower part of the bridge itself, inundating some of the little rooms that she had found so foolish.

By spending so much on the grounds, the fourth duke dissipated a great part of the Marlborough fortune. The sixth duke made a little money by letting tourists in for a shilling apiece, and the seventh duke sold off the fine palace library, including such treasures as the Bedford Book of Hours. By the time of the eighth duke the paintings by old masters were going too, their places taken in part by family portraits. Lady Randolph Churchill, the mother of Sir Winston and sister-in-law of the eighth duke, recalled that in the 1870's she and others of the family sometimes put on their dowdiest coats and hats to join the tourists in the great rooms. They were convulsed one day to hear one of the trippers exclaim: "My, what poppy eyes these Churchills have got!"

Lady Randolph happened to be walking in Blenheim Park on the evening of November 30, 1874, when labor pains warned her that the baby she was expecting might be born at any minute. She was hurried into the palace and put to bed in the nearest room, a small one kept for undistinguished guests. There, very shortly, Winston Churchill came into the world.

By the time Winston's cousin, the ninth duke, inherited the title in 1892, the financial affairs of the family were at low ebb. The palace had been nearly stripped of heirlooms, the lawns had gone almost to hay. In that crisis

*The fortunes of the Marlborough family were replenished by an infusion of American money when the unhappy Consuelo Vanderbilt wedded the ninth duke. She is shown here, front row, third from left, at an 1896 house party. Her husband is on the ground at lower right, and the Prince of Wales is seated in the center. In the snapshot at right, Consuelo's hat shades young Winston—a Churchill as renowned as the victor of Blenheim.*

the family fortune was saved by an American lady of indomitable will, Mrs. William Kissam Vanderbilt. Alva Vanderbilt had come to Europe to find a suitably aristocratic husband for her lovely daughter Consuelo. The ninth duke, young, handsome, and needy, was just what she had in mind. The duke was coolly amenable, but Consuelo had to be browbeaten into submission. In due course the Marlborough solicitor was sent to New York to deal with Mr. Vanderbilt on terms that, as the solicitor put it, "would profit the illustrious family." The terms were not announced, but the best guess was a dowry of some fifteen million dollars.

The family fortune restored, the ninth duke went about the improvement of the palace and grounds with zeal and taste. Capability Brown's natural settings were ripped up and replaced with formal gardens like those originally laid out by Vanbrugh and Henry Wise. New trees filled the gaps in the long rows of elms that lined the entrance road—planted, it was always said, in the battle formations of Blenheim. Water gardens were built on the western terrace overlooking the lake.

The new duchess, Consuelo, having spent her winters in her parents' Fifth Avenue mansion and her summers at Marble House in Newport, was no stranger to a life of magnificence. But even she was taken aback by the ceremonial of Blenheim Palace. In *The Glitter and the Gold* she described her arrival on a special train:

"The little station was festive and beflagged; a red carpet had been laid on the platform and the Mayor in his scarlet robes, accompanied by members of the Corporation, greeted us in a welcoming speech. Turning to me he said, 'Your Grace will no doubt be interested to know that Woodstock had a Mayor and a Corporation before America was discovered.' Feeling properly put in my place, I managed to give the awed smile I felt was expected, although a riposte was seething on the tip of my tongue. A carriage from which the horses had been unhitched was awaiting us and our employees proceeded to drag us up to the house. Somewhat discomfitted by this

means of progress at which my democratic principles rebelled, I nevertheless managed to play the role in fitting manner, bowing and smiling in response to the plaudits of the assembled crowds. Triumphal arches had been erected, schoolchildren were waving flags, the whole countryside had turned out to greet us, and I felt deeply touched by the warmth of their welcome. We stopped at the Town Hall where addresses on parchment written in a lovely illuminated script were given to us, and flowers were brought to me by the children. At last we reached the house, but here again ceremonies awaited us. Tenant farmers, employees and household servants were ranged in groups, and each had prepared a welcoming speech and a bouquet which had to be . . . fittingly responded to."

Blenheim's time of splendor reached a peak around the turn of this century in the ninth duke's hunting parties. On one such occasion five guns killed fifty-two hundred rabbits in a single day to set a world record. At another party in 1896, the Prince of Wales, soon to be Edward VII, was the guest of honor. The skills of any hostess would have been taxed by juggling the seating and sleeping arrangements for a hundred guests with a bewildering variety of titles and offices. Consuelo breathed a sigh of relief as they disappeared down the drive.

To her, as to so many others in its history, Blenheim was a burden. It had been a burden to Queen Anne, who came to regret she had ever begun it; to the first duke, who barely lived to occupy it; to Sarah, who never wanted it; to Vanbrugh, who had to put up with Sarah; to the ninth duke, who had to marry an heiress to keep it up. And Blenheim remains a burden to the present eleventh duke, who is in effect the caretaker of a national tourist attraction. None of this would have come as any surprise to Lady Lechmere in 1721. Commiserating with Sarah on her troubles with Vanbrugh, she wrote: "By what I have heard you say, some parts of Blenheim were so vast in ye designs that tho' they were formed by a man, they ought to have been executed by ye Gods."

*Anders Zorn painted this exuberant portrait of Mrs. Gardner in 1894.*

# Isabella Gardner's Fenway Court

*Mrs. Gardner, second from the right, entertains the gentry.*

One of Isabella Stewart Gardner's girlhood friends remembered a visit they made to the Poldi-Pezzoli palace in Milan when they were sixteen. Belle Stewart was enchanted by the Italian Renaissance paintings, the heavy carved furniture, the rich hangings and ornate silver. "If I ever have any money of my own," she declared, "I am going to build a palace and fill it with beautiful things."

In later years, when she was Mrs. John Lowell Gardner, friends learned to take Belle's fancies seriously. "What Mrs. Jack wants," one of them said, "you can be pretty sure she is going to get."

Belle Stewart was the daughter of David Stewart, an enterprising New York businessman of recent fortune. At a finishing school in Paris she became a friend of Julia Gardner of Boston and, when they returned to America, was introduced to Julia's brother Jack. No one ever said that Belle Stewart was a beauty, but she had a magnetism that captivated Jack Gardner as it captivated many men (but few women) throughout her life.

In both fortune and social standing Jack was the heir of two Massachusetts families that had prospered in the China trade, the Gardners of Boston and, on his mother's side, the Peabodys of Salem. After he and Belle were married in 1860 he settled contentedly into the life of a proper Bostonian, looking after his investments, lunching and often dining at his clubs, fussing over the wines for dinner parties at their house in Back Bay, growing more staid and more portly with the years. He was also intelligent, industrious, affable and, fortunately, tolerant.

Belle Gardner required a lot of tolerance. To the eagle eyes of Boston matrons her dresses always seemed to be fitted a little too tightly, the necks cut a little too low, the strings of pearls a little too long and showy. Where other ladies were content with a coachman, Belle drove out with two footmen on the box. She took such a fancy to the lion cubs at the Boston Zoo that she gave two of them a ride in her carriage, and once she led a grown lion around the zoo on a leash.

What scandalized Boston the most, however, as "Mrs. Jack" grew older, was her evident fondness for young men, usually young men connected with the arts. One of these, who became her lifelong friend, was John Singer Sargent, the most fashionable painter of the day. Belle was forty-eight and Sargent was thirty-two on a Sunday morning in 1888 when they were visiting Groton School, where her nephew was teaching. One of the students, a boy named Ellery Sedgwick, who later became an editor of *The Atlantic Monthly*, happened to be lying among the wrestling mats in the gymnasium, reading *Ben Hur*, when he looked up to see Sargent chasing Mrs. Jack around the floor. Just as the painter was about to catch her, young Sedgwick took flight for fear of discovery and jumped out the window, leaving the readers of his future memoirs forever tantalized by not knowing what happened next.

Bostonians naturally assumed the worst, not only with respect to Sargent but with respect to others, including the novelist F. Marion Crawford. When Sargent's painting of Mrs. Jack in a low-cut dress was exhibited at a Boston club, a member was heard to remark crudely (in a reference understood by anyone familiar with the White Mountains) that she was naked "all the way down to Crawford's Notch." The remark, which reached her husband's ears, inspired the only reaction that ever betrayed Jack Gardner's concern about his wife's reputation. He ordered that the painting be taken down and never shown again in public. Belle was unperturbed, although she did remark, when asked for a contribution to the Charitable Eye and Ear Infirmary, that she did not know there was a charitable eye or ear in Boston.

No matter how much they gossiped and carped at Mrs. Jack's behavior, proper Bostonians seldom refused her invitations. For she gathered into her circle not only the most brilliant of the talented young men but also the established intellectual luminaries of Boston and Cambridge. Among her closest friends and admirers were Henry and William James, Henry Adams, Charles Eliot

Norton, James Russell Lowell, and Oliver Wendell Holmes. The literary lions were as dazzled as anyone else by Mrs. Jack, and more gifted than others in their elevated flattery. Henry Adams began a letter, "Wonderful Woman!" Henry James wrote: "I think of you as a figure on a wondrous cinquecento tapestry—and of myself as one of the small quaint accessory domestic animals, a harmless worm, or the rabbit who is very proud and happy to be in the same general composition with you."

If Boston's social matrons felt it necessary to keep a perpetually raised eyebrow at Mrs. Jack, other elements in the population were quite delighted by her. Their sense of propriety was not offended when, on a Sunday morning in Lent, she drove down to the Church of the Advent with a mop and bucket and did her penance by swabbing down the steps of the church. When her carriage was caught in a mob during some labor troubles in South Boston, a voice rang out, "Don't worry, Mrs. Jack. I'll see you get through." It was her friend John L. Sullivan, then heavyweight champion of the world.

Foreigners, understandably, were sometimes taken aback by her customs. Once, during a trip to Italy, she dispatched a handsome bouquet of yellow roses with her compliments to the king, Umberto. Unused to receiving presents from ladies, His Majesty sent an equerry to ascertain just what the lady's intentions were. It took not only her husband but the U.S. ambassador to Italy to convince the court that Mrs. Jack was not an adventuress with designs on the king but simply an American who was accustomed to sending flowers to men she admired.

Mrs. Jack's male admirers, young and old, were of great help to her in what soon became the serious business of her life, the collection of great works of art. Sargent became her adviser on purchases, as did James McNeill Whistler, who had drawn a portrait sketch of her in London. Henry Adams found for her the magnificent stained glass windows which may once have graced the abbey of Saint Denis. Henry James and others kept an

eye out for noble English families that might be ready to part with the family treasures. Most important of all to Mrs. Jack was Bernard Berenson, whom she had taken up when he was a young fine-arts student at Harvard with long curly hair and soft eyes. Berenson went on to become the world's leading authority on Italian Renaissance art and Mrs. Jack's adviser and agent for years.

At first the paintings were intended—or so she said—simply for her own house in Back Bay. But they were purchased with a care and a sure judgment of quality that were seldom matched by buyers for the world's great museums. "I haven't enough money to buy second-rate things," she once said. "I can buy only the best."

Before she died Mrs. Jack had acquired the finest collection of Italian Renaissance paintings in the United States; it still ranks second only to that of the National Gallery, which received the collection of Andrew Mellon. Its single greatest treasure is Titian's *Rape of Europa*, bought through Berenson's skillful agency for twenty thousand pounds (then one hundred thousand dollars) from Lord Darnley. Rubens thought it the greatest picture in the world and painted a copy of it, which is now a treasure of the Prado in Madrid. Later Van Dyck, who had never seen the original, painted a copy of Rubens's copy, and Mrs. Jack bought *that*, too.

Perhaps the greatest bargain she ever got was Jan Vermeer's *The Concert*, one of only about thirty-six existing paintings by the Dutch master. When the picture came up for auction in Paris in 1892 both the Louvre and the National Gallery in London wanted it, but Mrs. Jack outbid them and got it for six thousand dollars. It became the cornerstone of her collection of works by Rembrandt, Raphael, Botticelli, Piero della Francesca, Rubens, Simone Martini, Mantegna, and other old masters.

In 1898 Jack Gardner died of a stroke at his club, appropriately enough. Between the inheritances from him and from her father, Belle found herself in possession of a fortune estimated at upward of five million dollars, sufficient to realize the ambition she had

Mrs. Gardner first met the future art expert Bernard Berenson when he was the natty Harvard undergraduate at left. He served her nobly throughout her career as a collector, but his signal triumph was the acquisition of the Rape of Europa, which hangs on the left in the Titian room below. His name dominates her list of acquisitions for 1895, reproduced at right.

cherished since girlhood. Now she would build her palace.

During their travels in Europe the Gardners had been picking up not only paintings but bits and pieces of old houses, palaces, and monasteries. Among these trophies were the mosaic floor of the palace of the Empress Livia near Rome, a doorway and two stone lions from Florence, and eight balconies from the Ca' d'Oro, most resplendent of Venetian palazzi. All of these would be used in the palace she planned to erect on the newly filled land of Boston's Back Bay. Since the land had recently been salt marsh, the palace would have to rest on pilings, even as the palazzi of Venice itself. The first pilings were driven in the summer of 1899.

Mrs. Gardner left the driving of the piles to the contractor while she took off on a final buying tour of Europe, but by spring of 1900 she was on the scene to supervise construction and never left it for any length of time until the palace was finished. She had an architectural design drawn to her specifications by William T. Sears, but it was continually revised as the building proceeded. First off, she decreed that the brick walls could not rest on a flat foundation but must be laid on an irregular surface of rough blocks so that they would seem to rise directly from the earth. Almost at once she ran into trouble with the building inspector in Boston, who insisted that such a large structure must have a steel frame. Mrs. Jack insisted that if marble columns would support a palace in Venice they would do so in Boston. At length, knowing that all of Boston was looking forward to seeing her "Eyetalian palace," she informed the inspector: "If Fenway Court is to be built at all, it will be built as *I* wish and not as *you* wish." As usual, she had her way.

During the next three years, in fair weather and foul, it seemed that Mrs. Jack was always on the building site. She took her lunch with the workmen, bringing her sandwiches and contributing ten cents a day for oatmeal to clarify the drinking water. When the workmen had trouble getting the right pink-and-white effect on the

*John Singer Sargent painted this final portrait of his old friend two years before her death.*

walls of the courtyard she seized two sponges and showed them how to slosh the paint on. On another occasion she wielded a broadax to demonstrate just how the timbers of the ceilings should be rough-cut in the old Italian style.

Among the Italian workmen who had been recruited for the job she took a liking to an ex-gondolier from Venice, one Theobaldo Travi, nicknamed "Bolgi," who impressed her as having the proper respect for the materials he worked with. Bolgi became her superintendent, and when Mrs. Jack found that he was also a cornet player, she worked out a series of signals for summoning the workmen she wanted: one toot for masons, two for steamfitters, and so on. Later, in her will, Mrs. Jack provided that Bolgi should be lifetime superintendent of Fenway Court.

During construction Mrs. Jack allowed only a handful of friends to take a coveted glimpse at the future palace, knowing that their reports would tantalize Boston society. Finally the palace was finished, and Mrs. Jack sent out invitations to a grand opening.

If Fenway Court had collapsed, as the building inspector feared it would, on New Year's night, 1903, it would have wiped out the entire social, financial, and governmental structure of Boston. As the guests alighted from their carriages they were ushered into the music room, at the far end of which Mrs. Jack had installed a horseshoe staircase. On the landing stood Mrs. Jack, triumphant in all her pearls, with two huge diamonds, the Rajah and the Light of India, swaying gently on springs set in her hair. Her guests, friend and foe alike, climbed up one side of the staircase, paid their respects to the hostess, and went down the other. Then they sat down for an hour to hear a concert by fifty musicians from the Boston Symphony Orchestra. Finally, at ten-thirty, the mirrored door to the courtyard was rolled back and the guests beheld the fairyland that Mrs. Jack had created. The pink walls, broken by the balustrades from the Ca' d'Oro, rose four stories to a glass roof. Here, in the midst of a bleak Massachusetts winter, was an enchanted garden of blooming flowers and tinkling fountains. Thousands of candles lit the courtyard and the art-filled rooms, still to be seen, that opened off it. Describing the reaction of the beholders, William James said that "it had a peculiar effect on the company, making them quiet and docile and self-forgetful and kind, as if they had become children" (although, as he added on second thought, children are just the reverse).

After her night of triumph Mrs. Gardner lived on at Fenway Court among her treasures for the twenty years that remained to her. On the outside wall a carved seal bore her personal motto: "*C'est mon plaisir.*" After she had a stroke at 79 she was carried about the palace in a Venetian gondola chair. Two years before Mrs. Gardner died Sargent came again to paint the finest portrait of his old friend, by then a wraith, white of hair and skin and wrapped all in white clothing.

By the terms of her will Fenway Court was endowed and left "for the education and enjoyment of the public forever." One provision of the will is that nothing may ever be moved from the place where Mrs. Jack put it. That has meant that when some paintings originally bought as the works of great masters have been ascribed to lesser artists, they still remain in places of honor, with only their cards of attribution altered. It has meant too that, unlike other museums, Fenway Court neither lends its paintings to other museums nor borrows theirs for display. But the strictures have had a compensating value. They have preserved Fenway Court not as simply a museum but as the home and creation of one remarkable woman. Thanks to the shrewd collaboration of Mrs. Gardner and Bernard Berenson, most of the important paintings are still recognized as the work of the greatest masters. In the history of art collecting there has hardly ever been a better investment. It is likely that a single painting—either the Titian or the Vermeer—would today bring at auction as much as Mrs. Jack paid for Fenway Court and everything in it.

# THE WINE OF ARCHITECTURE

*A fountain-ringed statue in Leningrad's Peterhof*

*Fountains for an estate, according to a 1712 book on
gardening, should include "Basins and large Pieces of
Water" with "Cascades, Gullets, Buffets, Sheets, Masks,
Bubbles, Sheafs, Spouts, Surges. . . ." The ebullient
list suggests the variety and ingenuity of the waterworks,
such.as the ones on these pages, that began to sparkle and
sing in the gardens of Europe in the sixteenth century*

The tricky watercourse above at the Villa Lante near Bagnaia, Italy, is designed to give the falling water the irregularities and random patterns of a river. The water spills from a large crayfish, the singularly unglamorous animal that appears on the coat of arms of the man who built the villa, Cardinal Gambera, Bishop of Viterbo.

Another cardinal, Ippolito II d'Este, consoled himself for his repeated failures to get elected pope by building some of the most elaborate fountains in the world at his Villa d'Este near Rome. Grandest of them is the Fountain of the Water Organ, opposite, which originally played a tune on pipes housed in the structure above it.

*Fountains often inspired bizarre whims in their builders, and many feature
statues that spray water from unlikely orifices. The spouting stag's head opposite
is in Hellbrunn Castle, whose eccentric gardens were built by an Austrian
archbishop for the express purpose of charming his guests. The oddities above are, clockwise
from top left: a grotesque water mask from Alessandro Farnese's Caprarola;
a glaring visage and, below it, a sphinx, both from the Villa d'Este; spewing dolphins
in Charles III of Spain's gardens of Caserta near Naples; a Nereid and a
merbaby from Peterhof, Czar Peter the Great's summer palace near Leningrad.*

OVERLEAF: *Actaeon is pursued by Diana's hounds before Caserta's great cascade.*

# 5 ARTISTS AS BUILDERS

Writers and artists have brought their special creative talents to the building of their own houses—sometimes with strange results. Walter Scott's ambition was to live like a medieval lord. Frederick Church imagined an Oriental palace on the Hudson. Horace Walpole fancied the "gloomth" of Gothic cloisters. Although some of them lost their fortunes in doing it, all of them brought their expensive visions to reality in brick and stone.

*Sir Walter Scott's hat, pen and inkwell, cane, seals, and notebook lie on the desk in his study at Abbotsford, his Gothic home.*

# Mark Twain's Hartford House

When Mark Twain came to build a house, he thought to profit from the mistakes the Lord had made in creating the world. "It is likely," he wrote, "that if more time had been taken, in the first place, the world would have been made right, and this ceaseless improving and repairing would not be necessary now. But if you hurry a world or a house, you are nearly sure to find out, by and by, that you have left out a towhead, or a broom-closet, or some other little convenience, here and there, which has got to be supplied, no matter how much expense or vexation it may cost." Mark Twain meant to take more care about his house than the Lord had taken about the world.

The place he had chosen for his home was a long way from the Mississippi River town of Samuel Clemens's boyhood or the roistering mining camps where he had begun his career as a writer under the name of Mark Twain. It was a little enclave of literary folk called Nook Farm in West Hartford, Connecticut. His new wife Livy liked it because it was a step up in gentility from Buffalo, where she had grown up. Clemens liked it because it was not as dull as Buffalo and the neighbors included such congenial literary spirits as Charles Dudley Warner and Harriet Beecher Stowe. Some of his western friends were frankly envious. As Mrs. Mary Fairbanks of Cleveland wrote him: "Don't you think heaven does lie somewhere near Hartford or Boston, and that if I am good I shall sometime go there to stay?"

The houses in Hartford were something else. Another friend, Alfred Bigelow Paine, described them in the decade following the Civil War as "mainly of the goods-box form of architecture, perfectly square, typifying the commercial pursuits of many of the owners." Clemens made it plain to his architect, Edward Potter, that he wanted a lot more than that. What their collaboration produced at 351 Farmington Avenue was a classic piece of General Grant Victorian architecture, replete with chimneys, porches, gables, balconies, verandahs, and a porte-cochère—the whole thing reminiscent in part of a medieval cloister and in part of a Swiss cuckoo clock. Behind all the cornices and curlicues it was a great, warm, dark, comfortable place to live. In all his travels through Europe and America, Clemens never saw a house he liked as much.

Before he was through building, however, Clemens must have envied the Lord for not having had to rely on hired help in the Creation. To his mother-in-law, Mrs. Langdon, he wrote: "I have been bullyragged all day by the builder, by his foreman, by the architect, by the tapestry devil who is upholstering the furniture, by the idiot who is putting down the carpets, by the scoundrel who is setting up the billiard table (and has left the balls in New York), by the wildcat who is sodding the ground and finishing the driveway (after the sun went down), by a book *agent*, whose body is in the back yard and the coroner notified. Just think of this thing going on the whole day long, and I am a man who loathes details with all my heart!"

By the time the Clemenses moved into the house in 1874 it had cost them $125,000, a heavy commitment for a writer in those days. Livy had private means, and Clemens was riding the tide of his first important financial success as the author of *Innocents Abroad* and *The Gilded Age*. But all through his most productive years the house would consume a great part of his income.

The house contained many spots that might have been expected to invite Mark Twain's perverse muse. There was a porch fixed up like a steamboat pilot house of his Mississippi years. There was a conservatory where Livy made him a writing nook amid the flowers and fountains. There was a study furnished with a divan copied after something in a Syrian monastery and a deep bay window looking out on the garden. But Mark Twain found that he could not work in any of these places. He was always lying down on the divan for a smoke ("Not more than one cigar at a time," he was quick to explain. "That would be excessive smoking.") or looking out the window at the falling snow. So he moved up to the billiard room

*Mark Twain sometimes worked in bed, surrounded
by comfortable clutter. "A little imp," he explained,
"whispers in my ear and tells me what to say." The
sketch was created by an admirer, who combined the
rumpled pillow and the writer's shaggy head
into an impish creature issuing its instructions.*

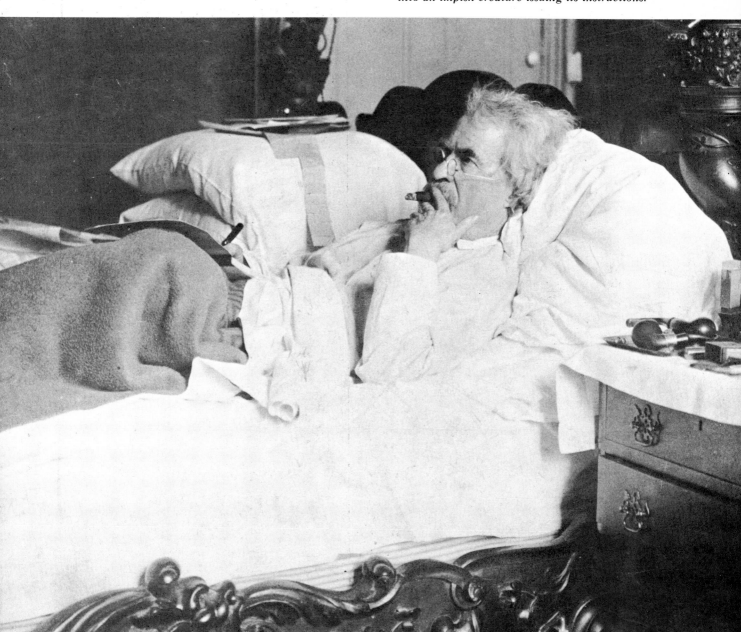

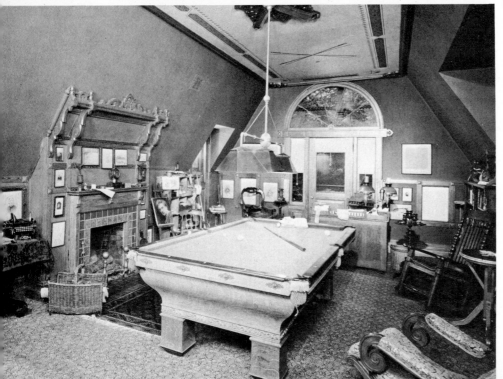

*Despite his wife's hopes that he would write in the conservatory, above, Twain preferred the billiard room, at left. There, between restorative bouts at the table, he wrote* The Adventures of Tom Sawyer *and* Huckleberry Finn. *The intricate decorations in the front hall, above left, all supervised by Twain, belie his professed hatred of detail.*

on the third floor, where he was able to sit with his back to the window.

It was here that Mark Twain called up the world of *Tom Sawyer* and *Huckleberry Finn* and *Life on the Mississippi*, the world of his own boyhood in its inspiration but distilled into the classic idyll of young, yearning America. It was an idyll far removed in time and place from the Hartford of his mature years. Livy never entered it. Even his oldest daughter Susy, who doted on her father as he on her, was not comfortable with the world of the rough, unruly Huck. The family had to make an effort not to agree with Louisa May Alcott, who complained: "If Mr. Clemens cannot think of something better to tell our pure-minded lads and lasses, he had best stop writing for them!"

Yet life in the Clemens household in Hartford was itself an American idyll of a different kind. A later generation would come to look back upon such a close family life in such a warm, supportive circle of friends with the same sort of nostalgic longing that Mark Twain had for Hannibal, Missouri. The Clemenses and their neighbors at Nook Farm lived on terms of such intimacy that they kept no fences, walked in and out of each other's houses unannounced, and often stayed for meals. Many evenings they gathered around the fireplace in the library, where Sam stood and read stories or poems with such verve that the younger listeners cheered and begged for more. At other times the Clemens children and their friends put on plays and pageants of their own invention, which included roles for the grownups. Clara, the second

daughter, remembered a particularly enjoyable evening:

"We were trying to enact the story of Hero and Leander. Mark Twain played the part of the impassioned lover obliged to swim across the Hellespont to snatch a kiss from his sweetheart on the other side of that foaming water. For this scene Father wore a bathing-suit, a straw hat tied under his chin with a big bow, and a hot-water bottle slung around his chest." Thus it was before television.

The Clemenses had seven in help. Clara recalled one of them vividly: "Our butler, George, was colored and full of personality. He had come one day to wash windows and remained for eighteen years. Everyone in the family liked him, although the only time he looked after anyone's needs at the table was when a large company of guests were invited to dine. On such occasions he would rise to great heights of professional service and throb with feverish excitement, as if he were acting a big role on the stage. When only members of the family were seated at table, however, he preferred listening to the conversation to passing them food. He explained that the intellectual inspiration he received in the dining room saved him from the bad effects of life in the inferior atmosphere of the kitchen. Often did we hear a prompt laugh filling the room from a dark figure at ease against the wall, before the rest of us at table had expressed our amusement at one of Father's remarks. George was a great addition to the family and afforded Father almost as much amusement as Father did George."

As the years went on, there were more and more guests

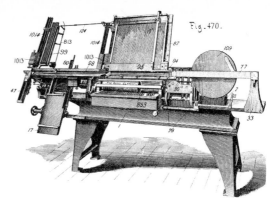

*Although the investments in the Paige typesetter, above, gobbled up most of his fortune, it was the death of his daughter Susy that finally persuaded a depressed Twain to offer his home for sale in 1902.*

for dinner. They included such celebrities as William Dean Howells, Thomas Nast, Edwin Booth, Generals Sheridan and Sherman, Sir Henry M. Stanley, Rudyard Kipling, and Bret Harte. They came for a meal or a night or a week, always sure of a warm reception and a spirited performance by the host. With such constant company, even Mark Twain, the most resourceful storyteller of the age, could not help repeating himself. His children, listening from the stairs, could mark the progress of the party: "Father is telling the beggar story; they must have reached the meat course."

By the 1880's, the cost of running such an establishment was getting out of hand. More than once the Clemenses had to take off for Europe, where they could live more cheaply for a season. Then in the late 1880's the financial roof fell in. Clemens had formed a publishing house that prospered on his own writing but lost money on other literary works. At the same time he had invested heavily in a typesetting machine that he felt sure would make him a fortune. By 1894 he was bankrupt.

Like Sir Walter Scott before him, Clemens was resolved to repay every penny he owed his creditors. The Hartford house was closed, and the Clemenses started off on the first of a long, weary series of lecture tours. That effort, together with a successful travel book, eventually cleared their financial accounts, but it could not restore their happy family life. While they were in England in 1896, they got word that Susy, then twenty-four years old, had died of meningitis.

Though the house was still theirs, Livy would never enter it again. Her husband wrote its epitaph:

"To us, our house was not unsentient matter—it had a heart, and a soul, and eyes to see us with; and approvals and solicitudes, and deep sympathies; it was of us, and we were in its confidence, and lived in its grace and in the peace of its benediction. We never came home from an absence that its face did not light up and speak out its eloquent welcome—and we could not enter it unmoved."

*Sir William Allan painted Scott in front of the gloomy Border landscape he loved.*

# Sir Walter Scott's Abbotsford

On a fine morning in late May of 1812 an odd procession wound up the valley of the river Tweed, some thirty miles south of Edinburgh. At its head was a carriage bearing Mrs. Walter Scott with her two youngest children and a governess. Scott and the older children rode on horseback. Behind them followed servants, driving the farm wagons and shepherding animals. "We had twenty-four cart-loads of the veriest trash in nature," Scott recorded, "besides dogs, pigs, poneys, poultry, cows, calves, bare-headed wenches, and bare-breeched boys." The neighbors, he went on, were most delighted by the sight of his "furniture in which old swords, bows, targets, and lances made a very conspicuous show. A family of turkies was accommodated within the helmet of some *preux* chevalier of ancient border fame and the very cows, for aught I know, were bearing banners and muskets."

It was a day that Scott had long looked forward to. From his salary as Clerk of the Court of Session at Edinburgh, the earnings of his first literary success, *The Lay of the Last Minstrel*, and a loan from his brother, Scott had enough money to buy a half-mile stretch of meadowland along the Tweed. For the time being, because of a bad investment in a printing and publishing company, the Scotts would have to make do in the farmhouse that stood on the property, but Walter's head was filled with plans for a grand house where he could live like a laird of old. The land had once belonged to the abbots of Melrose; a little way downstream was a ford where an ancient Roman road crossed the river. The estate would be known as Abbotsford.

To Scott this was hallowed land. He was descended from Border chiefs who had lived among the hills and valleys of southern Scotland since at least the thirteenth century and had earned their armorial bearings in the long troubles with the English. They were minor lairds but related to the great house of Buccleuch, whose head, the third duke, was Walter Scott's friend and patron. An earlier Walter Scott had rescued Kinmont Willie from Carlisle Castle, to become the hero of a famous ballad. Another Walter, the poet's great-grandfather, had vowed never to shave until the Stuarts were restored to the throne of Scotland and, since that never came to pass, had been recognized ever after as Beardie. To his great satisfaction, Scott owned the entire site of the 1526 Battle of Melrose, including Skirmish-field, on which the earl of Angus and the earl of Home fought over possession of King James V. Also part of the battlefield was the spot known as Turn-again, where the Scott clan had rallied and mortally wounded Kerr of Cessford, as recounted in a contemporary ballad:

> *Gallant Cessford's life-blood dear*
> *Reeked on dark Elliott's border spear.*

By upbringing as well as by birth Walter Scott was well fitted for his life work as chronicler and poet of medieval warfare and romance. He was born to a strict Calvinist father who practiced at the Edinburgh bar and an affectionate mother who sang her baby to sleep with old ballads. At the age of eighteen months, after an attack of polio that left him with a lifelong limp, he was sent off to regain his health on his grandfather's farm in Roxburghshire. An only child among old people who remembered the tales of the Border troubles from their own youth, he listened eagerly, learned early to read and recite, and was soon making up his own poems. Returning at the age of seven to Edinburgh, he was sent to the best schools and given plenty of chance to display his precocity to the well-placed friends of the family. This varied youthful experience, combined with a sunny disposition and a convivial nature, enabled Scott to move ever after with equal comfort among the scholars, the aristocrats, and the plain people of the country.

The love that Scott felt for the Tweedside where he bought his land in 1812 was based as much on its romantic historical associations as on its natural endowments. To visitors from across the border it seemed a barren country, covered mostly with heath. Indeed it was almost treeless, but Scott, in his imagination, already saw

*A turn-of-the-century photographer took this placid view of Abbotsford from the river Tweed.*

*This aerial view shows Abbotsford as it appears today.*

his property covered with a forest of oak. The first thing he did, upon taking possession, was to spread the word among his friends in England and Ireland that he wanted acorns. Shortly they began arriving by the bagful and Scott was showing his gardener how to plant them, not in rows but irregularly, as in nature.

By 1815 Scott had managed to fashion minor improvements in the farmhouse, providing a dining room for the family, a study for himself, and several rooms for guests. "I cannot," he said, "relinquish my border principle of accommodating all the cousins and *dunawastles* who will rather sleep on chairs and on the floor than be absent when folks are gathered together."

Two years later he was able to start his major building program. Abbotsford began to take on the appearance of a manor house, but Scott was already busy with plans for something more like a castle, with stone walls, a massive gate and courtyard, and a Gothic tower. Over the next eight years, as the earnings of his novels poured in, they were translated at once into walls and battlements. *Rob Roy, The Heart of Midlothian, The Bride of Lammermoor, Ivanhoe, The Talisman,* and all the rest, flowing from his pen in prodigious quantity, paid for carved fireplaces and stained glass windows. Scott had little difficulty justifying these expenditures. A friend wrote that he "thinks himself entitled to spend on castle building what he earns by castle building."

Scott filled the house with furnishings to match. There was a chair made from timbers of the house at Robroystone where Wallace was betrayed, escutcheons bearing the arms of families in the Scott ancestry, a folding lap desk made from planks of ships of the Spanish Armada wrecked on the Scottish coast, a suit of armor said to have come from Bosworth Field, where Richard III was defeated by Henry Tudor in 1485, a cast of the skull of Robert the Bruce. He was an insatiable collector of objects with historical associations. The library contained, among many other items, the following: a set of golden coat clasps in the form of bees, found in Napoleon's coach

*Scott filled Abbotsford with trophies of the gallant days he chronicled. The hall at bottom contains his extensive collection of arms and armor, and the romanticized painting in the library above it shows young Scott in the dashing uniform of the Royal Edinburgh Volunteer Light Dragoons, a unit formed during the threat of French invasion in 1796. The main hall, far left, with its hand-painted wallpaper, is in sharp contrast to the quiet study, at left, where he wrote.*

after the Battle of Waterloo; a piece of a dress of Mary Queen of Scots; an oatcake retrieved from the pocket of a fallen Highlander after the Battle of Culloden; a lock of the hair of Bonnie Prince Charlie; a pocketbook that belonged to the prince's savior, Flora Macdonald.

In 1820, to his great satisfaction, Scott received a knighthood from his friend and admirer King George IV. Now, as Sir Walter, a knight in title as well as in fancy, he could feel even more at home among the vaulted ceilings, mullioned windows, and rooftop parapets of his made-to-order medieval castle. Abbotsford was always overflowing with his own growing family, relatives, invited guests, and visitors who found some excuse to partake of his famous hospitality. Washington Irving, who stopped by for breakfast, was importuned to stay for five days. Many of the guests wondered how Scott could possibly get his writing done when he was so busy being a host. "If he is really writing 'Rob Roy,'" the painter Sir David Wilkie marveled in 1817, "it must be while we are all sleeping." That was, in fact, the truth. Scott customarily rose at five, put on his old green hunting jacket, and worked steadily at his desk until nine, when he joined the household for breakfast. After breakfast he attended to his wide correspondence and other affairs. By noon the day's work was done. When the weather was good he spent most of the afternoon outdoors, riding and fishing, planting his gardens, and seeing to the needs of a large estate. In the evening there were rarely fewer than twelve at table. The guests included members of the local gentry, English friends, and in later years distinguished visitors from abroad, such as Prince Leopold of Saxe-Coburg and Prince Gustavus Vasa of Sweden. After dinner the company was treated to games, music, and dancing as well as to the host's great stock of Scottish stories.

The high point of the year was the Abbotsford Hunt, usually held on October 28, the birthday of his son Walter Jr. All Scott's neighbors—yeomen and gentry together—were invited for a full day of coursing rabbits on the moors around Cauldshiels Loch and on the Gala

219

hills. The feast that followed was not soon forgotten: "a baron of beef, roasted, at the foot of the table, a salted round at the head, while tureens of hare soup, hotchpotch and cockeyleekie extended down the centre, and such light articles as geese, turkeys, entire sucking pigs, a singed sheep's head, and the unfailing haggis, were set forth by way of side dishes. Blackcock and moorfowl, bushels of snipe, black puddings, white puddings, and pyramids of pancakes formed the second course." What with bagpipes, the recital of ballads, and "quaighs of Glenlivet tossed off as if they held water," the festivity lasted far into the night. The wife of one of the revelers delighted Scott by telling him what her husband had said after stumbling to his room: "Ailie, my woman, I'm ready for my bed—and oh lass, I wish I could sleep for a towmont, for there's only ae thing in this warld worth living for, and that's the Abbotsford Hunt."

Two misfortunes brought the great days of Abbotsford to an end. One was Scott's declining health. Though he loved sports and had spent much of his life in the open, he came from a short-lived family. In his forties he began suffering attacks of acute pain from gallstones, for which his doctors had no treatment except bed rest, blistering, and bleeding. Then in 1825 he suffered financial disaster. The publishing firm of which he was part owner failed, and Scott found himself responsible for its debts. As a gentleman—and indeed by that time the first gentleman of Scotland—Scott could not contemplate bankruptcy. "My own right hand shall do it," he resolved. For a while he thought he would lose Abbotsford, but since he had deeded the estate to his oldest son, Walter, the house was saved. However, there would be "no more building; no purchases of land. . . ." For the rest of his life, in steadily declining health, he labored at his writing desk to pay off the mountain of debt. It was never fully paid, but Scott mercifully came to believe at the end of his life that he had cleared the account. After his death in 1832, Abbotsford eventually passed to the descendants of his daughter Sophia—who live there still.

# THE HOUSE THAT SHERLOCK HOLMES BUILT

William Gillette had already established himself as one of America's foremost actors when he first played the role of Sherlock Holmes in 1899. But the English detective made him immortal. It was Gillette who invented the enduring popular vision of Holmes—the saturnine man in deerstalker hat and Inverness cape. He played the role for thirty years, and put the money it brought him into something equally picturesque: a beetling twenty-four-room castle overlooking the Connecticut River near Essex. Gillette designed it himself and designed everything within the four-foot-thick walls as well. Intrigued by all things mechanical, he devised elaborate locks for the sturdy oak doors, a complex system of mirrors that let him check the living room from his bedroom, and chairs and tables that rolled back and forth on tracks. Outside the house, he laid track for a three-mile miniature railway, and delighted in careening along at twenty miles per hour while his anxious guests clung to their tiny cars. Today the castle and its furnishings remain intact and are open to the public. The State of Connecticut bought the land in 1943, after Gillette, in his will, had decreed that his executors should "see to it that the property did not fall into the hands of some blithering saphead who has no conception of where he is or with what surrounded."

*The fifty-by-thirty-foot living room is walled in fieldstone.*

*Nursing a pipeful of Holmes's beloved shag tobacco, Gillette relaxes in his most famous role.*

*Made of native stone and white oak, Gillette's castle was five years building and cost over a million dollars.*

# Frederick Church's Olana

*Frederick Edwin Church by Charles Loring Eliot*

"About an hour this side of Albany is the Center of the World—I own it." So wrote Frederick Edwin Church to a friend in July, 1869.

The tract of high land that he had bought on the eastern bank of the Hudson River is indeed as fine a piece of property as any artist could choose for his home. It overlooks a curve of the lordly river and commands, across the fertile valley, a view of the distant Catskill Mountains. The land itself is little changed from the time Church bought it. But upon its height now stands the great, unlikely Oriental mansion that Church built. The name he gave it, "Olana," meaning "our place on high," is derived loosely from the Arabic, as is its architecture.

Frederick Edwin Church is remembered today, when he is remembered at all, as the last of the painters of the Hudson River school that included Thomas Cole, Asher B. Durand, and George Inness. But there was a period of about ten years just before the Civil War when Church could fairly have been called the most illustrious painter in the United States. Even as late as 1863 *Harper's Weekly* commented that "it has been the happiness of Mr. Church to achieve a more popular reputation than any American painter since Allston. . . . He alone, with the confidence of success, exhibits his single works as they are completed. No other name, perhaps, among our artists would summon such crowds as his."

The son of a prosperous Hartford, Connecticut, businessman, Church had studied with Cole and accepted Emerson's challenge to create an art "worthy of the continent." His first major success, a finely detailed view of Niagara Falls, was dramatic but still realistic. In later paintings he undertook to improve the natural landscape by adding symbolic figures and echoes of ancient history. His huge panoramic *Heart of the Andes*, painted after a trip to South America, attempts to convey the spirit of that continent in a never-never scene of snow-clad peaks, tropical jungle, primitive Indians, a missionary's cross, and the ruins of Mayan civilization. When it was first shown in his New York studio it drew so

*Rich carpets and furnishings fill Olana's main hall.*

many viewers that police were needed to control the traffic. Visitors brought opera glasses to inspect its details above the heads of the throng.

In 1867 Church set off with his wife on a grand tour of Europe and the Middle East. The sights he saw, especially in Syria, Turkey, and the Holy Land, filled his pads with sketches for future paintings and filled his mind with ideas for the house that he was already planning to build. To a friend he wrote that he was bringing home boxes of "rugs—armour—stuffs—curiosities, etc. etc. etc." and "old clothes (Turkish), stones from a house in Damascus, Arab spears—beads from Jerusalem—stones from Petra and 10,000 other things."

Before beginning construction of a house on the land he had bought near the town of Hudson, New York, Church consulted two leading New York architects. But in the end he put aside their professional plans and, although he had no training as an architect, designed Olana, both inside and out, himself. "I give directions all day," he wrote, "and draw plans and working drawings all night." As his voluminous sketchbooks prove, he would try as many as ten designs for a newel post before settling on one of them.

It takes a brave critic to describe the architectural style of Olana. Here is what Professor David C. Huntington of Smith College, who led the movement to preserve the old house, makes of it: "In the pointed arches, the block-like massing, the steep-pitched roof of the tower, and the 'constructional' polychromy of the original house, one can make out the connections with Gothic Revival, Italian Villa, French Mansard, and Ruskinian Venetian stylistic idioms." The house is built of native stone, mostly tawny in color but with shades of red and blue. To get Arabic effects in the elaborate exterior wall patterns, he used brick in various colors, tiles, and carved wood. The main entrance, with its pointed arch, geometrical designs, and strips of blue tile, is reminiscent of the door to a Persian mosque.

The rooms of the house are arranged around a large central space which in the Middle East would have been an open court but, in deference to the New York climate, is roofed over to make a great hall with a stairway at the far end. Church fussed endlessly over the placement of every object, from Victorian overstuffed chairs and medieval suits of armor to Indian brass urns and Persian filigree peacocks. A missionary in Beirut was commissioned to buy rugs and the French consul in Teheran to select tiles for the fireplace in the master bedroom. Some of the furniture was made to order in India at a factory that Mrs. Church's cousin, Lockwood De Forest, had set up to supply the needs of wealthy Americans.

By the time the main house was finished, the art world had turned its back on Frederick Church and his landscapes of transcendental grandeur. Finding little demand for his canvases, Church switched his primary attention to planting and improving the three hundred twenty-seven acres of his estate, always for the purpose of "opening views" from the house or the drives or favorite spots of ground. To a friend he wrote philosophically, "I can make more and better landscapes in this way than by tampering with canvas and paint in the Studio."

After Church's death in 1900 his family continued to live at Olana until 1964. It took almost all of that time for the changing art world to get around to admitting that Church's sketches at least, if not his paintings, had some merit. By then even the architectural critics were beginning to look upon Olana as something more than an Orientalized Victorian monstrosity. By good fortune the family had thrown nothing out, but had packed away in the attics what they did not use. It was all there—the plans and sketches and letters and furnishings—ready to be studied and put back in place when Olana was saved from the wrecker's ball and made a New York State historic site in 1967. It brings back an exuberant era in the republic, when a man of wealth and taste could conceive of building his personal monument to the cultural treasure of the Old World in the magnificent natural landscape of the New.

During his single trip abroad, Church was smitten by the ancient city of Petra, with its "splendid colors in the rocks—ribbons of bright and beautiful colors winding and twisting and interlacing like marbled paper." The bright façade of the building, far right, shows how closely Church was able to approximate the effect of that glowing stone. At right is his studio balcony, below it one of his vistas framed in a Moorish arch, and, directly below, a detail of the complex and prankish stonework.

*Rubens sits with his first wife, Isabella, in a painting he did in 1609, the year of their marriage.*

# Peter Paul Rubens's Antwerp House

In a painting that hangs in the Alte Pinakothek in Munich, a seventeenth-century gentleman is shown walking in his garden with a young woman and a boy. The garden is beautifully planted and tended, with beds of tulips, clipped hedges, and potted orange trees. In the foreground a woman servant is feeding a peacock. The strollers are approaching an elegant little pavilion with marble columns, antique statues, and swirls of baroque carving. The man is handsome, with a touch of aristocracy in his dress and bearing. His attentive attitude toward the woman suggests that they are man and wife, but she is much younger than he, hardly more than a girl, and surely not old enough to be the boy's mother.

The painting gives us a true picture of the life and circumstances of Peter Paul Rubens. He was a man of wealth and a man of the world, a courtier and diplomat as well as a painter, a gentleman of great polish and charm. The young woman in the painting is his second wife, and the boy is the son of his first wife. The setting is the garden of his house in Antwerp, and the painter of the picture was Rubens himself.

The fates that so often afflict artistic genius with emotional miseries and material hardships spared Peter Paul Rubens. He was born to a Flemish family of substance and social standing, just on the edges of aristocracy. Peter Paul was blessed with an even temperament and a capacity for work that enabled him to turn out paintings of high quality in prodigious quantity. He had the head of a businessman, both in the running of a large studio and in the prices he charged his noble and royal clients. He became the most prosperous as well as the most famous painter in Europe.

Nevertheless, a cloud hung over the Rubens family during Peter Paul's childhood. His father, Jan Rubens, an Antwerp magistrate, had taken the side of the Protestants in opposition to the Spanish Catholic rulers of the Netherlands. To escape persecution, he had moved the family to Cologne, in Germany. Cologne, as it happened, was the headquarters in exile of the prince of Orange, called

*In this detail from one of his paintings, Rubens, now in his fifties, walks in the garden of his Antwerp home with his young second wife, Helen, and his son Nicholas.*

William the Silent, who was then leading the revolt of the Netherlands against Spain. While William was away campaigning, his spoiled young wife, Anne of Saxony, took Jan Rubens for her adviser, and eventually her lover. William knew of the affair but chose to ignore it until Anne became pregnant. Then Jan was arrested, and it seemed likely that he would be condemned to death. But Maria Rubens, Peter Paul's mother, pleaded so effectively for her husband's life that he was freed, and she took him back without reproach.

When Peter Paul was ten his father died, and his mother, who had clung to the Catholic faith, moved the family back to Antwerp. Three years later she sent her youngest son to be a page in a noble household, hoping that such service would lead to a career in government, but after a while Peter Paul threatened to run away unless he was allowed to study painting. He became an apprentice at the age of fourteen, and during the next seven years learned all he could from the Flemish artists, while impressing them with his precocious talent.

For an ambitious young painter in northern Europe the next step was a pilgrimage to Italy, which had been the fountainhead of painting since the Renaissance. In the spring of 1600 Rubens left Antwerp and got an appointment as court painter to the duke of Mantua, Vicenzo Gonzaga. The Gonzaga palace was filled with the fruits of assiduous patronage and collecting by the ducal family. Part of Rubens's job was to add to this collection by making copies of paintings owned by the duke and other great collectors.

Most of all he admired and studied Titian, spending many days in learning to mix and match the colors Titian used. In later years his work would show striking resemblances to that of Titian, especially in the use of color and the masterful handling of voluptuous human flesh.

His enlightened patron gave him other opportunities. For months at a time he was sent to live in Rome, where the art of the greatest masters was on display and where a new, flamboyantly compelling style, later to be called baroque, was being developed by younger artists. The new style appealed to powerful princes of the Church, who saw in it a means of expressing in art the renewal of Catholic faith after the attacks of the Protestant Reformation. It also appealed to Rubens, who made it his own.

Once Rubens was sent to Spain to present copies of paintings in the Gonzaga collection to Philip III. At the Spanish court he began his education in the practice of diplomacy, which was to be his second career.

When Rubens returned to Antwerp at the age of thirty, his reputation as a painter of unusual talent had preceded him. Within a year he married Isabella Brant, the daughter of an Antwerp civic official, a girl of eighteen. He accepted an appointment as court painter to the rulers of the Spanish Netherlands, Archduchess Isabella, who was a daughter of Philip II of Spain, and her husband, Archduke Albert. And he bought a solid old house on one of the canals.

At once Rubens began work on the structure, redesigning, rebuilding, and adding wings until he had an establishment of forty rooms. Very likely, he drew his own architectural plans, down to the finest details of balconies and balustrades, cornices, chimneypieces, niches for statues or busts, and fluted columns in the antique style. From what we know of the way he worked on paintings with apprentices, we can imagine him watching over every stroke of the builders' chisels, having the work done over and over until it met his exacting specifications. He had seen the fine carved interiors of palaces in Venice and Genoa and Rome. Nothing less would do for what he meant to be the showplace of the artistic capital of the North.

The most important addition to the house was a spacious studio with plenty of room for his canvases. "I am," he said, "by natural instinct better fitted to execute very large works than small curiosities." Some of his altarpieces are forty feet tall, and many of his other scenes are painted on a scale that fits them best for

232

palaces or modern museums. The studio, which is faithfully reproduced in a painting by his talented apprentice, Anthony Van Dyck, provided space for Rubens and several students to work at once. It was almost bare of furniture, for Rubens did not encourage anyone to sit down in working hours, neither himself nor his apprentices nor visitors. But in accordance with the custom of the day there was a visitors' galley where clients or guests—or even people who came in off the street—could stand and watch the painters.

Rubens generally had from six to eight apprentices in the house. They lived on the second floor of the studio and were expected to follow the master's schedule, with no nonsense about waiting for their genius to move them. The demands on his time were extraordinary, and in a letter written in 1611 to an engraver in Brussels who had recommended a new assistant Rubens candidly explained his situation: "I am so besieged that there are apprentices who have been waiting for years, under other masters, for me to be able to accept them. Truly, and without exaggeration, I have found it necessary to turn away more than one hundred aspirants, among them blood relatives and the sons of lifelong friends. Could your young candidate serve his apprenticeship elsewhere, I might be better able to find a place in my studio for him as a journeyman, it being somewhat more difficult to persuade graduate painters to remain in my service."

Work began in the morning as soon as there was light in the studio, and continued until dark. After that the apprentices were free, but Rubens usually retired to a small room, where he worked for another two or three hours on sketches for the next day's work. He painted rapidly and steadily. A Danish physician, Otto Sperling, reported in awe that during a visit to the studio Rubens kept on painting while at the same time dictating correspondence and listening to a reading from Tacitus in Latin.

Just how much of the work that Rubens signed was done by apprentices has long been a matter of dispute.

Probably they painted in many of the backgrounds and minor details. On lesser commissions they may have painted the full pictures, leaving the master with nothing to do except touch up the final product. But Rubens always made the original sketches, and it is probably safe to assume that on an important picture he painted the faces and other main elements, if not the entire canvas.

Whatever came from his studio bore the unmistakable marks of the Rubens style. He became the greatest master of baroque painting, as Bernini was the greatest master of baroque architecture. Rubens canvases, both religious and secular, are filled with powerful movement, dramatic lighting, vibrant colors, surging clouds, and swirling fabrics. Most striking to modern eyes are the nude female figures—great, billowing creatures rendered in every delicate shade of milk and blood and honey. Viewers have often wondered whether seventeenth-century ladies in the well-fed Netherlands really looked like that, or whether Rubens sought out the most buxom models he could find, or whether he gave them more in his paintings than nature had given them in life. Certainly it is true that excess was a characteristic of the baroque style and that even his Christ on the Cross looks like a weight lifter in comparison with the gaunt, ethereal figure of conventional Christian art.

The living quarters of the Rubens family, which came to include two sons and a daughter, were as handsomely furnished and decorated as the studio was spare. Ever since his years in Italy Rubens had collected ancient coins, statues, busts, and carved inscriptions. They were mingled in his rooms with pictures by his favorite painters—Titian, Raphael, Tintoretto, Veronese, and Brueghel—as well as his own canvases. At the long table in the dining room Rubens entertained the best families of Antwerp as well as frequent visitors from abroad. By the time he was fifty he commanded the highest prices of any painter in Europe, and he lived up to his income.

No painter ever had more royal and noble clients. For Charles I of England he painted portraits of the royal

family and members of the court as well as the ceiling of the banqueting house at Whitehall. For Philip IV of Spain he painted portraits and a series of paintings for the walls of the king's hunting lodge, the Torre de la Parada. For Marie de' Medici, the Queen Mother of France, he painted an allegorical story of her life in twenty-one splendid panels. So pleased was Charles that he conferred a knighthood on the painter, making him Sir Peter Paul Rubens.

Rubens's easy access to the courts of Europe did not escape the notice of his own ruler, the archduchess Isabella. Knowing him also as a man of intelligence, industry, and winning personality, she realized that he could be of use to her and to her royal cousin, Philip IV of Spain, in their delicate relations with other governments. Rubens's first assignment was to try to help bring about a reunion of the northern provinces of the Netherlands, which had become an independent republic, with the southern, Catholic, provinces, which were still under Spanish rule. Nothing came of this, but a few years later he was sent to London to help promote an alliance between England and Spain at the expense of France. He got on famously with Charles, a great art lover and collector, and scored a personal success in London. But the diplomatic assignment was essentially hopeless, and his efforts had no lasting effect.

Rubens had suffered cruel blows in his private life. His favorite child, Clara Serena, died of the plague at twelve, and his wife Isabella died, perhaps of the same cause, two years later. These tragedies, combined with his diplomatic activities, had inevitably distracted him from his artistic work. Now at fifty-three—the threshold of old age in those days—he was determined to retire to his studio and devote himself to painting. It was partly for that reason, he said, that he did not choose a second wife from among the ladies of the court, who might "blush to see me take my brushes in hand." But he was also honest enough to admit that "it would have been hard for me to exchange the priceless treasure of liberty for the

embraces of an old woman." The bride he chose was a girl of sixteen, Helen Fourment, the daughter of a silk merchant. The difference between his feeling for his first wife, Isabella, and his feelings for Helen may be imagined from the pictures he painted of them. Isabella appears as a pretty, composed young woman, attractively and fully dressed, the painter's partner and equal. Helen is the voluptuous darling of an infatuated husband thrice her age. She poses half nude, clutching a fur robe, and wholly nude as Venus in *The Judgment of Paris* and variously clothed as each of the ladies dallying with their suitors in *The Garden of Love.*

The last decade of Rubens's life was lived in happiness with Helen and the four children she bore him. He continued to live in Antwerp during the winter, but he bought as a summer place the Chateau de Steen, a moated and castellated manor house in the midst of farms and orchards. There he developed a new interest in the painting of landscapes and of peasant festivals reminiscent of Brueghel. He never stopped painting until his last months, when arthritis (confused at the time with gout) crippled his right hand. He died in 1640, presumably of a heart attack. Eight months later Helen bore her fifth child (his eighth), Constantia Albertina.

His will provided that all his sketches and drawings be kept intact for any of his sons who might become a painter or any of his daughters who might marry a painter. They were held for sixteen years, until the youngest daughter, Constantia Albertina, decided to enter a convent. Then the older children by both marriages, all burghers and wives of burghers, agreed with Helen, now herself remarried, to sell them at auction. Both of the houses were sold, and many of the furnishings disposed of. Today the Chateau de Steen is still in private hands, but in 1937 the Antwerp house was bought by the city for restoration as a museum. By the four hundredth anniversary of Rubens's birth in 1977 his admirers had re-created, with careful research and refurnishing, the house and garden of his lifetime.

# Gabriele D'Annunzio's Villa

Gabriele D'Annunzio was a short man with a bald head and almost no eyebrows, bulging eyes, beak nose, scrawny neck, yellowish skin, narrow shoulders, wide hips, tiny hands and feet, and sharp, brownish teeth. He was irresistible to women.

What was his secret? Let Isadora Duncan, the American dancer, bear witness: "I remember a marvelous walk I had with D'Annunzio. In a forest. We stopped and remained standing silently. Then D'Annunzio exclaimed, 'O, Isadora, it is only with you that one can be alone in the midst of nature. All other women destroy the landscape. You alone are part of it. You are a part of the trees, the sky, you are the Supreme Goddess of Nature.'"

Though he thought of himself as a prince, and eventually became one, D'Annunzio was born in 1863 into a bourgeois family of Pescara, on the Adriatic shore of Italy. By the age of seventeen he was writing poems to a girl named Griselda, whose mouth "opened like a pomegranate." He called her his "only, only, sole, unique, my only one," proposed marriage, was accepted—and departed for Rome. During the next several years he wrote poems, novels, and also a newspaper gossip column that won him entrée to the drawing rooms of principessas, contessas, and marchesas. Many of these ladies and their daughters were quite overcome by the crinkly-haired boy with his dashing style and his dazzling flights of talk. Within two years he married (to her parents' indignation) Maria, the daughter of the duke and duchess of Gallese. "When I married my husband," she said long afterward, "I thought I was marrying poetry itself."

Not long after their marriage, Maria discovered a love letter to her husband from the first of a long line of ladies who succumbed to his charms. Maria remained his wife and bore him three sons but gradually drifted out of his life. Over a period of fifty years D'Annunzio's conquests, of which he early lost count, ranged from waitresses to princesses to opera stars. The most renowned was the great Italian actress Eleonora Duse.

*D'Annunzio in his World War I uniform*

*Barbara Leoni*

*Eleonora Duse*

*Ida Rubinstein*

The scene of this tempestuous liaison was a villa called La Capponcina that D'Annunzio rented on a hillside at Settignano outside Florence. He chose the area, he said, "because great art can only be created where great art has been." The house came furnished, but the first thing D'Annunzio did was to pay the owner an extra fee to take everything out of it.

He began the process of redecoration by having the interior walls painted in different shades of gold. The rooms were hung about with silks and brocades, strewn with rugs and pillows, stuffed with heavy furniture, paintings, statuary, and all the objects that the poet had been collecting. The D'Annunzio style of decoration was thus described by Anthony Rhodes, his biographer: "Every object must be decorated with another object. On a chest will be a bust; on the bust, a jewel; on the jewel, a flower. On a table will be a piece of old velvet; on the old velvet, an embroidered stole; on the stole, a coat of arms; on the coat of arms, a glass cup; in the glass cup, an hourglass; in the hourglass, some grains of incense."

Here D'Annunzio lived for ten years with twenty servants, in a style that was never matched by the income from his writing. One of the reasons he needed so many servants, he once explained, was to keep his creditors out of the house.

The years he spent at Settignano were the most productive of his life. From his study there poured forth a prodigious quantity of poems and plays in which scenes of passion were mingled with carnage worthy of the Grand Guignol—all rendered in flamboyant lines that inflamed Italian hearts but did not travel well to other lands. When the creative fever was upon him he wrote in a frenzy through the night. Even the Duse, who brooked no hindrance from any other living soul, had to wait meekly in the courtyard, wrapped in her cloak, until he was finished. "His creative genius must be supported at all costs," she said.

The Duse had left her husband and child. She had reverently picked up pages of manuscript as they fell

*Maria D'Annunzio*

*Between writing and spasms of military heroics and marriage to Maria, above, D'Annunzio found time for noisy love affairs with the other women pictured here.*

*Marchesa Casati*

*Maria di Ramacca*

from D'Annunzio's pen, and made no protest when he sent a play, *La città morta*, containing a role that she cherished, to her archrival, Sarah Bernhardt. Her reward was to become the model for the heroine of *Il fuoco* (The Flame). In life Eleonora was four years older than D'Annunzio, but the heroine of the novel is twenty years older. The hero, modeled on D'Annunzio himself, takes her for a ride in a Venetian gondola, as D'Annunzio had often taken the Duse, but instead of extolling her beauty he spends the time observing her sagging chin and the wrinkles about her eyes.

So long as he was faithful to her, the Duse did not complain. Romance was her life. It was said that when they went on vacation to the Adriatic, after a night of poetry and love D'Annunzio would mount his horse, stark naked, at dawn, ride into the sea, and then swim back to shore, where the actress would be holding a purple robe to receive him. It was also said that they drank together from a virgin's skull by moonlight.

D'Annunzio's passion for women was matched only by his passion for Italy. He had been born in the time of the Risorgimento, when Garibaldi had conquered the Kingdom of the Two Sicilies and Victor Emmanuel II had unified Italy under the house of Savoy. For the spirit of nationalism D'Annunzio was a perfect mouthpiece. Italy, he proclaimed, was the new Rome. Italians were the purest of races. He, D'Annunzio, was the embodiment of the Italian spirit.

When World War I broke out, D'Annunzio was in France, where he had gone to escape his creditors and to bestow his genius on the theatrical world of Paris. To an Italy that was still trying to stay out of the conflict he had already appealed: "Oh, Italy, somnolent and inert, will you ever waken from your ignoble sleep?" The well-meaning but unheroic little king, Victor Emmanuel III, had been exhorted in these words: "Oh young King. . . . Bend the bow, oh King! Light the torch! Destiny has chosen you for great events."

In May of 1915, as Italy wavered on the brink,

*Piled with souvenirs of his scattershot career, D'Annunzio's Vittoriale hermitage, at left, on the shores of Lake Garda was designed as a monument to his genius. "Come and see my relics," he would say to visitors toward the end of his life. "Now I live only through my dead. . . ." The music room, below, was as well-stocked with relics as the rest of the house. For concerts, D'Annunzio had the room hung with either red or black silk, depending on his assessment of the mood of the music that was being performed.*

D'Annunzio set out for home, but before reaching the border he bound his eyes, lest the first sight of his native land be too dazzling to bear. He arrived in Genoa uttering apostrophes to "Victory, wild as the horse which crops the asphodel in the Roman desert. . . ."

A few days later Italy entered the war, and D'Annunzio although he was fifty-two years old, managed to get a commission in the army, with roving assignments also as a naval commander and an aviator. His military operations during the next three years might be described as parallel to those of the Italian armed forces but separate. His supposedly superior officers never seemed to have any clear idea of where he was or what he was going to do next. Sometimes he was dashing into an enemy harbor in a torpedo boat to fire at anything in sight. Sometimes he was flying over Trieste, Vienna, or Trent to drop leaflets or a package containing water from a sacred fountain of Rome or a laurel branch from the garden of the vestal virgins. No one could question his bravery, which won him many medals and cost him his right eye. At the time of the Armistice he was planning a flight to drop leaflets over Berlin. He had already plotted the route—not over one of the Alpine passes, which he disdained, but over Mont Blanc, the highest peak in Europe.

Like other Italian nationalists, D'Annunzio was outraged by the peace conference, which rewarded the other Allied powers but gave Italy nothing. Determined to right this wrong, D'Annunzio gathered a private army, made up mostly of past and present soldiers, and marched on Fiume, a city at the head of the Adriatic that had long been disputed by Italy and Austria. Meeting no opposition from the Allied occupying forces, he ruled Fiume for a year before the Italian government mustered enough political courage to chase him out.

One of D'Annunzio's allies in the comic-opera conquest of Fiume had been Benito Mussolini. When Mussolini came to power he created D'Annunzio prince of Monte Nevoso, and endowed the hero's new home at Lago di Garda with public funds. Once again

D'Annunzio set about the business of turning a rather modest villa into a theatrical setting for himself.

As the villa outside Florence had been a shrine to D'Annunzio the lover, his postwar home, called Il Vittoriale, now became a monument to D'Annunzio the fighter. The original house was enveloped in new rooms, all of them adorned with the master's favorite silks and damasks and brocades. But among the plaster casts of Roman statues, the gilded lions and grotesque masks and mounds of pillows, there now appeared flags and medals, swords and machine guns. The broken steering wheel of a motorboat reposed in front of a predella. From the ceiling of one room hung the little airplane in which D'Annunzio had raided Vienna. Thrusting through the cypress trees was the prow of the cruiser *Puglia*, which had carried some of his compatriots from Fiume.

When visitors came to see him at Il Vittoriale, the master would sometimes fire a few guns or press upon his guests some sacred relics of his life. D'Annunzio did little writing, but he kept on talking, grandly and incessantly, to a dwindling band of admirers and household servants. The local prostitutes, who now replaced the glamorous ladies of better days, were treated to hours of philosophical disquisition. In his private rooms, which he called The Priory, he often dressed in a monk's cowl, and sometimes he slept in a coffin. He lived on, a recluse and a legend, until 1938, and when at last he died his vigil was held by torchlight on the *Puglia*.

In deeding Il Vittoriale to the nation, D'Annunzio had proclaimed: "I give this as a testament of the spirit, immune from every illegal search or vulgar intrusion forever. Not only every house I have ever owned, not only every room I have ever lived in, but every object I have ever chosen and collected in the various ages of my life, has been for me a perpetual means of expression, a form of spiritual revelation—as were my poems, my dramas, my political and military acts." It is all there still, like the empty set of a road-company *Don Giovanni* after the show is over.

*Among the scraps of cloth from old battle flags and the dried flowers from old affairs that fill D'Annunzio's home are some startling large souvenirs. The biplane he flew over Vienna hangs in the rotunda, and the Puglia, a cruiser that figured in his chimerical Fiume expedition, rests in his garden. Mussolini, seen with D'Annunzio below left, admired the poet's bumptious nationalism and was a comrade in arms at Fiume. D'Annunzio worked in his crowded "office" below.*

# Horace Walpole's Strawberry Hill

Houghton Hall stands in the flat Norfolk country-side, big and solid and foursquare. It seems to fit the nature of the man who built it, Sir Robert Walpole, the great prime minister of England from 1721 to 1742, a hearty, red-faced, hunt-loving country squire. Robert Walpole's ancestors had been Norfolk squires for longer than anyone could trace them. His brothers were of the same stamp as he, and so were his two older sons. But not his youngest son, Horace.

From an early age Horace hated sports and rowdy play and shooting and bluff country gentlemen. He liked books and pictures and clothes and conversation. He was not only the youngest of Walpole's children but younger by eleven years than any of the others. Almost from the time he was born in 1717 his parents had been estranged. In effect an only child, Horace was brought up mostly in London and almost wholly by his mother until at nine he was sent off to Eton, and after that to Cambridge.

Thus he and his father were almost strangers when he was summoned down from Cambridge for his first visit to the mansion that Sir Robert had recently completed in Norfolk. One of his classmates, the poet Thomas Gray, wrote him in commiseration: "You are in a Confusion of Wine and Bawdy and Hunting and Tobacco . . . ." Actually, Horace had already developed considerable cunning in avoiding the things he disliked, so that he managed to enjoy the country and the great house while keeping clear of the hunters and drinkers and political place seekers who hung about his powerful father.

After Cambridge, in the aristocratic pattern of the day, Horace spent the next two and a half years on a grand tour of the Continent, in company with Gray. He returned to England in 1741, just in time to witness his father's political downfall. A new title—earl of Orford—was little consolation to Sir Robert for the loss of the great political power that he had held for more than twenty years. But Horace's own future was not affected. He was assured the distinction—boring though it may have been—of a seat in Parliament, representing one of the

family's pocket boroughs, and the prospect of an effort-less living from such picturesque sinecures as Clerk of the Estreats, Comptroller of the Pipe, and Usher of the Exchequer.

For the three remaining years of Sir Robert's life Horace lived with him in London and in the country. He still did not care for the company at Houghton. "Only imagine," he wrote "that I here every day see men who are mountains of roast beef and only seem just roughly hewn out into the outlines of human form, like the giant rock at Pratolino. I shudder when I see them brandish their knives in act to carve, and look on them as savages that devour one another." But he learned to like a horseback ride in the morning and he shared his father's love for the fine collection of paintings that Sir Robert had gathered at Houghton. Despite the total opposition of their temperaments, Horace admired his father, and Sir Robert for his part developed a fondness for the strange son who did more to brighten his old age than any of the other children.

After his father died Horace Walpole became for two years "the friend of London," spending his evenings at dinners and parties and masquerades, the theater, the opera, and the gambling clubs. Rather short and extremely thin, he entered a drawing room on tiptoes, "as if he were afraid of getting his feet wet." Hostesses loved him for his wit, his flights of conversation, his effusive flattery, his love of gossip, and his talent for spearing the fashionable figures of the day with a phrase ("Capability" Brown, the landscape architect, was "Lady Nature's second husband"). But he was not the complete dilettante or butterfly that many of his father's friends thought him. He was forming a life purpose that would satisfy his own tastes and make the most of his special talents and advantages. He would become the social and political chronicler of the age. His family connection and his dinner-table gifts were passports to society. His seat in Parliament and his acquaintance with political leaders put him close to the center of public affairs. His talents of

observation and writing were the tools he would need. Memoirs and letters would be his medium. Posterity would be his chief audience.

It was all very well to live in London during the season, but for summer weekends and for serious writing Walpole needed a country place. Even if he had liked Houghton Hall he could hardly have lived there, because his oldest brother had inherited the estate. In 1747 he acquired a piece of property near Twickenham on the Thames, eleven miles from London. Someone had named it Strawberry Hill, although it rose only thirty-three feet above the river. It had a fine, big lawn with a view of the passing pleasure boats and the commercial barges, "as solemn as Barons of the Exchequer." The new owner was pleased with his neighbors: "Dowagers as plenty as flounders inhabit all around." Walpole was good with dowagers.

As for the house—"Lord God! Jesus! What a house!" exclaimed his friend Lady Townshend when she first beheld it. "It is just such a house as the parson's where the children lie at the foot of the bed." So much the better, Walpole probably thought. He would not have to bother with preserving any part of it.

In a letter to his friend Sir Horace Mann, the British envoy to Florence, he declared his intention to build "a little Gothic castle" at Strawberry Hill. He was by no means the first to revive the Gothic style in the Georgian age. Pope had built a monk's grotto in his garden, and Lord Brooke had erected a neo-Gothic castle at Warwick. But Walpole approached the project with far more scholarly authority and greater artistic background. First of all, he constituted a Committee on Taste, consisting of himself and two idle but talented fanciers of the architectural past, Richard Bentley and John Chute. The members of the committee pretended to no knowledge of the techniques and practicalities of construction. They trusted a long-suffering builder named William Robinson to embody their notions in a structure that would keep out the rain and not fall down. Their part was to evoke

the feeling of the medieval age—to create, as Walpole put it, a delicious "gloomth."

It was never Walpole's intention to put up an authentically Gothic edifice. He would not have been able to afford it, nor would he have wanted to live in the drafty halls and cold stone vaults of a true Gothic castle. What he had in mind was to take notions from the great Gothic buildings of the English past and adapt them to an agreeable country house. Thus the tombs of the earl of Cornwall in Westminster Abbey and the duke of Clarence at Canterbury furnished models for the chimneypiece in the library at Strawberry Hill. The effect of carved stonework, in the rooftop battlements and elsewhere, was achieved by lath and plaster.

Just three years after the purchase, Walpole's Gothic additions had apparently attracted some notoriety. He wrote to Horace Mann because he "could not rest any longer with the thought of your having no idea of a place of which you hear so much. . . . Imagine the walls covered with (I call it paper, but it is really paper painted in perspective to represent) Gothic fretwork: the lightest Gothic balustrade to the staircase, adorned with antelopes (our supporters) bearing shields; lean windows fattened with rich saints in painted glass, and a vestibule open with three arches on the landing place, and niches full of trophies of old coats of mail, Indian shields made of rhinoceros's hides, broadswords, quivers, long bows, arrows and spears—all *supposed* to be taken by Sir Terry Bobsart in the holy wars."

When he came to design the gallery, the largest and most resplendent room in the house, Walpole left true Gothic far behind. His biographer, R. W. Ketton-Cremer, explains: "The extreme flamboyance of the room was due to the materials in which those features were executed. It is permissible to adapt the tomb of Archbishop Bourchier at Canterbury into a series of recesses in the gallery of a private house; but gold network over looking-glass is not the happiest medium in which to reproduce stone ribbing over a smooth stone surface. The fan-vaulting of Henry

Taking a hand in every detail of the design of Strawberry Hill, Walpole turned out a great supply of sketches like the ones at the right. From such chicken scratches did the long-suffering architects succeed in assembling the superb Gothic whimsy in the photograph below.

VII's chapel at Westminster may well be copied in the ceiling of the same gallery; but its effect is gravely diminished if the vaulting springs from a wall covered with the brightest crimson Norwich damask."

As fast as rooms were completed, they were decked out with the fruits of Walpole's years of compulsive collecting. As a youth on the grand tour he had written from Rome, "I am far gone in medals, lamps, idols, prints, etc." Later he came to possess twelve thousand prints and drawings of English heads and the country's finest collection of enamels and miniatures. He put them on display at Strawberry Hill, along with such curiosities as Cardinal Wolsey's red hat, the pipe that the Dutch admiral Tromp smoked during his last sea fight, a bust of the mad Roman emperor Caligula with silver eyes, and the spur that King William struck into the flank of his horse Sorrel at the Battle of the Boyne. He always regretted that he had allowed himself to be outbid for Oliver Cromwell's nightcap.

In a tower adjoining the gallery Walpole had a "charming closet" where he carried on the important business of his life—the writing of letters. He always had four or five main correspondents to whom he wrote, regularly and at length, on the society and politics and personalities of the day. They included Mann, Gray, Mme. du Deffand (who kept a Paris salon), and others remembered chiefly as Walpole's correspondents, such as George Montagu and the Countess of Upper Ossory. The recipients, in those days before the Xerox machine or even carbon paper, were under strict admonition to save the letters and return them on request so that Walpole could edit them for publication. It was serious work. Lytton Strachey was not far off when he said: "He did not snatch moments from life to write letters in: he snatched moments from letter-writing in which to live."

It would be impossible to draw a dividing line between his pleasures and his research. When he attended Parliament and dined with ministers, he was gathering material for an insider's chronicle of British politics. When he sat on his gilded sofa for hours at a time, gossiping with ladies of society, he was gleaning choice bits of social history concerning such matters as David Garrick's latest attack of gout and Lady Hertford's encounter with highwaymen on Hampstead Heath. Walpole only *seemed* to be frittering away his time. He was a Samuel Pepys without the financial necessity of working at the Navy office. He was Madame de Sévigné without the responsibilities of family life.

Indeed, Walpole had little to distract him from his work. Although he had a vast acquaintance and many whom he called friends, he had no strong emotional attachments. He liked pretty women, but only to talk to. By all evidence, he was devoid of physical passion for either sex. His attitude toward humankind is reflected in a comment he made about his traveling habits: "I always travel without company, for then I take my own hours and my own humours, which I don't think the most tractable to shut up in a coach with anybody else." Though he was constantly in society, Walpole traveled alone, in life as on shorter journeys.

After living for more than seventy years as a younger son, Walpole became in 1791 the head of a titled family. After his father's death the Orford title had descended, along with the estate of Houghton, to Horace's eldest brother, Robert, and then to Robert's son George. When George died young, both title and estate passed to Horace, who thus became the fourth earl of Orford. It was a burdensome inheritance, for the third earl had sold off the prime minister's fine art collection and allowed the mansion to fall into disrepair. "I am," lamented Horace, "the poorest earl in England." He spent much time struggling with the problems of ancestral property and greedy creditors and needy tenants at Houghton Hall, but he continued to live at Strawberry Hill.

Walpole's literary fame rests mostly on his letters and to a lesser extent on his more formal memoirs. But he wrote books as well and in his time was best known for his "Gothic" novel, *The Castle of Otranto*, which he dashed off during two months in 1764. The imaginary castle of Otranto is Strawberry Hill stripped of its rococo decoration, inflated to fearsome size, and filled with chilling horrors. Fearful that he might be laughed at, Walpole published the novel anonymously, but quickly claimed authorship when it became a success. *The Castle of Otranto* set the style for a literary genre that has had many followers and persists in watered-down imitation to this day.

Various collections of Walpole's letters were published after his death, but with many careless omissions and arbitrary changes. Then, in the 1930's, a remarkable scholarly enterprise was set in train by Wilmarth Sheldon Lewis, a wealthy member of the Yale faculty. Under Lewis's obsessive direction everything that Walpole wrote in more than seventy prolific years, down to the last scribbled note to his gardener, has been collected, arranged, and annotated, at Lewis's personal expense. This literary undertaking has required a staff of assistants and resulted in a shelf of thirty-nine published volumes, with more to come. Though some may regret that the effort was not expended on a greater writer, it has established Walpole as the premier source for a knowledge of English social and political life in the eighteenth century.

Strawberry Hill has been almost as fortunate. After Walpole's death in 1797 at the age of seventy-nine the house remained in the family for almost a century. Although most of the contents, including the collections of art and curiosities, were sold at a great auction in 1842, the house was maintained and even enlarged by Lady Waldegrave, a famous Victorian hostess. Finally, in 1888, it passed into the hands of a Roman Catholic order, the Congregation of St. Vincent de Paul, which has maintained it with scrupulous care and restored the gallery after it was hit by a German fire bomb in 1941. Visitors are received and shown around by the latter-day residents, even as they were shown about by Walpole in his lifetime.

# A WORLD OF FOLLIES

*Soaring buttresses arch above Rendlesham Lodge in Surrey.*

*Follies, as the name suggests, serve no practical function;
as buildings, they are simply picturesque indulgences of
the owners' taste. A perfect example of these monumental
fantasies, Rendlesham Lodge's flying buttresses rise
majestically to support—nothing. The sampling of follies on
the following pages indicates the capriciousness—and the
occasional foolish splendor—of these engaging aberrations.*

When, in the mid-1700's, British Admiral George Anson was lucky enough to capture
the richest Spanish treasure ship ever taken by the Royal Navy, he put his prize money to
good use by building this huge arch on his Staffordshire estate commemorating his
round-the-world voyage. Not one to grab all the glory for himself, the admiral
also built a monument nearby dedicated to a cat that accompanied him on his journey.

The eerie ruin rising up through the Dorset mist at left was built to be precisely
that—an eerie ruin. The admiration of things Gothic in the eighteenth century
often got carried to such lengths, and the English countryside is still dotted with
hermits' cells, ruined abbeys, and the like. A Mr. Stuart built this seven-story
folly and, although he claimed it was an observatory, he never put it to that use

Forty miles north of Rome near
Bomarzo lies the strangest garden
in the West, a fantastic place
where huge, grotesque statues
stand listing in tangled vegetation.
It was built in the sixteenth
century by a shadowy Italian
nobleman named Pierfrancesco
Orsini, for reasons that have
long been forgotten. The gaping
mouth above is called the Gate
of Hell, the elephant is crushing a
Roman soldier, and the dragon
is holding two fierce beasts at bay.

The world's gaudiest follies are undoubtedly the gardens filled with weird animals and contorted figures that a Chinese millionaire named Aw Boon Haw built in Singapore and Hong Kong during the 1930's. Mr. Aw developed Tiger Balm, a patent medicine reputed to cure anything from toothache to venereal disease. Enough people believed in its efficacy to enable Aw to donate some twenty million dollars to various philanthropies— and to build his public gardens. Some of the figures represent various Eastern religious themes, others, the wonders of Tiger Balm. "Obviously," says the novelist Anthony Burgess, "this garden is the externalisation of everybody's unconscious, Chinese, Indian, Malay, European alike. In a pit a man in shining scarlet trunks wrestles happily with a great white snake. If that sort of thing isn't everybody's unconscious, what is?"

his two trades—carpenter and gardener—he built this wooden fantasy garden from fragments of fruit crates

# 6 EASTERN POTENTATES

When Darius the Great of Persia built
Persepolis he was raising a monument
to his absolute, near-divine power. But
the heirs of other Oriental rulers—the
sultans and Moguls and shahs—thought
first of their pleasures. Behind plain
walls of mud or brick they created oases
of luxury and ease, filled with flowers and
perfumes and splashing fountains. Of the
kings of Granada it was said that Allah
took the Alhambra away from them because
they had made it too much like Paradise.

*The Court of Myrtles is the most celebrated*
*of the pooled gardens at the Alhambra, the*
*palace of the Moorish rulers of Granada.*

# Darius the Great's Persepolis

*Shielded forever from the fierce Persian sun, Darius surveys his city; above him flies the winged disk of Ahura Mazda, divine protector of the Achaemenid kings. The great beasts at left, part man and part bull, guard the Gateway of All Lands, built by Darius's son, Xerxes.*

For more than two thousand years the ruins of Persepolis have stirred the minds of dreamers and poets. In the eleventh century the Persian poet Omar Khayyam mused on the fate of the Persepolis:

*They say the Lion and the Lizard keep*
*The courts where Jamshid gloried and drank deep.*

Jamshid? Jamshid was a myth, a king only in Persian legend. The builder of Persepolis was Darius, third of the Achaemenid dynasty that established the Persian Empire in the sixth century B.C. That much we know from Herodotus, who traveled far and wide in the empire, though he never got as far as Persepolis.

Not until the seventeenth century do we have an eyewitness report from a responsible Italian traveler, Pietro della Valle. In 1620 he pitched his tent by a small stream below the ruins and made a detailed survey of the site. At that time there were twenty-five of the tallest columns standing (there are thirteen today). Protruding also from the sand were the bases of fallen columns, sections of stone walls, the side pillars of a gate bearing sculptures of lions, and a majestic staircase leading up to the stone terrace on which the buildings had stood. Many of the carvings of figures on the exposed surfaces had been chipped away by zealous Moslems, who thought it a sacrilege to represent the human form in art. But otherwise the site had remained almost untouched, the sands drifting ever higher over it.

At last, in 1931, the archaeologists came. Representing the Oriental Institute of the University of Chicago, they were led by a German scholar, Ernst Herzfeld, who went about the job of examining and clearing the ruins with energy and efficiency.

The site of Persepolis is a tableland at the foot of the Elburz mountains. Perhaps it appealed to the Persian monarchs for its very remoteness, which befitted their own remoteness from the people, or perhaps for its closeness to the mountains from which they had come. "I will not live on the plains," Cyrus, founder of the Achaemenid dynasty, had said. "Soft lands breed soft people."

On the site they had chosen the builders leveled a series of spacious terraces, stretching from the mountains to a retaining wall that dropped fifty feet to the valley floor. Upon these terraces they raised the complex of ceremonial buildings that Darius had decreed. Parsa to the Persians; the Greeks named it Persepolis.

On the south side of the terrace, where the thirteen tallest columns still stand, the archaeologists began their excavation. In the first season of work they uncovered the foundations of a large square building that they called the apadana, or audience hall, a term borrowed from a similar building at Susa. Under the pavement in a corner of the floor they found a stone box containing one gold and one silver plaque, each inscribed with the same message to posterity from "Darius the Great King, King of Kings: This is the kingdom I hold: from the Scythians who are beyond Sogdiana, thence unto Kush; from India thence unto Sardis, which Ahura Mazda, the greatest of the gods, bestowed on me."

Here was confirmation, in the king's own words, of what the Greek chroniclers had said: that Persepolis was built, or at least begun, by Darius. In the following seasons of work the archaeologists uncovered the floors of the other buildings and attached to them names that rested on considerable guesswork. These include the throne hall (or perhaps museum), which once had a hundred columns, the treasury, the palace of Darius, and the larger palace of his son Xerxes.

Among the ruins the archaeologists found a vast number of clay tablets inscribed with cuneiform writing. Most of the inscriptions concerned business affairs: the wages of the laborers who built Persepolis, the prices paid for materials, and so forth. Of personal matters or historic events there was scarcely a word beyond the formal titles of the kings. For information about Darius it is necessary to go to the face of a cliff at Behistun on the caravan route from Ecbatana to Babylon. Here, for all who passed to read, is Darius's own testament. The message, four hundred fourteen lines long, is inscribed in adjoining

blocks of Old Persian, Elamite, and Babylonian, the three languages used in the empire during his reign. When the words had been chiseled out of the stone, the surrounding surfaces were polished as smooth as glass, presumably so that no one could ever scale the cliff to damage the inscription. The message read in part as follows: "I was not a Lie-follower, I was not a doer of wrong. . . . According to righteousness I conducted myself. Neither to the weak nor to the powerful did I do wrong. The man who cooperated with my house, him I rewarded well; whoso did injury, him I punished well."

In the Behistun inscription Darius tells how he came to the throne by overthrowing a usurper named Gaumata who had killed Smerdis, the younger son of Cyrus: "The people feared Gaumata the pretender greatly, thinking that he would slay the people who had previously known Smerdis. . . . No one dared say anything about Gaumata the Magian until I came. Then I with a few men slew Gaumata the Magian and those who were his foremost followers." After reciting his further exploits in putting down rebellions and killing nine other conspirators, he adds: "Let what has been done by me convince you; do not think it is a lie." And a little farther on: "This is true, not false."

Since the time of the Greek historians, readers of this testament have remarked on the insistence with which the author demands belief for the story of how he obtained the throne. The phrases seem to be directed at persons who might have heard a contrary report. And indeed there has always been a cloud over Darius's succession. Cyrus, the first king, had left his throne to Cambyses, his eldest son. Cambyses led an army into Egypt, where he died. It was during his absence from Persia, according to Darius's story, that the usurper Gaumata killed Cambyses's rightful heir, his younger brother Smerdis, and seized the throne. Darius, a distant cousin of Cyrus and Cambyses, then overthrew the usurper and took the crown. That was Darius's story, but not everyone believed it. Some theorize that Darius

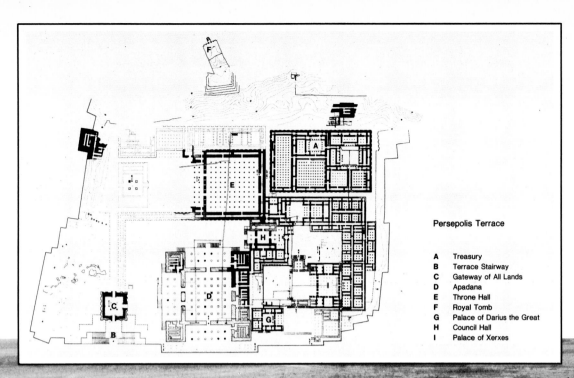

Persepolis Terrace

A   Treasury
B   Terrace Stairway
C   Gateway of All Lands
D   Apadana
E   Throne Hall
F   Royal Tomb
G   Palace of Darius the Great
H   Council Hall
I   Palace of Xerxes

himself was the usurper and invented the tale to justify his own action.

However that may have been, Darius made good his claim to the throne and ruled the empire for thirty-six years, passing it on to his own son. The Greek historians generally support his own estimate of his qualities and capabilities. As a general under Cambyses he commanded an elite corps called the Ten Thousand Immortals, the finest striking arm of his day. As king he consolidated the conquest of Egypt and pushed the eastern border of the empire to the banks of the Indus River. He built a canal to connect the Red Sea with the Nile and the Mediterranean, partly on the route of the present Suez Canal. He established firm control of the conquered provinces, or satrapies, each ruled by a Persian satrap closely bound to the imperial house.

One of the Persian monarchs' means of maintaining control over the many subject peoples, so recently independent and so reluctantly Persianized, was to make the imperial person an awesome figure, elevated far above all other humans, only one step below the great god Ahura Mazda. It was probably in pursuit of this aim that Darius decided to build Persepolis. He scarcely needed another court, having sumptuous palaces at Susa, Babylon, Pasargadae, and Ecbatana. But Persepolis would be his own creation, set far apart on a height, like the king himself.

From the masses of clay tablets and the evidence of the stones themselves, archaeologists have been able to reconstruct in some detail the process of building. The first step, begun in about 520 B.C., was to install beneath the terrace a network of massive conduits to provide drainage. Because the openings in the conduits are fitted precisely to structures built at a later time, the excavators concluded that Darius planned the entire complex in advance of construction, although much of it was not completed in his lifetime. In the nearby mountains workmen quarried blocks of stone by drilling holes and inserting wooden wedges, then soaking the wedges with water until they swelled and split the rock. The stone

blocks were shaped with chisels into tapering drums which were hauled up inclined planes and placed end on end, with the help of blocks and tackle, to form columns. The slender columns of the apadana, including their fluted bases and elaborately carved capitals, are sixty-five feet tall. The crossbeams and roof were made of wood, covered by straw mats and a layer of earth and gravel.

Though Persepolis stood far apart from the other great cities of the empire, it was linked to them by a network of fine, straight highways. Over them couriers riding in relays could cover the seventeen hundred miles from Sardis in Lydia to Susa in seven days. In a phrase that later found its way to the United States Postal Service, Herodotus wrote, "Not snow, nor rain, nor heat, nor gloom of night stays these couriers from the swift completion of their appointed rounds."

It was over one of these roads that Darius moved his court from Susa, the administrative capital of the empire, to Persepolis for a period of one month each spring, the time of the Persian New Year. From all the satrapies of the empire delegations then gathered to swear their loyalty to the monarch and present him with gifts. On an appointed day the golden throne was carried out of the apadana, probably onto the western portico.

From their camp on the plain below, the leaders of the delegations mounted the ceremonial stairs to the terrace. The sculptures on the walls of the staircase are thought to mirror the members of the procession: first among the gift-bearers come the nobles of the realm—Persians in their flowing gowns and crown-shaped headgear, Medes in their leather trousers and dome-shaped felt hats. Then come the delegates of the subject nations: Babylonians bringing lengths of fabric and leading a prize bull; an Elamite carrying a lion cub; Assyrians with animal skins and live rams; Ionians with bolts of cloth and vessels made of precious metals; Bactrians with a camel; Scythians and Armenians with fine horses; an African with elephant tusks; Indians carrying containers filled perhaps with pure gold dust.

*A Mede holds hand to mouth in homage.*

*Assyrians offer a sleek bull.*

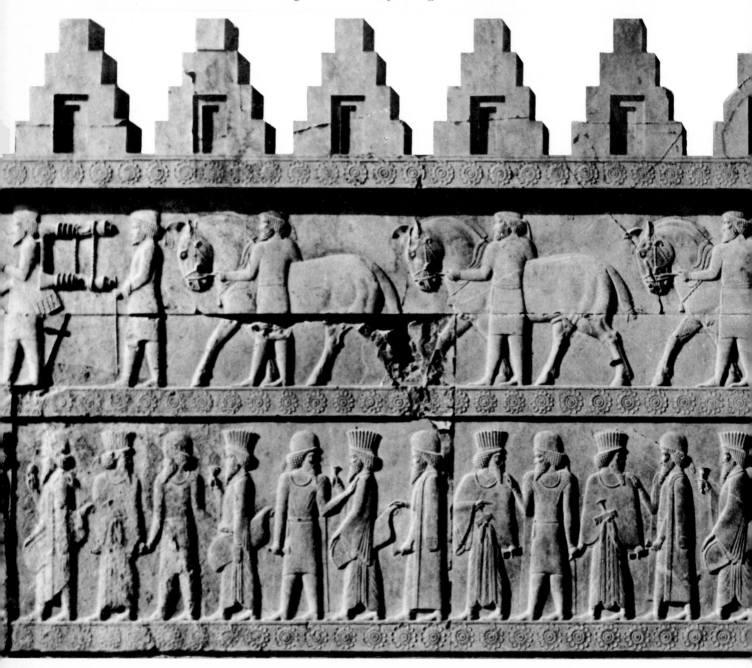

*Lydians carry vases, possibly of gold.*

*To mark the Persian New Year each spring, dignitaries from the more than fifty satrapies and client states that made up the empire converged on Persepolis, there to renew their oaths of fealty to the "one king of many, one lord of many . . . the great king, king of kings, king of the countries possessing all kinds of peoples, king of the great earth far and wide." The foreign delegations—and the lavish gifts they brought with them—are exhaustively catalogued on the apadana walls, left. Nearby are carved symbols of the king's omnipotence, including, below, the snorting horses that drew his chariots into battle and his Median and Persian soldiers, who had together conquered most of the ancient world.*

To hold the gold and silver and jewels that poured in from the subject lands, Darius erected the building called the treasury. Some of the other structures on the terraces were begun during Darius's reign, and all were completed by his son Xerxes. Thus the building of Persepolis was accomplished during the fifty-odd years in which the Persian Empire reached its zenith—and suffered the defeats that foreshadowed its doom.

Ever since Cyrus had established Persian control of the Greek cities on the coast of Asia Minor they had been in sporadic rebellion against the satrap of Sardis. In 490 B.C. Darius sent an army of twenty-five thousand men on six hundred ships to punish their mother cities in mainland Greece. At Marathon the Athenian army attacked and drove them back into the water, inflicting such damage that the fleet retreated to Persia.

Ten years later Xerxes arrived with a much larger invasion force—perhaps two hundred thousand troops— at the Hellespont, which separates Europe from Asia. A bridge of boats was constructed, only to be wrecked by a violent storm before the army could cross. In a rage Xerxes ordered the strait to be lashed with whips in punishment. After that the Hellespont offered no further resistance and, after crossing over a second bridge of boats, the Persians marched south into Greece. Despite the Spartans' heroic defense of the pass at Thermopylae, the Persians reached Athens and burned the buildings of the Acropolis. But then the Persian fleet was routed in the Bay of Salamis. In haste the Persians retreated to the Hellespont and crossed back into Asia, never to return.

Despite this repulse, for more than a century the Persian monarchs continued to rule their vast empire. At Persepolis the annual ceremonies were carried out with full pomp and panoply. But a concerted attack by Alexander of Macedon doomed the empire. Beginning in 334 B.C. Alexander marched through the satrapies of the Persian Empire, west to Egypt and then back to Babylon and Susa. On February 1 of the year 330 B.C. he arrived at Persepolis and found it, like the other centers, unde-

*On the staircase that leads to the palace of Xerxes
a snarling lion buries its fangs in the throat
of a rearing bull—perhaps a reference to the
triumph of good over evil. Below the struggling
beasts, servants bear more presents to the king.*

fended. While his soldiers sacked the buildings, he seized the imperial treasure, thirty-six hundred tons of silver and two hundred forty tons of gold, together with great quantities of jewels and precious objects.

On an evening a few weeks later Persepolis went up in flames. Some say that Alexander burned it as an act of deliberate policy, in retribution for the burning of the Acropolis by Xerxes. Some say that he was in his cups, banqueting in the apadana with his officers, when a courtesan named Thais egged him on to apply the torch. The flames roared through the wooden roofs, leaving only blackened walls and columns.

In the long centuries of its desolation the very remoteness of Persepolis offered a measure of protection to what was left. Gradually the very existence of the Achaemenid rulers faded from memory. Moslem geographers of the twelfth century labeled Persepolis "Takht-i-Jamshid," the Throne of Jamshid, after a mythical ruler of ancient Iran. Three hundred years later a Christian traveler, Josapha Barbaro, speculated that one of the statues represented King Solomon of the Bible, and discerned on the head of another statue the miter of the Christian pope.

It was during the nineteenth century that Persepolis worked its greatest magic on the minds of visitors from the West. By that time scholars had learned its history from Greek authors, but archaeologists had not yet stripped away the covering sands. Here and there a few statues and carvings brought vividly to light after more than two thousand years the glories of an ancient empire. At the head of the ceremonial staircase stood the Gateway of All Lands, still guarded by the massive figures of two winged bulls with human heads. Standing also, as it stands today, on a doorjamb of the palace was the carving of a crowned and bearded man, plunging his dagger into the vitals of a beast with a lion's head and a scorpion's tail. The beast is probably a representation of Ahriman, the god of evil, eternal enemy of Ahura Mazda, god of light. The man, remarkably untouched by time, is Darius, the great king.

# Shah Jahan's Red Fort

Shah Jahan did not come to the throne of Mogul India without a struggle. As Prince Khurram, he was the third son of the Mogul Jehangir and naturally feared that his eldest brother, Prince Khusrau, would be preferred for the succession. Both Khurram and Khusrau were commanders of armies, but Khurram got the upper hand and had his brother executed. When he succeeded to the throne as Shah Jahan in 1627, he immediately took the necessary precautions to make sure that what happened to Khusrau could never happen to him. He ordered the execution of all his remaining brothers, half-brothers, nephews, and every other male relative who might challenge his right to the throne.

Shah Jahan was, nevertheless, a man of the most exquisite sensibilities. To his court at Agra and later at Delhi he welcomed artists from all over India and foreign lands, rewarding them with gold and jewels. He spent many of his happiest hours working over designs for palaces, mosques, and public buildings. The Great Moguls, of whom Shah Jahan was the fifth, may have come by their refined tastes, as well as their bloodthirstiness, through natural inheritance. They claimed Timur the Lame, Tamerlane, the fearsome Mongol conqueror, as an ancestor. The most famous structure that Timur ever built was a great mound of his defeated enemies' skulls. But he and his heirs, the Timurid kings, made their Asian capital, Samarkand, one of the most resplendent centers, for a time, of Moslem culture.

The first of the Great Moguls, known as Baber (Tiger), began life as a prince of Fergana in west central Asia. At the age of eleven he succeeded his father and at fourteen led an army to the conquest of Samarkand. But while he was away from Fergana his throne was usurped by a half-brother, and the Uzbeks drove him out of Samarkand. Undaunted, Baber raised another army, led it across the twelve-thousand-foot passes of the Hindu Kush, and conquered Afghanistan. From the mountains he swept down through the Khyber Pass and in one day of furious battle (April 21, 1526) made himself master of northern India.

The Tiger of the north was not much pleased by his vast new kingdom. Here is what he wrote in his memoirs: "Hindustan is a country of few charms. Its people have no good looks; of social intercourse, paying and receiving visitors there is none; of genius and capacity none; of manners none; in handicraft and work there is no form or symmetry, method or quality; there are no good horses, no good dogs, no grapes, muskmelons or first-rate fruits, no ice or cold water; no good bread or cooked food in the bazaars, no hot baths, no colleges, no candles, torches or candlesticks . . . there are no running waters in their gardens or residences. These residences have no charm, air, regularity, or symmetry . . . peasants and people of low standing go about naked . . . the towns and country of Hindustan are greatly wanting in charm."

Baber's successors, however, adapted quite happily to the soft life of the Indian lowlands. To relieve the heat they built splendid formal gardens, with fountains and running streams, and enclosed these tiny Edens within walls of sumptuous palaces. They covered their weapons with gold leaf, and wore huge diamonds and rubies, and filled their harems with voluptuous girls. They rather liked to watch their enemies trampled to death by elephants, and passed judgment on criminals at the dinner table, ordering one to have his arms and legs cut off, another to be disemboweled, a third to be strangled. But they treated their Indian subjects, so long as they did nothing to offend the ruler, with tolerance, even advancing them as equals in the government. The third Mogul even married an Indian princess, as did the fourth, so that Shah Jahan was three-quarters Indian.

As a young prince Shah Jahan had married the beautiful daughter of his father's vizier, or prime minister. She was not his only wife (he had already married a Persian

*Shah Jahan slays a lion in the Mogul cameo above and, in a more contemplative moment at right, rests on one of the seven jeweled thrones from which he ruled India.*

*The emperor's private apartments, the Khas Mahal, stood inside Agra's Red Fort.*

princess for reasons of state), and he never lacked a harem, but Mumtaz Mahal ("Chosen One of the Palace") was his true love. Shah Jahan had hardly come to the throne when his lovely queen fell ill and died. The chronicles of the court tell that the ruler locked himself in his rooms, taking neither food nor drink, that for eight days only the sound of moaning was heard, and that during that time his hair turned white. When he came out it was to lay plans for the Taj Mahal.

When the Taj Mahal was begun, Shah Jahan's residence was the sandstone Red Fort at Agra, constructed by his grandfather, Akbar. The Moguls ruled from twin capitals, Agra and Delhi, both located on the banks of the Jumna River and joined by a one-hundred-twenty-mile-long avenue of stately trees. After redoing much of the palace at Agra in marble, Shah Jahan decided to build an even finer residence at Delhi. Like the one at Agra, the Red Fort at Delhi takes its name from the ruddy sandstone of its outer wall, but many of the buildings within the enclosure are built of pure white marble. Carved in the marble are the words: "If there is a paradise on earth, this is it, this is it, this is it."

The Red Fort covers an area roughly three thousand by eighteen hundred feet. It is a collection of buildings, courts, and gardens, all enclosed within the wall. It served not only as the residence of the king but also as the administrative seat of Mogul India, a military barracks, and a court of justice. Visitors to the palace entered through the Lahore Gate and proceeded through a stately arcade to the central court. Nobles might come this far on their horses or their elephants but had then to dismount and approach the Hall of Public Audience on foot.

In the architecture of the Mogul palaces one can see the legacy of their nomadic ancestry. The buildings are not planted on the earth with solid walls, like the palaces and fortresses of Europe. The roofs rest on pillars, as tents were held up by poles. The sides are often left open to the breeze, with movable screens to keep out the sun or rain. Until fairly late in Mogul times the seat of government

was called the *urdu*, which was the Turkish word for horde and thus by extension the place where the horde settled down, for a night or a century. Not until after the Moguls began building in marble did they use the word *mahal*, or palace.

But if these marble palaces echo the feeling of nomadic tents, their actual design and ornamentation derive from Persia. It was there that the fierce nomads lived long enough to absorb an older and higher civilization on their way to India. The bulbous domes of the mosques and palaces, the minarets, the delicate marble filigree, the glazed tiles and bright mosaic floors reflect their Persian origin. They bear little relation to the native stone palaces and temples of old India.

While the public parts of the Red Fort were sufficiently splendid to dazzle any visitor, the peak of refinement and delicacy was reached in the private areas. Extending the length of the palace on the river side were the emperor's own quarters, his private reception rooms, and the harem, all artfully arranged around courtyards and gardens. Through this section of the fort ran a canal, with water diverted from the upper Jumna River and called the Canal of Paradise. It provided the means for Mogul designers to exercise their unmatched genius for combining water with marble. Among the many fountains, the jewel is perhaps the one in the Rang Mahal, or Painted Palace. It consists of a shallow marble basin seven yards square, carved in the shape of a lotus flower with such skill that, when seen through the running water, the petals seem to be waving gently. In the center a tiny stream of perfumed water rises from the blossom of a single silver lotus on a slender stem.

Shah Jahan's day in the Red Fort began an hour or so before sunrise. By the light of candles he donned his robes and jewels and walked through the "moonlight garden" of the harem to his private mosque, where he knelt toward Mecca and spent some two hours in prayer. Then, as the sun rose, he stepped out onto a marble balcony beneath which a crowd was always gathered for

*Scrub jungle has grown up at the base of Agra's Red Fort walls, where battling elephants once delighted the emperor.*

The Red Fort at Delhi, left, was still the home
of a Mogul figurehead when an Indian artist
painted the nostalgic view below in 1820. It
recalls the empire's gaudy height. Ordinary
citizens entered through the distant gate and
ventured only as far as the Hall of Public
Audience (its roof, edged with brightly colored
tenting, is at the center). Here they presented
their grievances to the emperor and timorously
withdrew. They had reason to be fearful: Mogul
justice was swift and stern. Those found guilty
of capital crimes were crushed by elephants;
adulterers were strangled. The emperor's apartments
were in the foreground, cooled by the river
breezes that whispered through the pierced marble
windows. The emperor himself is seen entering
the Hall of Private Audience at right foreground,
his royal head shaded by a servant's fan.

a glimpse of the imperial person. Sometimes he would also visit the Jasmine Tower to review the palace elephants and judge any newly captured beasts for their looks and fighting qualities. An elephant fight was the greatest spectacle of the Mogul court. At the emperor's pleasure, two of the great beasts, decked in ornaments and bells and ridden by their keepers, were led out onto the fighting ground. Rearing and trumpeting, they fought until one succeeded in downing the other, whereupon they were separated by flaming pinwheels. The riders were injured more often than the elephants.

When the entertainment was over, the emperor proceeded in state to the Hall of Public Audience. The great reception hall stood in the courtyard and was open on three sides. To enhance the imperial majesty and at the same time offer protection against any would-be assassins, the throne was recessed in an alcove and raised on a platform against the wall on the fourth side. Ranged about the alcove were princes of the imperial family, the prime minister, and groups of high officials and courtiers standing in strict order of rank. To the sound of drums and trumpets Shah Jahan took his seat on the throne.

Shah Jahan had seven thrones, six of them for everyday use. The seventh, used for important occasions, was the Peacock Throne, perhaps the most magnificent ruler's seat that ever existed. It was not in the shape of a chair, like a standard Western throne, but was a raised platform on which the emperor sat cross-legged beneath a canopy. The throne was covered with gold and studded thickly with diamonds, rubies, emeralds, and pearls, all worked into the most intricate designs. A court poet recorded that "the world had become so short of gold on account of it that the purse of the earth was empty of treasure."

At the morning session on the throne, the emperor received and sent dispatches to officials of the empire, issued orders, authorized the expenditure of public funds, made appointments, and dictated letters. Not all the messages that reached his ear bore upon the fate of the empire; the court records show that Shah Jahan was kept

informed of such matters as bleeding and purgatives administered to high nobles, as well as dreams they thought significant. On Wednesdays the emperor heard complaints and decided criminal cases. Theoretically, any subject could lay his case directly before the ruler, and Shah Jahan is on record as wondering why more did not avail themselves of the privilege. Possibly they lost the habit during his father's time when, as recorded by an English visitor, "right before the King standeth one of his sheriffes, together with his master hangman, who is accompanied with forty hangmen wearing on their heades a certaine qyuilted cap, different from all others, with an hatchet on their shoulders; and others with all sorts of whips being there, readie to do what the king commandeth." In Shah Jahan's time, as in Jehangir's, justice was often administered on the spot.

After holding public court, the emperor moved to the Hall of Private Audience. There, with his chief ministers, he set the policies of the state, received foreign ambassadors, and planned military campaigns. It was also in this hall, the most beautiful of the public rooms, with its intricately carved marble columns, that new paintings were exhibited to the ruler and new building plans presented for his approval. By then it was time for the chief meal of the day, which the emperor took in the harem with his family and his favorite women. No strangers were ever invited to this private banquet, and accounts are rare. But a Spanish friar, Father Manrique, claimed to have observed a similar banquet in Lahore when Shah Jahan was entertained in 1641 by his father-in-law, Asaf Khan.

Father Manrique, according to his own story, was smuggled into a gallery above the banquet hall by one of the harem eunuchs. The food was brought by eunuchs in golden vessels and served to the emperor by two beautiful girls, who knelt on either side of him. So numerous were the dishes and so elaborate the ceremonies of dining that the meal lasted four hours. Entertainment was provided by twelve dancing girls, whose "lascivious and suggestive dress, immodest behavior and posturing" the good friar chose to "pass over in silence . . . as matter unfit for Christian ears." The emperor, however, showed more interest in three bowls of diamonds, rubies, and other gems that came with the dessert.

After his midday meal and a brief siesta the emperor held a sort of household court in the harem. It should be borne in mind that the harem was not the glorified massage parlor of Western imagination. It was the residence of his wives, his ex-wives, his female relatives, and his young children, as well as his current favorites. Among the ex-wives were daughters and nieces of other princes, whom he had married for dynastic reasons and presently divorced in order to stay within the Moslem quota of four wives at one time. In addition, the harem was home to various aging ladies who had been part of his father's harem. In such a closed community of females, who rarely left the palace and met no men except the eunuchs who served them, there were constant demands and disputes that only the emperor could settle. When the business of the harem had been attended to, the emperor went to prayers again and then held a final session with his ministers to clean up official business. He had put in much more than an eight-hour working day when he retired to eat a light evening meal and listen to music and to readings from the memoirs of the family founder, Baber. And so to bed by ten o'clock.

This routine was interrupted when the emperor went forth on his favorite elephant to visit his provinces or make war or hunt the tiger. Five days of festivity marked the emperor's birthday. At that time the courtyards were covered with awnings of red velvet embroidered with gold and supported by poles sheathed in gold and silver. On the great day the emperor was seated on one side of a scale while the other side was piled with gold and jewels to balance his weight. This treasure was then distributed to charity, but the imperial hoard was more than replenished by gifts from the nobles and provincial governors.

Toward the end of his reign, as he came to contem-

*Mogul court pageantry was played out against settings rarely surpassed for opulence anywhere on earth. At the far left, Shah Jahan's grandfather, Akbar the Great, and Akbar's son, Jahangir, sit blissfully surrounded by a few of the emperor's eight hundred concubines. At near left, Shah Jahan himself, hung with gems and ropes of giant pearls, plays host to an embassy from Persia. Long-abandoned Mogul monuments still retain their grandeur: below is the Hall of Public Audience in the Red Fort at Delhi.*

The marble apartments Shah Jahan had built for himself in the Red Fort at Agra became his prison for the last eight years of his life. The helpless captive of his son, Aurangzeb, he spent his days being ministered to by the women of his harem (who had conveniently been imprisoned with him) and gazing wistfully at his beloved Taj Mahal, seen here glimmering from across the Jumna.

plate his own mortality, Shah Jahan conceived a plan to build a black marble tomb for himself to match the white one he had built for his wife. It would stand across the river Jumna from the Taj Mahal and would be connected to its mate by a bridge of solid silver. But this romantic dream was frustrated by the rebellion of his sons. Shah Jahan had made the mistake of giving them command of armies and now, excited by a false rumor that the emperor was dying, they set out to contest the throne. When Aurangzeb, the third son, emerged victorious, he confined his father to the palace at Agra (the first Red Fort) and proclaimed himself emperor. Then, following the pattern his father had set, he killed off his three brothers and all other male relatives who might threaten his rule. Shah Jahan remained a prisoner until his death eight years later in 1666. He slept where he could look out at the Taj Mahal, and he kept a jealous interest in the Red Fort at Delhi. When he learned that Aurangzeb had built a fortified tower before the main gate he felt as if his son had desecrated the palace.

This was the least of the indignities visited upon the Red Fort in subsequent years. In 1739 the Persian conqueror Nadir Shah sacked Delhi and carried off the Peacock Throne, which was subsequently broken up. (A smaller version, which may contain some of the original stones, now serves the present shah of Iran.) During the troubles that came with the collapse of the Mogul power and the establishment of British rule in India, the gardens were left to run wild and the floors were piled with debris, and some of the marble slabs were shipped off for sale in London. After the Sepoy Rebellion in 1857 the British occupied the Red Fort, building military barracks in the gardens and walling up the Hall of Public Audience as an arsenal. Toward the end of the nineteenth century an enlightened viceroy, Lord Curzon, made an effort to refurbish the palace. Even today, without the sparkle of jewels or the tinkle of running fountains, it retains its power to evoke the splendors of the Mogul Empire.

*Inlaid precious stones decorate the glorious domes of the Taj Mahal.*

*Shah Jahan and his bride lie reunited in the tomb's dark, dazzling heart.*

# TOMB FOR A BELOVED QUEEN

When it came to family matters, Shah Jahan was not a conventionally sentimental man: he bought his throne with blood, most of it shed by his male relatives. But he seems genuinely to have loved his favorite wife, Mumtaz Mahal, and only months after her death in 1631 thousands of workmen began quarrying white marble for her great tomb. No one knows who designed it. Historians have variously credited an Italian goldsmith and a Turkish architect, but it is now thought more likely that the bereaved emperor himself— and the artisans who did his bidding— were responsible. The building is almost purely Persian in its design and in its emphasis on perfect symmetry: only the stylized lotus petals that cap its domes are a concession to its Indian setting. It took an army of twenty thousand workers twenty-one years to finish the complex. Shah Jahan was deposed in 1658, too soon for him to have begun his own mausoleum: a black marble twin of the Taj that was to have been built across the river, linked to it by a bridge of silver.

*An identical marble minaret graces each corner of the Taj Mahal.*

*The modern furnishings of this room in the newly renamed Lake Palace Hotel are a Western decorator's dream of what might once have graced a prince's bedchamber at Udaipur. The real princes favored Victorian styles, the more ornate and overstuffed the better.*

# A PALACE IN A LAKE

*The Maharana of Udaipur, stripped of power, at his former palace*

For seven centuries the heart of Hindu resistance to the Moguls lay among the stony hills and sandy deserts of what is now the north Indian state of Rajasthan. Here lived the Rajputs, a martial people ruled by fierce and quarrelsome princes who, when they were not warring upon one another, hurled their mounted legions and armored war elephants into battle with the Moslem interlopers again and again. The rulers of Mewar were almost always in the forefront of the fighting: they believed that they were directly descended from the god-king Rama, and it was their proud boast that they alone among the Rajput royal houses had never given a princess in marriage to the Moguls and had never bowed before the Mogul throne. The Mewar rulers were also tireless builders. Their white-walled capital of Udaipur, with its palaces and gateways and manmade network of blue lakes is one of the handsomest cities in India. Perhaps the best known of all the Udaipur palaces is the Jag Nivas, built by Maharana Jagat Singh in 1740 on an island in the center of the largest lake. Each year when the summer heat descended on the city, the prince and his court boarded a royal barge and glided out to this sprawling, marble-capped complex of open pavilions and hidden gardens to keep cool. Members of the once-invincible royal family of Udaipur are now ordinary citizens of democratic India, and to make ends meet they have transformed their island palace into a glossy, fifty-five-room hotel. The stillness of the ancient lake is now broken daily by the clatter of a motor launch, hauling visitors to the halls where the descendants of India's tenacious defenders once lived.

*The Jag Nivas, now a hotel, mirrored in the waters of Pichola Lake*

*The first ten sultans of the Nasrid dynasty are
portrayed on the ceiling of the Hall of Ambassadors.*

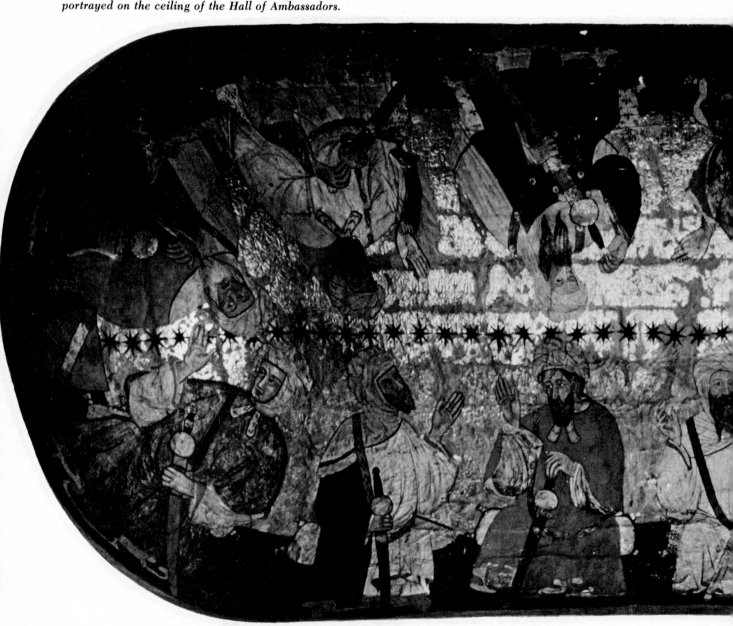

# Ibn al-Ahmar's Alhambra

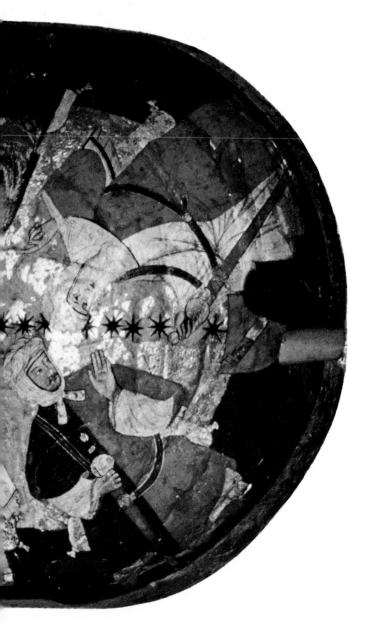

The stark, red-brown walls of the Alhambra, rising above the Spanish city of Granada, offer little hint of what lies within. This is partly because it was built as a fortress by sultans who feared that it would one day be attacked by their Christian neighbors, and hoped that future sultans would have the resolution to defend it. But also it embodies the oldest tradition of Arabic architecture, which hides interior delights behind the barest of mud-brick facades. The walls of the Alhambra enclose a fairyland of gardens and fountains and gorgeously decorated chambers which, in the time of its glory, was not surpassed on earth. An old legend tells that Allah finally took it away from the Moors because they had dared to make it too like Paradise.

When the Alhambra was built in the thirteenth century, the old conquering drive of Islam had long since been spent. Six centuries had passed since the first wave of fanatical Arabs, reinforced by Berber converts from North Africa, had swept up on the shores of the Spanish peninsula. The Moors, as Europe called them, had found a Spain torn and weakened by rival factions in the Visigothic kingdom. Within three years they had made themselves masters of the whole peninsula, save only the rugged mountainous region of the northwest.

The Moorish drive did not stop at the Pyrenees but swept on into France. It was finally halted in 732 at Tours by Charles Martel, the grandfather of Charlemagne, in a battle that Western historians mark as one of the great turning points of history, ranking with the Greek defeat of the Persians at Marathon in 490 B.C. and the repulse of the Turks at the gates of Vienna in A.D. 1683. In Moslem history it does not loom so great. Middle Eastern chroniclers treat it as the last skirmish in a border campaign that failed because of dissension among Moorish factions back in Spain. In any case, the Moors retreated behind the Pyrenees, where they ruled a dominion that lasted longer than the ancient Roman Empire, longer than the period of time that has now elapsed since the discovery of the New World.

*Fountains and pools and cool, lush gardens like those that grace the Alhambra, right, and the nearby Generalife—the summer villa of the Nasrid kings—were greatly prized by Islamic builders in Spain and elsewhere.*

Though the Moorish conquest had been spurred by religious fervor, the Moors showed tolerance toward both Christians and Jews. At a time when the light of learning burned low in the rest of Europe, they established in Spain a culture in which the arts and sciences flourished. From all over the continent scholars came to learn from the mathematicians and medical scientists and natural philosophers of Moorish Spain.

While the Moors ruled almost all of the Iberian peninsula, they were never quite at home on the high, bare central plateau. Their heartland was the soft southern region called Andalusia, where they built their great cities of Seville and Córdoba and Granada. To the sons of the desert this fertile land, with its flowing streams and luxuriant fields and orchards, was one vast oasis. Their villas were scattered, in the words of one Arab writer, "like Oriental pearls in an emerald setting."

In such a clime the martial spirit flagged. From time to time it was revived by new waves of desert warriors from North Africa, but only to subside again under a different dynasty. In the eleventh century the caliphate was broken up into small competing states, one of which was Granada. To the Christians, some of whom had clung to virtual independence in the far northwestern corner of the peninsula, the decline of Moorish militancy spelled opportunity. The Reconquest took more than four hundred years, but by the thirteenth century the Christians had taken the greater part of the peninsula and were moving against the divided sultanates of Andalusia. The sultan of Granada was ibn-al-Ahmar, the first of the Nasrid dynasty, a ruler much beloved by his people but no reckless warrior. Assessing the strength of the Christian forces, he went to Ferdinand III of Castile and offered, in return for peace, to become the vassal of the Christian king. The offer was accepted, and Granada won a two-hundred-year respite from complete subjugation.

It was at this unheroic moment in Moorish history that ibn-al-Ahmar began work on the walls of the Alhambra. He chose for its site a natural acropolis, a last rocky spur of the Sierra Nevada thrusting into the plain at Granada. Its northern wall plunged straight down to the bank of the Darro River. Its southern battlements faced the bare slopes up which an attack would have to come. (The tall English elms which now grace those slopes were planted centuries later by the Duke of Wellington when he used the Alhambra as his headquarters during the Napoleonic Wars.) Water was brought to the citadel by an aqueduct and stored, against any future siege, in cisterns cut from the rock. As matters turned out, the Alhambra was never besieged, and served as a refuge for succeeding sultans only in minor troubles with dissident Moorish factions.

The Alhambra is not laid out according to a carefully ordered plan, as European castles and palaces customarily are. The prevailing unit of architecture in the Arab world is the courtyard with surrounding arcades and apartments, often planned and erected piecemeal. The result is likely to be an irregular complex of these units placed in whatever relationship to each other was dictated by their several purposes. At the western end of the promontory, where the walls were steepest, stood the Alcazaba, which would have been the last-ditch stronghold in case of war and served as a military headquarters and barracks in time of peace. To the west, but still within the walls, was a town filled with the houses and shops of the people who served the royal court and government. This town has long since been cleared away, leaving hardly a trace, but another, incongruous architectural element has been added on the hilltop. In the sixteenth century Charles V built within the walls a stone palace of European Renaissance design, intruding on the courtyards and blocking the view of the sultan's palace.

The sultan's palace itself is divided into three parts. One side was devoted to government offices and courts of justice. It was the practice of the sultans to hold court twice a week to hear the pleas of their people, as their desert forebears had listened to tribesmen before their tents. In the second section of the palace official visitors were conducted through the Court of Myrtles, with its

long pool and colonnades, to the Hall of Ambassadors, the grandest of the palace rooms. Having little military power, the sultans expended great effort on diplomacy and the reception of powerful visitors.

Beyond the official rooms were the private quarters of the sultan and the royal family. The harem, with its gardens and pools and staff of eunuchs, was, at least in outsiders' imaginations, the heart of the palace. It was the place where, Chateaubriand wrote, the sultans "tasted all the pleasures and forgot all the duties of life."

A vizier of the fourteenth century, ibn-al-Khatib, left a vivid description of the ladies of the court. They were, he wrote, "lovely, being moderately plump with firm, voluptuous curves and long sleek hair. Their mouths smell good and they are given to wearing fresh-scented perfumes. They are lively, move with grace, and speak with elegance, charm, and wit. Tall women are, however, a rarity. In our day they have reached the extreme limits of what can be achieved in the arts of the toilette and coiffure, harmonizing these with different-colored layers of fabric, vying with one another in lavish displays of embroidered cloth-of-gold and brocade and other alluring finery, and in a word, carrying luxury to the point of lunacy. . . ."

The center of the private section of the palace was the Court of the Lions. With the folk memory of the desert possibly in their minds, the Moors treated water as the pearl of architectural design. A courtyard with its shimmering pool was a manmade oasis, surrounded by slender columns that might almost be the trunks of palm trees. Water is everywhere, not commonly rising in tall jets or splashing in grand fountains like those of most European countries but flowing in little rivulets and dripping over stones or held in pools, as if every drop were treasured.

The glory of Moorish building lies not in the structures themselves but in the fine details of decoration. Floors and the lower parts of walls, which had to withstand wear, were covered with delicate, colorful mosaics. In keeping with the Moslem taboo against representation of

*Ornately filigreed walls like this one were impressive on formal state occasions, while the Court of the Lions, right, provided privacy. There, in the heart of the harem, the sultan and his concubines could meet with only the unconvincing beasts in the middle as witnesses.*

the human figure, there were hardly any paintings of people (except on the ceiling of the Hall of Ambassadors, which was painted in the last period of the sultanate, probably by artists imported from Christian Spain). Even animals were seldom depicted, and then crudely, as in the sculptures of the lions which, for all their collective beauty, look individually rather like spaniels. In place of representational paintings, the Moors used intricate geometrical designs and floral motifs, and they developed calligraphy into a high art. Walls are covered with inscriptions endlessly worshipping Allah, praising the sultans, and proclaiming the delights of nature.

Most wondrous of all are the vaulted ceilings made of little cells sculpted in stucco and forming a giant honeycomb. No two cells in these intricate ceilings are exactly the same. To Théophile Gautier, who lived in the palace for several months in 1842, they looked like "a cluster of soap bubbles which children blow with a straw."

The Moorish state of Granada owed its charmed existence for almost two hundred years not so much to its own efforts as to the disarray of the independent Christian kingdoms that vied with each other in the rest of the Spanish peninsula. But in the fifteenth century King Ferdinand II of Aragon and Queen Isabella of Castile, having united their kingdoms by marriage, set out to unify all of Spain. In 1491 they arrived with their army outside Granada with plans to besiege the Alhambra.

The sultan, twenty-first in the line of Nasrid rulers, was a young man known to the West as Boabdil. As a boy he had been imprisoned by his father on suspicion of disloyalty and might have been killed if his redoubtable mother had not lowered him by a rope made of her own and her ladies' sashes from a tower of the palace. Boabdil was made of weaker stuff. When he looked out upon the Christian encampment, he decided that the Moorish cause was lost and sent a message of surrender. We have an eyewitness report by a visitor who had come to see Ferdinand and Isabella in their camp on another matter. Christopher Columbus wrote: "On the 2nd of January

High above Granada, the Alhambra's hilltop is crowded with history. The crenelated towers and ramparts at the right are all that remains of the Alcazaba, a ninth-century fortress built on the site of a Roman temple. The Alhambra itself, foreground, with its formal gardens and tile-roofed towers, was once even larger. But Charles V— who loathed what he called "the ugly abomination of the Moors— tore down some of it in the sixteenth century to make way for the grandiose unfinished Renaissance palace in the background.

[1492] I saw the royal banners of Your Highnesses planted by force of arms on the towers of the Alhambra . . . I saw the Moorish king issue from the gates of the city and kiss the royal hands of Your Highnesses."

It was a great day for Columbus because Isabella, in the flush of final victory over the Moors, decided to finance Columbus's voyage of exploration.

For Boabdil, it was the ignominious end of eight hundred years of Moorish rule. As the sultan rode off to exile in Africa he stopped for a moment on a rise of land for his last tearful look at the lovely place he had lost. "You do well," said his unforgiving mother, "to weep like a woman for what you could not defend like a man."

The terms of surrender were generous, promising those Moors who chose to remain in Spain the rights to their lives, property, and religion. But tolerance was foreign to the nature of the Spanish rulers and the Spanish church. Even before the fall of Granada, Ferdinand and Isabella had driven the Jews from their realm. Soon they were hounding the Moors in similar fashion, first requiring them to turn Christian and then expelling them anyway. The city of Granada, once a citadel of learning and culture, lapsed into provincialism. For a while the Spanish sovereigns used the Alhambra as a summer palace; Philip V redid some rooms, put up Catholic shrines, and spent his honeymoon there. But it fell into disrepair and soon became the haunt of beggars, thieves, and gypsies.

It was Washington Irving, more than anyone else, who saved the Alhambra from total decay. On a horseback trip through Spain he arrived at Granada on a spring day in 1829 and took up residence in the run-down Moorish palace. His felicitous account of his three-month stay not only entranced his American and European readers but opened the eyes of Spanish authorities to the historic treasure they had neglected. Here is a sample passage:

"The moon . . . has gradually gained upon the nights, and now rolls in full splendour above the towers, pouring a flood of tempered light into every court and hall. The garden beneath my window is gently lighted up; the orange and citron trees are tipped with silver; the fountain sparkles in the moonbeams, and even the blush of the rose is faintly visible.

"I have sat for hours at my window inhaling the sweetness of the garden, and musing on the chequered features of those whose history is dimly shadowed out in the elegant memorials around. Sometimes I have issued forth at midnight when everything was quiet, and have wandered over the whole building. Who can do justice to a moonlight night in such a climate, and in such a place! . . . Every rent and chasm of time, every mouldering tint and weather stain disappears; the marble resumes its original whiteness; the long colonnades brighten in the moon beams; the halls are illuminated with a softened radiance, until the whole edifice reminds one of the enchanted palace of an Arabian tale."

Though the Moors were long gone by Irving's time, their blood flowed in the veins of many Andalusians. Their buildings still dominated the landscape; their music could still be heard in the streets; their words had entered the language. In some legends of Andalusia they had never left. Irving set down the tale of an old soldier who met up on the road with a horseman wearing ancient Moorish garb. At the horseman's invitation the old soldier mounted behind him on his big horse and they set out at a gallop. The horse seemed to fly through the night, his feet scarcely touching the ground, past Segovia, past Madrid, over hills and rivers until they came to the mouth of a cave in the mountains. They joined a throng of other horsemen and, passing through the rocky entrance, found themselves in a vast cavern. There on a golden throne sat a Moorish king, surrounded by a host of mounted warriors. It was the army of Boabdil, held under a powerful spell until the day when Allah should release them to regain their kingdom.

The tale was old when Irving told it. But, looking out from the walls of the Alhambra to the silvery peaks of the Sierra Nevada, it is easy to believe that the Moorish army still await the day of their return to Granada.

# MOVABLE DREAM HOUSES

Hi Esmaro *slices through a tranquil sea.*

*Even in transit, rich and powerful people have surrounded themselves with elegant, eye-catching examples of custom-made comfort. The sleek two-hundred-and-sixty-seven-foot vessel above, for instance, was built in 1929 to the careful specifications of manufacturer Hiram E. Manville, father of the much-married Tommy. As the pictures in this portfolio indicate, with money and imagination a person can travel on land, by sea, or in the air without surrendering the illusion that one is amid the familiar luxury of home.*

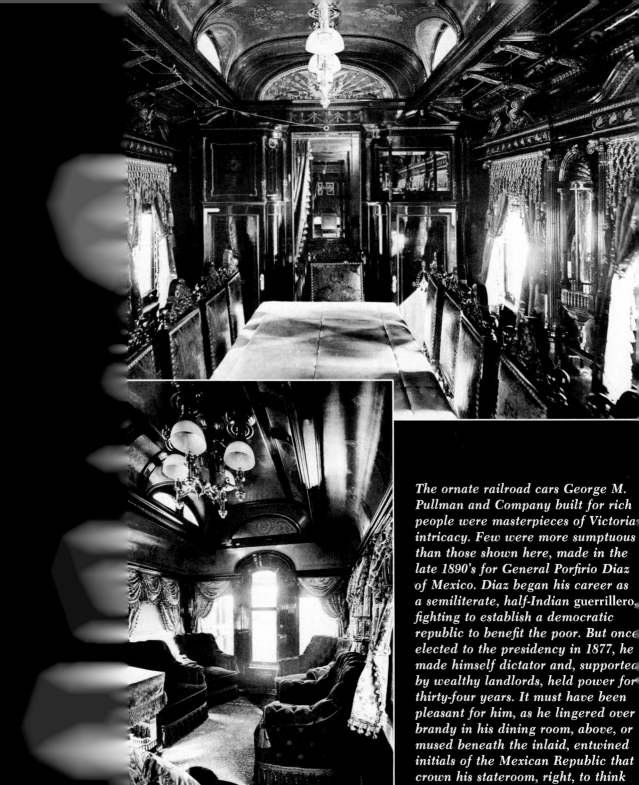

The ornate railroad cars George M.
Pullman and Company built for rich
people were masterpieces of Victorian
intricacy. Few were more sumptuous
than those shown here, made in the
late 1890's for General Porfirio Diaz
of Mexico. Diaz began his career as
a semiliterate, half-Indian guerrillero,
fighting to establish a democratic
republic to benefit the poor. But once
elected to the presidency in 1877, he
made himself dictator and, supported
by wealthy landlords, held power for
thirty-four years. It must have been
pleasant for him, as he lingered over
brandy in his dining room, above, or
mused beneath the inlaid, entwined
initials of the Mexican Republic that
crown his stateroom, right, to think
back over just how far he had come.

The elaborate furnishings in the main salon, seen below, and the card room and master stateroom, below right, aboard the steam yacht Cambriona overflow with furniture expensively upholstered in chintz and Edwardian plush. Launched in 1930, the two-hundred-thirty-four-foot Cambriona was the pride of Walter O. Briggs, who began work as a laborer and went on to found a company that manufactured automobile bodies and to buy the Detroit Tigers.

Private jets may be the last word in mobile ostentation. An Arabian businessman paid ten million dollars to buy and redecorate the Boeing 727 shown here, with its sprawling lounge, gold-plated bathroom faucets, and double bed. Of course, even airborne palaces need repairs from time to time, but the determinedly anonymous owner of this one need not worry: he has four other jets in his hangar.

# 7 PRINCELY AMERICANS

The men and women who appear in this chapter had little in common—except that, as builders, they shared the instincts of aristocrats. Thomas Jefferson's Monticello was the home of a planter, a scholar, and a self-taught architect. The Breakers and Marble House and Biltmore proclaim the rise of the Vanderbilts as the social leaders of a new industrial plutocracy in the Gilded Age. William Randolph Hearst's San Simeon was built by a man who lived more like a prince than perhaps any prince of his time.

*A tycoon's whim re-created this bit of baroque Spain on a dusty hilltop in southern California. Here is the entrance to the Casa Grande, publisher William Randolph Hearst's "house" at San Simeon.*

# Thomas Jefferson's Monticello

The marquis de Chastellux, on a visit to Monticello in 1782, was struck by the harmony between Thomas Jefferson and the site he had chosen for his home. "It seemed," the marquis wrote, "as if from his youth he had placed his mind, as he had done his house, on an elevated situation, from which he might contemplate the Universe."

It was unusual in those times for a Virginia planter to build his home on a hill. The great houses commonly stood on low ground, close to the river landings from which the tobacco was shipped. But Jefferson, since his college days, had known where he wanted to live. It was a hill on his father's property, no more than half an hour's horseback ride from his birthplace, the family plantation of Shadwell in Albemarle County. Often at dusk he would cross the little Rivanna River by canoe and climb to a great oak on the hill where, if he had had luck with his gun, he might roast a partridge for supper.

Jefferson was twenty-four in 1767 when he began work on the building project that would occupy many of his happiest hours for the rest of his life. The first thing was to clear the mountaintop, so that the house might command views in every direction. This was done, and a kiln was built to make bricks from the local clay. In the self-sufficient manner of the plantations, bricks, boards, plaster, and even nails would be made on the premises.

The design was Jefferson's own. Although he had been managing the family lands since his father died, and was carrying on a law practice besides, he had found time to give himself an education in architecture. His greatest inspiration came from the four volumes of Andrea Palladio, the Italian Renaissance architect, who had himself gone back to ancient Roman temples and villas for his models. But in Jefferson's hands the monumental Palladian style was adapted to the gentle Virginia countryside and to his own ideas of what made for agreeable living.

By January of 1771, when he married a young widow named Martha Wayles Skelton, only one room at Monticello had been finished. It was a small, square, brick

*This 1789 bust of Jefferson was made by Jean Antoine Houdon.*

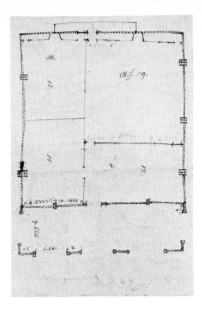

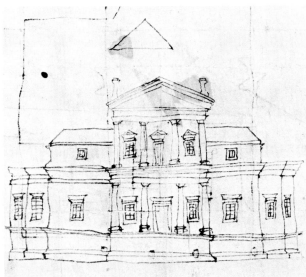

pavilion, which stands by itself at a distance of one hundred feet from the main house and which was serving Jefferson at that time as study, bedroom, and dining room, all in one. After their wedding at The Forest, the Wayles plantation, Tom and Martha set out in a snow-storm to drive to Monticello, but as the snow piled up they had to leave their carriage and mount the horses to go on. By the time they arrived, late at night, the fires were out, the slaves abed. Rather than waken them, the bridal couple had a bottle of wine and spent a cold night in what is now romantically called Honeymoon Cottage.

The Monticello that Jefferson planned and built in the following four or five years was substantially different from the building that stands today. The house was only half the size but had two full stories, with Grecian columns on the façade of both floors. At first Jefferson planned two low wings, stretching out to the north and south, to house the kitchen, dairy, ice house, wine cellar, and other service areas. Then he had the inspiration of sinking these wings below the level of the house, so that they opened on the shoulder of the hill but did not block the view from the main house. These wings were covered by verandahs that led to the Honeymoon Cottage at the south and a matching pavilion at the north. It was an ingenious plan that kept the sounds and odors of the service quarters away from the main house but provided easy access through an underground arcade.

In planning his house as a thing of beauty as well as utility, Jefferson was unusual in his time. He held a low opinion of the buildings he had seen in Virginia: "The genius of architecture seems to have shed its maledictions over this land. Buildings are often erected, by individuals, of considerable expense. To give these symmetry and taste would not increase their cost. It would only change the arrangement of the materials, the form and combination of the members. This would often cost less than the burthen of barbarous ornaments with which these buildings are sometimes charged. But the first principles of the art are unknown, and there exists

*Monticello occupied Jefferson's mind for almost sixty years. The first home, shown above in a plan and elevation drawn in 1767, was reconstructed along grander, more classic lines (below) between 1796 and 1806. Changes were still being made twenty years later.*

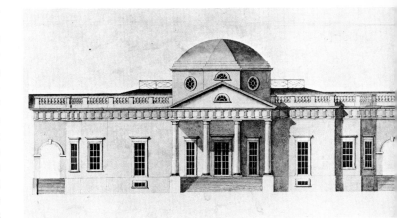

scarcely a model among us sufficiently chaste to give an idea of them."

This may seem a harsh judgment on some of the small, handsome colonial buildings then standing in Virginia as well as the northern colonies, but it was shared by other educated men of the Enlightenment, in Europe as well as America. The marquis of Chastellux was so carried away by Monticello that he wrote: "It may be said that Mr. Jefferson is the first American who has consulted the Fine Arts to know how he should shelter himself from the weather."

Monticello was a holding of some five thousand acres, with fields planted mostly to wheat and tobacco and worked by upward of two hundred slaves, some inherited from Jefferson's father and more from his father-in-law, John Wayles. It is remarkable that he could find time for managing his property, much less for architecture. For in those years most of his energies were taken up with the struggle for American independence.

During the final days of his term as wartime governor of Virginia he barely escaped being taken prisoner by the dashing British cavalry commander, Colonel Banastre Tarleton. On the morning of June 5, 1781, a courier arrived at Monticello to warn him that a troop was on its way to capture the author of the Declaration of Independence. Through his telescope Jefferson could see the dragoons milling about the square at Charlottesville, only a few miles away. After finishing breakfast and telling his slaves what to do, he mounted his horse and rode off to join his family at a neighboring plantation. The household silver was hidden in a hole under the portico, where Caesar, one of Jefferson's favorite slaves, crouched beside it for the next eighteen hours without food or water. In obedience to the orders he carried, the British captain did no more than search the house and then, after looking respectfully into Jefferson's study, locked the door and handed the key to another slave.

For a brief period after the war Jefferson was able to devote more time to the pursuits which established his reputation as a "universal man." As a botanist he collected and classified the plants of his native state. As a paleontologist he studied fossils and sponsored the excavation of a mastodon's bones. As an ethnologist he studied the lives and history of the Indians and carried out one of the first archaeological digs of an Indian burial mound. As an agriculturist he invented an improved version of the moldboard plow and adopted such advanced practices as crop rotation and contour plowing, both then new to America. He compiled many of his observations in his *Notes on the State of Virginia*, a work which contained much new scientific information and dispelled some fanciful ideas then prevalent in Europe. One of these, conceived and propounded by the great French naturalist Buffon, was that animal life in the New World, as measured by everything from moose's antlers to Indians' penises, was smaller than in Europe. Jefferson took delight in shipping Buffon the skin and skeleton of the biggest moose he could get hold of.

Jefferson believed, as he wrote later, that "nature intended me for the tranquil pursuits of science." But after his wife died in 1782 his friends found him so disconsolate that they urged him to return to public life, and in 1785 he accepted an appointment as minister to France. During the next five years he was entranced by much that he found there, and not least by the architecture. This was his reaction to the Maison Carrée, an ancient Roman temple preserved at Nîmes, as expressed in a letter to a cousin of Lafayette's:

"Here I am, Madam, gazing whole hours at the Maison Quarée like a lover at his mistress. . . . This is the second time I have been in love since I left Paris. The first was with a Diana at the Chateau de Laye-Epinaye in Beaujolais, a delicious morsel of sculpture. . . . This, you will say, was in rule, to fall in love with a female beauty, but with a house! It is out of all precedent. No, Madam, it is not without a precedent in my own history. . . . I was violently smitten with the Hôtel de Salm, and used to go to the Tuileries almost daily, to look at it. . . ."

No detail of life at Monticello was too small for Jefferson to worry over: "There is not a sprig of grass," he wrote, "that shoots uninteresting to me." His sketch at left shows just how he wished his damask curtains hung. He wanted his three-storied house to seem one-storied from the outside, and so the guestroom windows on the second floor (right) were cut low to seem like extensions of those below them. A pillared tunnel was carefully hidden beneath the south promenade, below, and through it slaves hurried hot food from the nearby kitchen.

When he returned to America in 1789, Jefferson's new architectural views found expression at Monticello. For one thing, he had developed a strong preference for single-story buildings, with long and graceful lines, in contrast to the massive shape of Palladian structures. Nothing would do but to tear down the upper part of Monticello and start over. During the next year or so the house resembled a brickyard, and the premises were so hazardous that Jefferson's daughter Martha fell through a floor into the cellar (without injury). The master was unperturbed: "Architecture is my delight, and putting up and pulling down one of my favorite amusements."

As seen today from the outside, Monticello appears to be a single-story building surmounted by a central dome. Actually there is a second floor of rooms surrounding the dome, and an attic above that, but these are concealed by the tall windows and balustrade. The upper rooms served as bedrooms for Jefferson's ever-present overnight guests. Just what he had in mind for the handsome circular room beneath the dome is a mystery; at his death it was being used as a storeroom. In line with his concept of a single-story house, Jefferson gave short shrift to staircases. Instead of the broad, sweeping flights that grace so many southern mansions, the Monticello stairs are narrow and twisting, as if the owner begrudged the space they took.

Jefferson had hardly time to finish the reconstruction before he was called to Washington to serve, during the next twelve years, as Vice-President and then President. It was not until 1809 that he was free at last to settle down at Monticello, the place where "all my wishes and, as I hope, my days will end." He rose, as always, at sunrise, spent an hour or so at his desk, and then went about the work of a plantation owner. One of his slaves remembered him "singin', always hummin' a tune" as he rode his horse about the estate.

Jefferson never wavered from his view that slavery was an evil, corrupting alike to the slaves and the owners. "The whole commerce between master and slave," he observed, "is a perpetual exercise of the most boisterous

passions, the most unremitting despotism on the one part, and degrading submissions on the other." In his younger days he had fought for statutes that would free the children of slaves and had first used the phrase "All men are born free" in a court case involving a black man. But he did not free his own slaves, believing, or so he said, that they would not be able to get along on their own. Meanwhile, he was a kind master, refusing to sell a slave if it meant breaking up a family and sometimes buying one to reunite a family. A few he freed, or allowed to run away, but these were mostly members of the Hemings family, and according to the persuasive evidence presented by his recent biographer, Fawn Brodie, were Jefferson's own children by Sally Hemings (who was herself the daughter of Jefferson's father-in-law John Wayles and thus half-sister of Jefferson's dead wife). By the time he was an ex-President he was ready to leave the cause of emancipation to others. To ask him to undertake "this salutary but arduous work," he wrote to Edward Coles, "is like bidding old Priam to buckle the armour of Hector. . . . This enterprise is for the young. . . ."

In retirement Jefferson had time to invent and use the ingenious devices that so intrigue visitors to Monticello. There is the calendar clock above the entrance that marks the days of the week by the slow descent of cannonballs. There are the double doors to the parlor that open simultaneously when one of them is pushed. There are the dumbwaiter for raising wines from the cellar, the polygraph for writing two letters at once, the music stand that opens up for four players, the special passageway for the removal of chamber pots.

The house was a virtual museum of objects reflecting Jefferson's limitless range of interests. George Ticknor, a visitor from Boston, was struck by the "strange furniture" on the walls of the entrance hall: "On one side hang the head and horns of an elk, a deer, and a buffalo; another is covered with curiosities which Lewis and Clark found in their wild and perilous expedition. On the third, among other striking matters, was the head of a mammoth. . . .

On the fourth side, in odd union with a fine painting of the Repentance of St. Peter, is an Indian map on leather, of the southern waters of the Missouri, and an Indian representation of a bloody battle, handed down in their traditions."

Now Jefferson had time to pursue his architectural interests. He designed houses for many of his friends and neighbors, including Madison and Monroe, and even inspired a Palladian barn on one Virginia estate. His most important work was the design of the University of Virginia, including the rotunda, the serpentine walls, and the grounds. Much of his time was taken up with correspondence and with visitors. One who warmed his heart was his old comrade of Revolutionary days, the marquis de Lafayette. Thomas Jefferson Randolph described how his grandfather walked to greet Lafayette as he emerged from his carriage. Jefferson, he said, "got into a shuffling quickened gait until they threw themselves with tears into each others arms—of the 3 or 400 persons present not a sound escaped except an occasional suppresst sob, there was not a dry eye in the crowd—altho invited into the house none would enter."

Less than two years later Jefferson was dead. As a plantation, Monticello too was finished. It was soon sold by Jefferson's daughter, Martha Jefferson Randolph, and during the nineteenth century the house passed through two periods of neglect that almost brought it to destruction. In the 1830's one owner tried unsuccessfully to establish a silk farm, plowing up Jefferson's lawns to plant mulberry trees. During the Civil War the Confederate government seized the house and sold most of its furnishings at auction. After each of these crises Monticello was saved by members of the Levy family, the first time by Commodore Uriah Phillips Levy of the United States Navy and the second time by his nephew, Jefferson Monroe Levy. Thanks to these devoted Jeffersonians, the house was preserved until 1913, when funds were finally raised by the Thomas Jefferson Memorial Association to restore it as a national monument.

*A visitor to Nutt's estate thought it resembled "an English gentleman's country seat," except for its pagoda-like house.*

*This portrait of Haller Nutt hangs at Longwood.*

# WAR CASUALTY

Most ante-bellum southern planters' homes ran true to classic revival form: big, pillared, square, and stately. Dr. Haller Nutt, a physician and plantation owner of Natchez, Mississippi, wanted something different. He found it in *The Model Architect*, published by Samuel Sloan in 1852—an "Oriental Villa," octagonal in plan and capped with a fanciful Turkish dome. After corresponding with Sloan, in 1859 Nutt set his slaves to work on the mansion he called Longwood. Two years later he imported a skilled crew from Philadelphia to finish the job. The exterior was nearly complete when the Civil War broke out and the Philadelphians fled north. Nutt himself died three years later. His widow hung on in the half-finished house for three decades, trying to raise the money to realize her husband's dream. But Longwood was never finished, and when in 1971 the Pilgrimage Garden Club of Natchez took over the empty, overgrown husk in order to preserve it, the members found tools and lumber and old packing cases in the basement where Nutt's northern workmen had dropped them more than a century before.

*Longwood's octagonal shape is clearly seen from the air.*

*Wooden "fancywork" like this was shipped in from Philadelphia.*

# The Vanderbilts' Houses

I n the brick house at No. 10 Washington Place the old Commodore lay dying. This was the house he had built after he made his first few millions in the hard, rough business of running ferries and riverboats around New York Harbor. To his poor wife Sophia, who had never wanted to move from their old home on Staten Island, it had seemed impossibly grand. But compared to the uptown mansions of the Astors and the Goelets and the Stewarts, it was neither very big nor very fashionable.

Inside the house in the winter of 1876, Cornelius Vanderbilt's relatives came and went in a vigil that had been going on then for more than half a year. Sometimes the young wife he had married after Sophia died would lead them in singing the multimillionaire's favorite hymn, "Come ye sinners, poor and needy." Outside the house financial reporters from Wall Street waited for medical bulletins, knowing that the Commodore's rallies and sinking spells would be reflected in the price of New York Central stock. In response to reports of his death, the old man would roar down from the top of the stairs, "It's a damned lie."

But die he did, on January 4, 1877. And four days later the family gathered to learn what would happen to the greatest fortune in the United States. To his eight aging daughters, whose children did not bear the Vanderbilt name, he left a few hundred thousand dollars apiece. To support the younger of his two surviving sons, Cornelius Jeremiah, a wastrel and a forger, he set aside just two hundred thousand, and only the *income* from that. His young widow got half a million. For the tax collector, in those golden days, there was nothing. For lifelong servants and distant relatives, small remembrances. For charity, nothing. Almost all the rest—ninety-five million dollars of it—went to his older son, William Henry, with smaller amounts to William Henry's sons.

The fortune was kept intact. Family control of the New York Central was assured. And the money was freed

*Alva Vanderbilt, costumed for the fancy-dress ball with which she opened her Manhattan palace (right, workmen in front of the "everyday" entrance) in 1883, preened for a photographer.*

*This is the stately façade of Marble House, William K. Vanderbilt's gleaming summer "cottage" at Newport.*

from the old man's iron grip. What, the world wondered, would his heirs do with it?

The answer was not long in coming. They would spend it. And they would spend it, above all else, for houses. They would become the greatest house-building family in American history.

First off the mark was Alva Smith Vanderbilt, the new young wife of Willliam Henry's son, William Kissam, known to one and all as Willie K. Alva was the daughter of a cotton planter from Mobile, Alabama, a belle of local society. She knew exactly what she wanted—the position of New York's social leader, then held, almost as if by divine right, by Mrs. William Backhouse Astor. To make her bid, Alva must have the finest house in the city.

The money was there—two million dollars under the Commodore's will, with the assurance of much more to come from her father-in-law. Next, she needed an architect, and she found him in the person of Richard Morris Hunt, the first American trained at the Ecole des Beaux-Arts in Paris, with ideas as grandiose as Alva's own. Between them they planned a palace to be built on Fifth Avenue at Fifty-second Street.

The site that Alva chose was on the geographical frontier of New York society. The families of old wealth were settled in their mansions along both sides of Fifth Avenue from Washington Square to the Forties. The Astors, who had been new money a generation earlier,

were entrenched at Thirty-fourth Street, where the Empire State Building now stands. By the end of the first roaring decade after the Civil War, the Vanderbilts, as the leaders of the new industrial plutocracy, began staking their claims to the blocks between what is now Rockefeller Center and Central Park. Before the building spree was over, members of the family would erect ten houses along what came to be known as Vanderbilt Strip. Already Alva's father-in-law had built twin mansions between Fifty-first and Fifty-second streets.

These were the houses to beat, and Alva was the young woman to beat them. Breaking with the New York tradition, she and Hunt decided that the William Kissam Vanderbilt house would not be of local brownstone but of gray limestone. Hunt took his inspiration, and many details of design, from two French architectural landmarks, the chateau of Blois and the house of the great medieval financier Jacques Coeur at Bourges. The result, after three years of construction, was a mansion of great, though derivative, elegance, graced by a steep slate roof, a pinnacled tower, and a profusion of carvings, balconies, and bow windows.

With its vast rooms and its entrance hall that reminded visitors of Milan Cathedral, the house could not be said to have a homey feeling. In later years the Vanderbilts' daughter Consuelo recalled the white marble staircase with a shudder: "I can still remember," she wrote in *The*

*The Marble House ballroom richly mirrors the tastes of Alva Vanderbilt and her architect, Richard Morris Hunt.*

*Glitter and the Gold*, "how long and terrifying was the dark and endless sweep of stairs as, with acute sensations of fear, I climbed to my room every night, leaving below the light and its comforting rays."

Yet to architectural connoisseurs of the day it was Hunt's masterpiece. Charles Follen McKim, of McKim, Mead & White, paid the ultimate tribute to his rival's work. He told friends that he liked to walk up Fifth Avenue just to gaze at the mansion. "I can sleep better at night," he said, "knowing it's there."

On the evening of March 26, 1883, the Vanderbilts opened their palace with a costume ball, for which Willie dressed as the duc de Guise, a sixteenth-century French nobleman, and Alva as a Venetian princess, bearing stuffed doves. While police held back a crowd of onlookers, twelve hundred invited guests descended from their carriages and walked up a maroon carpet to be admitted by servants in livery of the same Vanderbilt colors. They spent the night dancing, feasting, watching the performance of elaborate quadrilles by the younger guests, and spotting familiar faces under such disguises as Louis XIV, Daniel Boone, the Goddess of Ice, Romeo, Juliet, and Electric Light.

It was a social triumph, and Alva was accepted as heiress presumptive to Mrs. Astor's throne. For a brief time she basked in her glory, but this was the Gilded Age, and social laurels were not to rest upon. The operative principle was well stated by Thorstein Veblen, the sour social economist of the time:

"Wealth is now intrinsically honorable and confers honor upon its possessor. . . . But as fast as a person makes new acquisitions and becomes accustomed to the resulting new standard of wealth, the standard forthwith ceases to afford appreciably greater satisfaction than the old standard did. . . . The tendency is constantly to make the present pecuniary standard the point of departure for a fresh increase of wealth. But in order to gain and hold the esteem of men it is not sufficient merely to possess wealth. The wealth must be put in evidence. . . ."

In accordance with this principle Alva Vanderbilt, having built the greatest house in America, promptly built another—a white marble summer "cottage" at Newport. This time Louis XIV's Grand Trianon was the model, but to make it even grander Alva and Richard Hunt added a row of columns copied (and somewhat enlarged) from those of the Temple of the Sun at Baalbek. Furniture, paintings, statues, mosaics, and objects of art began to arrive from Europe in such quantity that a special wharf and a warehouse were required to receive them. By the time it was finished, the house had cost two million dollars in old money (say fourteen million today) and the furnishings nine million dollars (say sixty-three million).

Such an establishment did not run itself. In the dining

room each of the solid bronze chairs weighed seventy pounds and required a strong footman to move it. The front doors were left without outside handles, in the confident expectation that a servant would always be standing there to open them. In addition to the household staff, the Vanderbilts required a coachman and grooms to get about and a small army of gardeners. At a time when they could be had for under two dollars a day, the cost was not unduly burdensome.

Meanwhile, in the competition to build white elephants (Henry James used the phrase to describe the Newport cottages), Alva's sister-in-law, Mrs. Cornelius Vanderbilt II, could not be left behind. Her husband was, after all, the elder brother and the chairman of the New York Central. In the year that Marble House was completed the Cornelius Vanderbilts began construction of The Breakers, a cottage that outdid even Marble House in the splendor of its design, the ornateness of its furnishings, the number of artisans who worked on it (five hundred), and the number of house guests it could accommodate (sixty).

These and other showy shelters were occupied during about two months in the summer. In late June the social families began arriving, by land and sea, with their servants, their horses, and their house guests. Some came in their private railroad cars or even, if they happened to own a railroad as the Vanderbilts did, in their private trains. Others came in their yachts, tying up at their own docks or, if their vessels were too big to get into the harbor, as Mrs. Richard Cadwalader's four-hundred-eight-foot *Savarona* was, anchoring offshore. Mornings were spent at their rigidly guarded bathing spot, Bailey's Beach. In the afternoons the reigning ladies of the colony went driving behind fast horses in their cabriolets and *grandes daumonts* on Ocean Drive, taking care to bow ceremoniously the first time they passed social equals, to smile thinly the second time, and look away the third.

Evenings were the test of a hostess's means and ingenuity. Ten-course meals were served, often on solid gold

*Cornelius Vanderbilt II, above, built The Breakers at Newport (exterior, below) at an initial cost of ten million dollars. He spent an additional five thousand each season just to paint the surrounding fence.*

*The coffered ceiling, gilt paneling, and carved pillars of The Breakers' salon were crafted to order in France.*

319

dinnerware. But the winning hostess was the one who added imagination to riches. At one memorable dinner, according to Cleveland Amory, the guests sat down to a table with a sand pile running down its center. At each place was a tiny silver pail and shovel. Digging in the sand with all decorous speed, the guests uncovered such favors as diamonds, rubies, emeralds, and sapphires.

"I know of no profession, art, or trade," observed Alva Vanderbilt, "that women are working in today, as taxing on mental resource as being a leader of Society."

If one were to pick the pinnacle of the Gilded Age it might well be the summer of 1895, when both Marble House and The Breakers were open and running in all their glory. It was during that summer that Alva brought off her proudest coup by arranging the marriage of Consuelo to the Duke of Marlborough. Since the beautiful Consuelo was in love with someone else, Alva did not hesitate to lock her up in the house, rage at her, and suffer a series of dramatic "heart attacks," until Consuelo, fearful for her mother's life, agreed to marry the unloved duke.

The heyday of the preposterous cottages was nearly over. By the following summer Cornelius Vanderbilt was ailing, and The Breakers was quiet. Alva had scandalized society by divorcing Willie K. and marrying Oliver Hazard Perry Belmont, a noted society whip. She held on to Marble House, but took up residence at her new husband's grand, odd Belcourt, where the horses lived on the first floor and the family on the second. Having no more social pinnacles to scale, Alva turned her formidable energies to the cause of women's rights. The last great affair she staged at Marble House, in 1909, was not a ball but a huge suffrage rally.

Though the Newport cottages are the most spectacular residences of the Gilded Age, they are not in fact the greatest of the Vanderbilt houses. That distinction belongs to Biltmore, the French Renaissance chateau built by George Washington Vanderbilt II in the mountainous country near Asheville, North Carolina. As the youngest of William Henry Vanderbilt's nine children, George inherited only ten million dollars, as compared with Cornelius's sixty-seven million and William K.'s sixty-five million (all from an estate that William Henry had doubled to two hundred million dollars). A quiet young man, with a love of books and nature but little taste for society, he bought a tract of land in the Blue Ridge Mountains of North Carolina and engaged a trio of talented experts to plan his estate: Richard Morris Hunt, the family architect, to design the house; Frederick Law Olmsted, the country's foremost landscape architect, to lay out the grounds; and a young man named Gifford Pinchot to manage the forest.

Hunt's philosophy of architecture was best expressed in his advice to his son: "The first thing you've got to remember is that it's your client's money you're spending. Your business is to get the best results you can following their wishes. If they want you to build a house upside down standing on its chimney, it's up to you to do it, and still get the best possible results." With such an attitude, Hunt got along famously with his clients, and George Vanderbilt was one of the easiest to get along with. To facilitate the construction Vanderbilt built a private spur of the Southern Railroad from Asheville and erected a village to house the one thousand workmen. After five years he was the owner of the largest private house ever built in the United States. Gobelin tapestries, Dürer engravings, and a collection of twenty thousand books offer testimony that its owner was the most schol-

arly and cultivated of the Vanderbilts. His favorite room was the lofty baroque library, where he engaged in the odd pursuit of translating works of modern literature into ancient Greek.

Vanderbilt had had the idea of turning his whole domain into a park, but Olmsted talked him out of that. The soil was poor, he pointed out, and the forest had been reduced to scrub by wholesale cutting of the best hardwoods. It would take too long to turn the whole place into a park on the European model, with stately trees and roaming herds of deer, as Vanderbilt had dreamed. Instead of a park, Olmsted advised, "such a land in Europe would be made into a forest, if it belonged to a gentleman of large means as a hunting preserve for game, mainly with a view to crops of timber."

So a forest it became—the first scientifically managed forest in the United States, with young Pinchot as forester. By selective cutting and careful soil management Pinchot began to upgrade the woodland and still made a small profit on the operation. His work excited the envy of the secretary of agriculture, J. Sterling Morton, who remarked ruefully that "Vanderbilt employs more men than I have in my charge" and that "he is spending more money than Congress appropriates for this department." Pinchot left Biltmore in 1893 and went on to become the first chief of the United States Forest Service.

After George Washington Vanderbilt's death in 1914, most of the Biltmore estate—one hundred twenty-five thousand acres by that time—was given by his widow to become the nucleus of the Pisgah National Forest. The house, like many of the surviving Vanderbilt houses, is now a public monument. Perhaps the most imposing Vanderbilt shelter still left in family hands is the mausoleum on Staten Island, where all the generations of Vanderbilts since the Commodore have been buried. With most of the money spent or scattered, many Vanderbilts today live in less than splendid homes, but in death they can still join their ancestors in the tomb designed to old William Henry's specifications: "roomy and solid and rich."

# PARADISE LOST

George Boldt had two dreams: to run a grand hotel and to build an equally grand castle reminiscent of those he had seen as a boy in Germany. He came alone to America in 1865 at thirteen and first found work as a dishwasher in a New York City hotel. He rose quickly in hotel management, and his skill gained him such wealthy friends as William Waldorf Astor, whom he persuaded to build a supremely luxurious hotel. When the Waldorf opened in 1893 with only thirty-two guests, critics dubbed it Boldt's Folly. He persisted though, and by the late 1890's he owned the combined Waldorf-Astoria and other corporations as well. With his wife, Louise, whom he adored, he often vacationed in the Thousand Islands, and in 1900 he bought Hart Island in Alexandria Bay on the St. Lawrence. On it he planned to build a three-hundred-room castle as a gift to his beloved wife. Renaming it Heart Island, he also reshaped it into a heart by constructing a five-hundred-foot-long, gently curving lagoon. The castle's construction required a small army of skilled craftsmen;

at one point two thousand of them. On one end of the island they built a small medieval castle. Beneath the conic roofs capping its circular towers were servants quarters, a powerhouse, and a set of Westminster chimes played from a keyboard hidden in the castle's main drawing room. Boldt planned to supply the island via an underground tramway running from the castle to a dock. But the dream of paradise vanished in 1902 when Louise died suddenly. Boldt ordered the workmen to leave the island at once. He made no plans to safeguard the castle or the precious furnishings still uncrated in its cavernous rooms. The grief-stricken man never visited Heart Island again. Today much of this huge structure remains an empty shell, walls scrawled with graffiti left by a half century of curious visitors. Thieves have looted many of the furnishings, though even today crates of carved wood stand unopened. And in 1962 even the dignity of solitude vanished when the Treadway Corporation acquired Heart Island to operate as a daytime tourist attraction.

*George C. Boldt*

*Louise Boldt*

*Boats entered the lagoon at Heart*

*Island through a miniature Arc de Triomphe. The Alster Tower on the shore is a model of a Rhine River castle.*

*The Ringlings once kept an authentic gondola—later destroyed by a hurricane—moored on an offshore islet.*

# VENETIAN CIRCUS

"I just want a little bit of a place," John Ringling told his architect when they sat down to design a house for the shore-front property that Ringling had bought on Sarasota Bay. But the architect soon discovered what the proprietor of "The Greatest Show on Earth" meant. During their European travels Ringling and his wife, Mable, had fallen in love with the doges' palace in Venice. They also admired the three-hundred-foot tower that Stanford White had designed for Madison Square Garden, and they thought that a duplicate would look good on top of the doges' palace. Thomas Martin, the architect, tried to talk the Ringlings out of the tower but succeeded only in persuading them to reduce its height. Just getting to talk to Ringling was a problem. The impresario's day did not begin until three o'clock in the afternoon, when he rose, breakfasted, then spent the next three hours bathing, dressing, and being shaved in an ornate barber's chair. But Mable Ringling showed up almost every morning with a satchel of sketches and paintings that she had paid Italian artists to do for her. While she made most of the architectural decisions, her husband had an old carnival man's dislike of paying bills. Only after Mrs. Ringling interceded for him was Martin paid for his design, whereupon he quit. With another architect, Dwight James Baum, the Ringlings began building in 1924 the mansion that Mable christened Ca' d'Zan—Venetian dialect for "house of John." Under the pressure of economy the resemblance to the doges' palace faded considerably. Baum had to eliminate the impressive arcades that had been planned for the west front, and the heavy walnut doors were given the look of great age by pounding them

*Mable and John Ringling beam down from the gaming-room ceiling.*

with cobblestones wrapped in burlap. Despite the economies the palace turned out to be something of a bravura masterpiece. Ringling kept in winter residence a musical ensemble called The Czechoslovakian Band of Prague, Bohemia. On gala evenings he concealed it aboard his yacht, the *Zalophus*, anchored offshore. When darkness fell it suddenly lit up, and the band burst into music. But the show at Ca' d'Zan had a brief run. In June of 1929 Mable Ringling died, and shortly thereafter the market crash set off an abrupt decline in Ringling's fortunes. Ca' d'Zan was only five days away from the auctioneer's block when, on December 9, 1936, Ringling died. Florida took over the palace and grounds and preserved them as a tourist attraction.

# William Randolph Hearst's San Simeon

*Actress Marion Davies was the hostess at San Simeon and William Randolph Hearst's mistress for thirty-two years. They rarely discussed marriage, but she did not seem to mind: "Why should I run after a streetcar," she asked, "when I was already aboard?"*

The finest room at San Simeon, or so its owner always felt, was the refectory, a baronial hall where guests dined at a long set of tables brought from a sixteenth-century Italian monastery. High above their heads, and just below a vaulted ceiling from another Renaissance monastery, hung twenty flags of the parishes of Siena. The walls were covered with Flemish tapestries depicting scenes from the Book of Daniel. Amid all this splendor guests were sometimes surprised to find at their places paper napkins and bottles of ketchup and mustard with the labels on.

It was not just another whim of William Randolph Hearst's. He had them there because they brought back memories of other days, when San Simeon was no more than a campsite on his father's ranch. When Hearst was only two years old his father, George, took some of the money he had made in mining and began buying Spanish land grants in California. As his fortune grew—from silver, copper, and most of all from the great Homestake gold mine—he added to the ranch until he had forty-eight thousand acres along the coast near San Luis Obispo, midway between San Francisco and Los Angeles. Often he would take his young son on horseback trips into the wild, mountainous country, sleeping in tents or under the open sky. Their favorite campsite was the highest hill, which was covered with tall cypress trees and commanded a sweeping view of the Pacific.

A generation later William Randolph Hearst often brought his own five sons to Camp Hill, as they came to call it. The place had not changed, but the camping arrangements had. Now a pack train brought in tents for as many as forty or fifty people and ranch workmen set up a pavilion where guests ate their meals, played games, and at night watched movies. Already the future pattern of life at San Simeon was taking shape.

Hearst never lost his love for the wild ranchland or for daylong horseback rides and picnics. But as time went on he developed other tastes that kept pace with, and sometimes outran, his large, increasing fortune. By World

War I he had built a newspaper empire that made him the country's most powerful publisher. Meanwhile, the ranch was enlarged by further purchases until eventually it covered two hundred seventy-five thousand acres and stretched for fifty miles along the California coast. It was during a cookout at Camp Hill in 1917 that Hearst brought forth a plaster model and told his guests: "This is the house I will build right at this very spot."

Just what that model looked like, except that it was Spanish and had twin towers, no one now remembers. Julia Morgan, who built the model, served Hearst as architect and decorator for the next twenty-four years, but it was Hearst who made the plans, Miss Morgan who refined them and carried them out. They started with three guesthouses—each of them big enough for any ordinary family of wealth—which became known as La Casa del Monte, La Casa del Sol, and La Casa del Mar. The top stories of these villas were level with the hilltop terrace, their lower stories clinging to the hillside. Then, on the crest, work was begun on the Casa Grande. Brickworks and tileworks were established on the premises to make the materials. Over a period of thirty years there never were fewer than twenty-five and sometimes as many as a hundred and fifty men at work on construction. Nothing at San Simeon was built exactly according to plan; everything was changed as it went along; and after thirty years, when Hearst left the place, it was still unfinished.

When the towers were almost built Hearst climbed up to the top level and was delighted by its view of the sea and mountains.

"I would like my living quarters right here," he said.

"But, Mr. Hearst, this is the roof," said Miss Morgan.

"Then put on another story," ordered Hearst. "We'll call it the Celestial Suite."

The same thing happened with the Neptune Pool, an outdoor swimming place so vast and luxurious that a Roman emperor might have thought it showy. After taking a few swims, Hearst emerged to say, "I think it will look better larger." Advised that this would run the

*"I'm not saying it's right," Hearst remarked of his relationship with Miss Davies. "I'm saying that it is."*

In this aerial partial view of the
San Simeon complex, the Neptune
Pool is below; at right is La Casa
del Sol; the Casa Grande is just
out of camera range at the top.
Despite San Simeon's grandiose size,
Marion Davies recalled, "W. R. didn't
like anyone calling it a castle.
It was always 'the ranch.'"

*Whenever the master of San Simeon was in residence, he received his dinner guests in the assembly room, its walls glowing with the Flemish tapestries he and his legion of agents had amassed in Europe. Hearst sat at the near end of the room and shook hands with each awed visitor in turn.*

cost up above a million dollars, he merely shrugged. The pool was enlarged, so that it now holds three hundred forty-five thousand gallons of mountain spring water and is good for sailing small boats.

One thing that governed much of the design of San Simeon was Hearst's passion for collecting. He seems to have developed that passion as early as the age of ten, when his doting mother, Phoebe Apperson Hearst, took him on a small boy's grand tour of Europe. On that trip he exhibited two very different but lasting personality traits. One was a talent for mischief: he got into constant trouble with hotelkeepers and local police by such pranks as fishing for goldfish in the Tuileries Gardens (a gendarme caught him), burning alcohol in his hotel room (the room caught fire), and shooting a toy rifle at a hotel ceiling (the plaster fell). At the same time he displayed a precocious interest in works of art, especially those concerned with ancient battles and romance. He brought back his first collector's trophies: stamps, coins, beer steins, porcelain, Swiss clocks, and the like. In her diary of the trip his mother recorded two reactions that prefigured the mature Hearst: when he saw the paintings in the Louvre he wanted his mother to buy them all; after he toured Windsor Castle he said, "I would like to live there."

Later, as a young newspaper publisher, Hearst began making frequent buying trips to Europe. His tastes ran to heavy medieval and Renaissance furniture, armor, antique silver, tapestries, Oriental rugs—the furnishings of ancient castles and palaces. But he also indulged sudden whims for snuffboxes, stuffed owls, spinning wheels, and mummies. Once when his wife, Millicent, visited the Bronx warehouse where he stored many of his trophies, she remarked: "I think he went out and bought things whenever he was worried."

It was not just single objects that Hearst bought. He had a special passion for the ceilings of historic Italian and Spanish buildings, which he had taken down and moved in sections. Eventually he was buying whole buildings. At Sacramenia in Spain he bought a twelfth-century monastery and then constructed a narrow-gauge railroad to get it out. The monastery was taken apart, stone by stone, put in numbered crates and shipped to a Bronx warehouse.

Some of Hearst's treasure never got beyond the Bronx warehouse, but the pieces he liked best were shipped to California. Visitors to the ranch remember seeing lines of packing crates stretching for half a mile along the road below San Simeon. Hearst wanted his trophies around him, and his house therefore had to be adapted and enlarged to accommodate them.

None of the rooms at San Simeon was thought of as a gallery. All served the purposes of a powerful man who worked hard and entertained lavishly. One of the most successful rooms is the Gothic study in the north tower, where Hearst carried on his work as the owner of his twenty-two newspapers, nine magazines, two wire services, five radio stations, and great quantities of real estate. Each morning copies of all of his papers were flown in and arranged on racks for his inspection. The press lord would spread them on the floor, one by one, and turn the pages with his bare toes, reading the headlines and often whole stories. At his side was Joseph Willicombe, his secretary. To Willicombe he dictated his comments, criticisms, and suggestions, which went to his editors in telegrams that began, "The Chief says. . . ."

At seven-thirty each evening Hearst would step into the carved mahogany elevator—it had originally been a confessional in a French church—that carried him down from the tower to the assembly hall on the ground floor to greet his guests. Over the years Hearst was host at San Simeon to many of the great figures of the 1920's and 1930's—Churchill, Lindbergh, Mayor Jimmy Walker of New York, George Bernard Shaw, and Presidents Coolidge and Hoover. But the regulars on the guest list were the friends of his mistress, Marion Davies.

Miss Davies had met Hearst, according to her own account, in 1919, when she was a dancer in the *Ziegfeld*

*Follies.* In the ensuing years he devoted a large amount of his time as well as some seven million dollars to establishing her as a Hollywood musical star. Hearst remained married to his wife, who presided over the family Christmas in the still-uncompleted Casa Grande as late as 1925. But thereafter Millicent Hearst lived in New York, and Marion Davies, who was some thirty-four years younger than Hearst, became the chatelaine of San Simeon.

An invitation to San Simeon was one of the top status symbols of the movie colony. First would come a call from a social secretary with words of advice: no need for specialized gear such as riding clothes (the ranch would provide them) and no personal maids or valets, please, the ranch was well supplied. The guests met at Glendale station on Friday afternoon to board Hearst's special train for the five-hour trip to San Simeon. Coming up the coast, long before they reached the little station at San Luis Obispo, they would see high above them the castle towers, brilliantly lit in the night to welcome them. From the station cars would drive them up "La Cuesta Encantada," the Enchanted Hill, passing on the way through Hearst's private zoo, where signs warned Animals Have the Right of Way, and where at times the cars would be held up by wandering camels, yaks, or llamas.

During the day, guests were free to do what they wished: swim in the outdoor or indoor pool, play tennis or croquet, ride, fish, or walk. There was only one rule, no drinking in the rooms, and only one fixed engagement: seven-thirty in the assembly hall. Between that time and dinner at nine, each guest was offered one drink—no more. Guests found Hearst a courteous and affable, if somewhat intimidating, host. He would fix a guest with his wide, pale-blue eyes and listen intently—but only so long as he was interested. It was the gay, warm-hearted Marion who kept the parties going with talk, games, and dressing up in costumes. After dinner every night in the year, except when there was some special festivity, a movie was shown in the projection room.

*At a 1937 dinner in the refectory at left, jammed with artifacts, Hearst is at center right; Marion Davies has just left the chair across from him. Hearst's mania for collecting—the bed at top was Cardinal Richelieu's—was such that when he died in 1951, his warehouse, above, was heaped with unpacked treasures.*

One of the enduring legends, perpetuated by Orson Welles in *Citizen Kane,* was that Hearst could not bear the mention of death. Guests often came to his table in fear that, by some slip of the tongue, they might violate the famous taboo. What they observed at San Simeon was not a morbid fear of death but an extreme, sometimes quixotic, concern for life in all its forms, animal or vegetable. Not only were elephants and antelopes given the run of the Enchanted Hill; mice had the freedom of the castle. Marion Davies tells in her memoirs of a time when, after saving a mouse from his dog, "W. R." spent half an hour digging it a hole and lining the hole with soft leaves. That night, Marion goes on, "he went out to check and came back and said, 'The mouse is fine. Nice and warm.' That mouse was warm because W. R. had taken a scissors and cut off part of the little blanket I had on my chaise lounge. He had ruined my lovely blanket just to keep that mouse warm."

Hearst could not bear to see a tree cut down. And since he wanted the trees precisely fitted into his evolving landscape plans, gardeners were kept busy moving them from one spot to another. One ancient oak offered such a problem that, before being moved thirty feet, it was encased in a large concrete flowerpot—at a cost of forty thousand dollars. In his gardening as in his newspapers, Hearst liked striking effects. He was capable of having the flower gardens completely replanted overnight in order to astonish his guests with seemingly endless beds of lilies on Easter morning. He behaved, his wife once said, as though he and San Simeon would last forever.

In his peak years Hearst was spending money at a rate never matched by any other American and by few kings or rajahs. W. A. Swanberg, his best biographer, estimates the annual expenditure, for both living and collecting, at about fifteen million dollars. Even in the worst years of the Depression, when salaries on the Hearst papers were being sharply cut, life at San Simeon went on unchecked. But the spree could not last forever. By the middle 1930's some of his newspapers were deeply in the red and

his whole publishing empire was in debt to the banks.

Hearst had never worried about money, and he did not want to think about the very real prospect of bankruptcy. John Francis Neylan, his top business executive, explained to a court: "Money as such bores him. His idea of money is that it is something to do something with. He is a builder. He wants to build buildings. He wants to build magazines. He wants to develop ranches. He builds hotels in New York. His idea is to build, build, build all the time. I have said repeatedly that in his make-up there is just almost a blank space in relation to money."

But finally Hearst had to listen, and when he did he accepted his plight in good spirit. The collecting was stopped. The losing papers were sold. Hearst gave over control of his publishing empire to a trustee. At San Simeon all construction work was halted and the entertaining sharply reduced. For two years during the Second World War the great house was closed.

It was the war—ironically, since Hearst had opposed it—that floated the sinking empire. In the booming war and postwar economy advertising revenues increased, the banks were paid off, and Hearst was master of his own house again. But life at San Simeon was no longer an endless house party. Hearst was in his eighties now and, although his editorial mind was as sharp as ever, heart trouble slowed his step and made his hands tremble. The voice, always high and thin, could scarcely be heard when he called his editors on the telephone. His doctors wanted him closer to medical care. Marion, still in her fun-loving forties, found San Simeon without its hordes of guests a lonely place. And so in 1947 Hearst sadly closed the doors of his Casa Grande and was driven down the Enchanted Hill to end his years in Marion's house in Beverly Hills.

The castle stood empty as long as Hearst lived, and when none of his sons could afford to take it on it was given to the State of California. Tourists now come by the busload to marvel at the home of a man who lived more like a prince than any prince of his time.

# MAGNIFICENT BUILDERS

By the time Wilt Chamberlain came to build a house with his basketball earnings, he felt that he had had enough of too-low ceilings, too-short beds, and too-small rooms. The retreat that he constructed in the mountains near Bel-Air, California, is scaled throughout to his seven-foot-one-inch frame. In the picture on the opposite page he is standing on a balcony under the soaring roof of the living room. For nocturnal relaxation there is a mirror-paneled bedroom with a huge fur-covered water bed, above. In the dining room, below left, the sixteen-foot crystal chandelier and the seventeen-thousand-dollar set of chairs have excited only envy and admiration in the movie colony. But conservationists are sometimes pained by the fur throw on his bed, made from the soft muzzles of fifteen hundred arctic wolves. Chamberlain likes it to be known that he bought the fur from Alaska hunters who had already killed the wolves for government bounties.

The new wealth of the Arab world is reflected in these rooms of a town house in the republic of Kuwait. The owner, shown in the picture at left, is Abdlatif al-Hamid, one of the most enterprising new money managers in the Middle East. Young Mr. al-Hamid, who belongs to an old merchant-banking family, got his education in the United States, studying international affairs at Harvard. Like many of his peers in the Arab countries, he divided his time between private finance and the handling of Kuwaiti government oil revenues. As a financier, he is head of the Kuwait Investment Company, with assets in excess of $130,000,000 and properties ranging from cement plants in Canada to cattle feed lots in Idaho, as well as a luxury resort on the island of Kiawah off the South Carolina coast. As a government official, he runs the Kuwait Fund for Arab Economic Development. Since his country is little more than a sandy crust over a vast dome of oil, with annual revenues of over eleven thousand dollars per Kuwaiti, it has plenty of money to place abroad where it will do the most good. The management of this huge program keeps Mr. al-Hamid away from home much of the time. His wife, Fattda, takes these long absences of his philosophically: "My father was a captain of a ship, like most men were then. He sailed to India and Africa and once he was away for a whole year. My mother spent her life waiting for his ship; I spend mine waiting for Abdlatif's plane."

Air travelers approaching Palm Springs, California, may look down upon a manmade oasis of grass, trees, and ponds, set in the middle of the desert. It is the estate of Walter H. Annenberg, the multimillionaire publisher (Daily Racing Form, TV Guide) and former ambassador to the Court of St. James's. The house, seen behind Walter and Lee Annenberg on the opposite page, is built of the palest pink stucco. The foyer, right, has pale green walls to display some of the owner's notable paintings, and a water garden to set off Rodin's statue of Eve. From the air the spacious house is almost lost in the lush golf course, a charmed spot for three Presidents (Eisenhower, Nixon, and Ford) as well as such celebrity neighbors as Frank Sinatra and Bob Hope.

One feature of modern mansions, almost unknown before the twentieth century but almost universal today, is the swimming pool. This architectural development has been carried to its extreme in the one-hundred-and-sixty-foot room at left in the house built by Octaviano Longoria, a Mexican financier, and his American wife, Jeanette, seen reclining there in clothes of her own design. The house is a white limestone block built in a basic H shape standing on a hill outside Mexico City. Its central space is filled by a marble pool beneath a movable plastic roof. At one end of the pool is the living area, where the mistress of the house has represented eighteen countries in furnishings like the zebra-covered bench from Goa. At the far end is the dining area, roomy enough to seat fifty guests and where a party of three hundred for supper and dancing is not unusual. Five bedrooms, a sitting room, kitchen, study, and hunt room all open off the pool.

Perhaps the only true palace built
in recent years stands in a valley
just south of the Elburz mountains
in northern Iran. It is the Pearl
Palace, residence of Princess Shams,
sister of the shah. Although it
shimmers like something out of The
Arabian Nights (bottom, left),
it was designed by an American,
William Wesley Peters, Chief
Architect of the Frank Lloyd Wright
Foundation at Taliesin West. The
interior design and color selections
were supervised by Mrs. Frank Lloyd
Wright. The palace complex takes
its inspiration from the princess's
fondness for pearls and the full
moon and the two architectural
forms associated with the
Middle East—the dome and the
ziggurat. Under the larger of the
two domes—which is one hundred
and twenty feet in diameter—are the
reception hall and, on lower
levels reached by a spiral ramp,
the dining hall, library, and family
rooms. The smaller dome, seen on the
opposite page, encloses a swimming
pool and lounge. Below the ziggurat,
lighted by clerestory windows, are
the private rooms of the princess

# ACKNOWLEDGMENTS

The Editors would like to thank the following people for their special contributions to the book: Olivia Buehl, Helen C. Dunn, Susan Green, Elaine Golt Gongora, Richard Hannemann, Robin Kenny, Georgia Little, Myra Mangan, Laura Lane Masters, Joyce O'Connor, Kate Slate, Trip Spencer, Mary Tomaselli, Geoffrey Ward, Henry Weincek, and Marian Weston.

The Editors wish to thank the following people and institutions for their generous aid in pictorial research: Airesearch Aviation Co., Los Angeles: R. A. Graser, Thomas S. Parker; Bibliothèque Nationale, Service Photographique, Paris: Madame Le Monnier; Blenheim Palace: Paul Duffie; Peter S. Bryant; The Cosanti Foundation: Mrs. Paolo Soleri, Linda Caputo; *Country Life*: Sarah Hann; Devonshire Collections, Chatsworth: Thomas C. Wragg; *Du*, Zurich; Editions Arthaud, Paris: O. Tridon; Il Vittoriale degli Italiani, Gardone Riviera; Koppers Company Inc., Pittsburgh; Life Picture Service: Hannah B. Bruce, Jean Reynolds; Mark Twain Memorial, Hartford; Massachusetts Historical Society: Louis Tucker; Musées de la Ville de Bourges: E. Meslé; The National Trust: Francesca Barron, Deborah Newlove; Juan O'Gorman, Mexico City; *Progressive Architecture:* Barbara McCarthy; Clive B. Smith, Mexico City; Olive Smith; Thames and Hudson, London: Elizabeth Clarke; Thomas Jefferson Memorial Foundation, Monticello: William L. Beiswanger; University of Virginia, Alderman Library: Gregory A. Johnson; Weidenfeld and Nicholson, London: Sara Elliott; William L. Whitwell, Roanoke; Winchester Mystery House, San Jose: Carol B. Miller.

## PICTURE CREDITS

*Credits for illustrations from left to right are separated by semicolons; from top to bottom by dashes.*

**CHAPTER ONE:** 8—Escudo de Oro, Patrimonio Nacional. 10, 11—Musées Nationaux, Louvre. 12, 13—Photo Bulloz; Archives Photographiques—Copyright reserved. 14–15—Belzeaux/Rapho-Photo Researchers—Musées Nationaux, Paris; Bibliothèque Nationale. 16, 17—Adam Woolfitt/Woodfin Camp and Associates. 18—Musées Nationaux, Versailles. 19—Copyright reserved—Musées Nationaux, Paris— Musées de la Ville de Bourges. 20—Musées Nationaux, Paris (2)—Giraudon. 21—Nationalmuseum, Stockholm—Lauros/Giraudon. 22—Bibliothèque Nationale. 23—Musées Nationaux, Versailles. 24—Adam Woolfitt/Woodfin Camp and Associates. 25—Sotheby-Parke Bernet and Co. from the Collection of the Earl of Rosebery, Mentmore; Photo Bulloz. 26—Edwin Smith courtesy Weidenfeld and Nicolson Archives (2)—Wadsworth Atheneum, Hartford. 27—Culver Pictures. 28-29—New York Public Library from *Notes on Haiti*, volume 1, by Charles Mackenzie. 29—Russ Kinne/Photo Researchers. 30—Bradley Smith/Photo Researchers. 31—Fritz Henle/Monkmeyer. 33—Richard Meek. 34—The Metropolitan Museum of Art, bequest of Annie C. Kane, 1926. 36-37—Biblioteca de Palacio, Madrid. 38-39—Courtesy of the Marquess of Salisbury, Hatfield House. 40—Bradley Smith/Photo Researchers. 41—Prado, Madrid. 42—Bradley Smith/Photo Researchers. 43—Dimitri Kessel/*Life* Magazine © 1963 Time Inc. 45—Derek Fell. 46—Georgina Masson, courtesy Thames and Hudson. 47—Edwin Smith—Claude Arthaud, Paris with Studio Richard-Blin. 48—Edwin Smith—Ted Polumbaum. 49, 50—Edwin Smith. 51—Editorial Photo Archives. 52-53—Dimitri Kessel/*Life* Magazine © 1946 Time Inc.

**CHAPTER TWO:** 54—Adam Woolfitt/Woodfin Camp and Associates. 56—Museo Nazionale, Rome © Leonard Von Matt. 58—E. Richter, Rome. 59—Roma's Press. 60—Scala. 61—Fototeca Unione, Rome. 62—From *Diocletian's Palace* by Nada Miljkovic. 62-63—From *Ruins of the Palace of the Emperor Diocletian at Spalatro* by Robert Adam, photo by Paulus Leeser. 64—Bayer. Verwaltung der Staatl, Schlösser, Gärten u. Seen. 67—Ewing Krainin, courtesy Pan American World Airways. 68—Herpich and Son. 70—Nymphenburg Palace, Munich. 71—Alan Clifton/Black Star. 72—Claude Arthaud, Paris with Studio Richard-Blin. 73—Nat Norman/Photo Researchers. 74—Pierre Strinati. 75—Courtesy Bruckmann Verlag, Munich—Photo Kempter. 76—Baltimore Museum of Art. 78—Erich Hartmann/Magnum. 79—Trustees of the British Museum, photo by John Freeman Group—The Royal Pavilion, Art Gallery and Museums, Brighton. 81,82,83—The Royal Pavilion, Art Gallery and Museums, Brighton. 84—The Cooper-Hewitt Museum, The Smithsonian Institution's National Museum of Design. 85—The Cooper-Hewitt Museum, The Smithsonian Institution's National Museum of Design—The Royal Pavilion, Art Gallery and Museums, Brighton. 87—Tony Howarth/Woodfin Camp and Associates. 88—Musée Condé, Chantilly/Giraudon. 89—Archives Photographiques, Paris. 90—André Martin. 91—André Martin—Trustees of the British Museum, photo by John Freeman Group. 92-93—Bruno Barbey/Magnum. 94—Jeremy Witaker. 95—Bibliothèque Nationale—André Martin. 97—Clemens Kalischer. 98—N. Jane Iseley, courtesy the Preservation Society of Charleston—Derek Keath/*Du*. 99—Helga Photo Studio. 100-101—Alinari. 102—Courtesy The Museum of Modern Art, New York—Foto Marburg. 103—Claude Arthaud, Paris with Studio Richard-Blin.

**CHAPTER THREE:** 104—George Leavens. 106—Mildred F. Schmertz. 108–109—Frank Lloyd Wright Memorial Foundation; Ezra Stoller © ESTO. 110-111—Ezra Stoller © ESTO—Pedro E. Guerrero. 112-113—Frank Lloyd Wright Memorial Foundation. 114—Frank Lloyd Wright Memorial Foundation; The Chicago Tribune; Wisconsin Historical Society; Frank Lloyd Wright Memorial Foundation. 115—Frank Lloyd Wright Memorial Foundation. 116–117—Courtesy Juan O'Gorman; Eliot Elisofon/*Life* Magazine © Time Inc. 118-119—Eliot Elisofon/*Life* Magazine © Time Inc.; Courtesy Juan O'Gorman (4). 120-121—Julius Shulman; Herb Greene. 122—Farrell Grehan/Photo Researchers. 124-125—Courtesy Philip Johnson; Ezra Stoller © ESTO; Farrell Grehan/Photo Researchers—Ezra Stoller © ESTO. 126-127—Site plan courtesy Philip Johnson. 126—Gene Maggio/*The New York Times*—Ezra Stoller © ESTO. 127—Ezra Stoller © ESTO—Russ Kinne/Photo Researchers—Farrell Grehan/Photo Researchers. 128—Gene Maggio/*The New York Times*. 129,130—Ezra Stoller © ESTO. 131—Courtesy Richard Foster. 132—Ezra Stoller © ESTO (2)—Courtesy Richard Foster. 133—From *Popular Mechanics* © 1968 by the Hearst Corporation. 134-135—From *Arcology: The City in the Image of Man* by Paolo Soleri, courtesy M.I.T. Press, Cambridge; no credit. 136—Edward Beaty. 137—Stuart Weiner. 138-139—The Cosanti Foundation, photo by I. Pintar (2); plan courtesy The Cosanti Foundation. 140—Musée Etrange, photo by R. Guillemot. 141—Sir John Soane Museum. 142-143—Sir John Soane Museum, photo by John Freeman Group. 145—From *All Their Own*, by Jan Wampler, John Wiley Co., © 1977. 146—© Georg Gerster/Rapho–Photo Researchers. 147—© Georg Gerster/Rapho–Photo Researchers—© Georg Gerster, Rapho–Photo Researchers; Roger-Viollet, Paris; Photo Edouard-Studio des Grands Augustins. 148—© Gianni Tortoli/Photo Researchers. 149,150 From *All Their Own*, by Jan Wampler, John Wiley Co., © 1977. 151—Emma Landau. 152—Craig Aurness/Woodfin Camp & Associates. 153—Stephen Green-Armytage/The Image Bank.

**CHAPTER FOUR:** 154—S. Knecht, Tours. 156—Offentliche Kunstmuseum, Basel. 158—S. Knecht, Tours. 159—Roger-Viollet, Paris. 160—Uffizi, Florence/Giraudon. 161—Archives Photographiques, Paris. 162-163—Alain Perceval. 164—National Portrait Gallery, London. 165—Trustees of Chatsworth Settlement and His Grace the Duke of Devonshire—The National Trust; Victoria and Albert Museum. 166-167—the National Trust. 168, 169—The National Trust. 170-171—Edwin Smith. 173—The National Trust. 174—Erich Hartmann/Magnum. 175—Trustees of the Chatsworth Settlement. 176—Winchester Mystery House. 177—Koppers Company Inc., Pittsburgh. 178—Koppers Company Inc., Pittsburgh (2)— Winchester Mystery House (2). 179—Winchester Mystery House; Koppers Company Inc., Pittsburgh—Koppers Company Inc., Pittsburgh; Winchester Mystery House (2). 180—Jeremy Whitaker, courtesy His Grace the Duke of Marlborough. 181—Edwin Smith. 182-183—Bryan Heseltine. 184—Commissioners of the Royal Hospitallers, Chelsea. 185—*Country Life*. 186—Edwin Smith. 187—The Bodleian Library, Oxford. 188—A. F. Kersting. 189—Jeremy Whitaker, courtesy His Grace the Duke of Marlborough. 190—*Country Life*. 191—From *The Glitter and the Gold* by Consuelo Vanderbilt Balsan © 1952. 192 through 197—Isabella Stewart Gardner Museum, Boston. 199—Susan McCartney/Photo Researchers. 200—Dimitri Kessel/*Life* Magazine © 1948 Time Inc. 201—Edwin Smith. 202—Claude Arthaud, Paris with Studio Richard-Blin. 203—clockwise from top left: Edwin Smith; Dimitri Kessel/*Life* Magazine © 1948 Time Inc.; Bernard G. Silberstein/Rapho-Photo Researchers; M. Audrain, courtesy Editions Arthaud; Gurinenko and John Dayton, courtesy Weidenfeld and Nicolson. 204-205—Edwin Smith.

**CHAPTER FIVE:** 206—Tony Howarth. 209—Culver Pictures. 210 through 213—Mark Twain Memorial, Hartford. 214—The Scottish National Portrait Gallery. 216-217—Culver Pictures; British Tourist Authority. 218-219—Claude Arthaud, Paris with Studio Richard-Blin. 220-221—Culver Pictures. 222—Gillette Castle State Park, Hadlyme; Culver Pictures. 223—G. E. Kidder Smith. 224—Olana Historic Site. 225—Frank Lerner. 226—Henri Dauman © 1965. 228—Helga Photo Studio. 229—Helga Photo Studio for *The Magazine Antiques*. 230, 231—Alte Pinakothek, Munich. 232, 233—British Museum, photo by John Freeman Group. 234—Gementebestuur Antwerp. 235—Foto A. De Belder, Antwerp. 236—René Dazy, Paris. 237—Vittoriale degli Italiani; René Dazy, Paris; Roger-Viollet, Paris—Roger-Viollet, Paris—Vittoriale degli Italiani (2). 238,239—Vittoriale degli Italiani. 240—Vittoriale degli Italiani—H. Paillasson, courtesy Editions Arthaud—René Dazy, Paris. 241—Vittoriale degli Italiani. 242—Courtesy of Commander C. Campbell Johnson, Brighton. 244—A. F. Kersting. 246, 247—A. F. Kersting. 247—The Lewis Walpole Library, Farmington, Connecticut. 249—Anthony Rumsey. 250—Edwin Smith. 251—Linda Bartlett/Photo Researchers. 252—C. Baugey, Paris. 253—Gabinetto Fotografico Nazionale, Rome—Georgina Masson, courtesy Thames and Hudson. 254—Charles Moore/Black Star—Marie J. Mattson/Black Star; Charles Moore/Black Star—Spectrum Colour Library; Marie J. Mattson/Black Star. 255—Spectrum Colour Library. 256-257—Jan Wampler.

**CHAPTER SIX** 258—George Holton/Photo Researchers. 260—Inge Morath/Magnum. 261—Dimitri Kessel/*Life* Magazine © 1951 Time Inc. 263—The Oriental Institute, University of Chicago—Holle Verlag, Germany. 264—Henri Stierlin, Geneva. 266-267—Roger-Viollet, Paris (3)—The Oriental Institute, University of Chicago. 268-269—Inge Morath/Magnum. 270—Bibliothèque Nationale. 271—The Metropolitan Museum of Art, gift of Alexander Smith Cochran, 1913. 272—Marie J. Mattson/Black Star. 273—Kosok/Black Star. 274-275—George Holton—India Office Library, photo by John Freeman Group. 276—The Metropolitan Museum of Art, gift of Alexander Smith cochran, 1913; Curators of the Bodleian Library, Oxford. 277—J. Niepce/Rapho-Photo Researchers. 278-279—David Carroll. 280—Fritz Henle/Photo Researchers. 281—Louis-Frédéric/Photo Researchers; Burt Glinn/Magnum. 282—Paolo Koch/Photo Researchers. 283—Alex Low/The *Daily Telegraph* from Woodfin Camp and Associates—George Holton. 284-285—Oronoz, Madrid courtesy *Newsweek*. 286—Spanish National Tourist Office. 287—John Lewis Stage/The Image Bank. 288—Adam Woolfitt/Woodfin Camp and Associates. 289—Clockwise from top: Adam Woolfitt/Woodfin Camp and Associates (2); Herschel Levit (2). 290—Adam Woolfitt/Woodfin Camp and Associates. 291—John Lewis Stage/The Image Bank. 292-293—Oronoz, Madrid courtesy *Newsweek*. 295—Morris Rosenfeld & Sons. 296—Collection of Lucius Beebe (2)—Pullman-Standard photo from the Arthur Dubin collection. 297—Collection of Lucius Beebe. 298, 299—Morris Rosenfeld & Sons. 300, 301—Courtesy Airesearch Aviation Company.

**CHAPTER SEVEN:** 302—G. E. Kidder Smith. 304—Museum of Fine Arts, Boston. 305, 306—Massachusetts Historical Society. 307—Thomas Jefferson Memorial Foundation, photo by Ed Roseberry—Thomas Jefferson Memorial Foundation. 308-309—Thomas Jefferson Memorial Foundation—Thomas Jefferson Memorial Foundation, photo by Ed Roseberry. 310-311—Collection of Mr. Thomas Jefferson Coolidge. 312—Wayne Andrews. 313—Mabel Lane; Milly McGehee—Mississippi Department of Archives and History. 314—The New-York Historical Society. 315—Culver Pictures. 316—G. E. Kidder Smith. 317—Farrell Grehan/Photo Researchers. 318—© Arnold Newman. 319—Brown Brothers—Farrell Grehan/Photo Researchers. 320 through 323—Courtesy Biltmore House and Gardens, Asheville, N.C. 324—Brown Brothers; UPI. 324–325—New York State Department of Commerce. 326—Ringling Museum/Sarasota. 327—John Lewis Stage/The Image Bank. 328—Culver Pictures. 329—Brown Brothers. 330–331—Rene Burri/Magnum. 332—Gjon Mili. 334—James Abbe. 335—Hearst San Simeon State Historical Monument—Gjon Mili. 337—Tom Dunham. 338-339—Ralph Crane/*Life* Magazine © 1972 Time Inc. 340–341—Tony Howarth/Woodfin Camp and Associates. 342-343—Robert Phillips © 1978. 344-345—Fred J. Maroon/Louis Mercier. 346,347—Prince Shahbaz Pahlbod, except bottom left, courtesy Taliesin, Stephen Nemtin.

# INDEX

*Numbers in boldface refer to illustrations.*